DEXYS YOUNG SOUL REBELS

MIDNIGHT

RICHARD WHITE

RUNNERS

DEXYS YOUNG SOUL REBELS
MIDNIGHT RUNNERS

RICHARD WHITE

OMNIBUS PRESS

LONDON / NEW YORK / PARIS / SYDNEY / COPENHAGEN / BERLIN / MADRID / TOKYO

Exclusive Distributors
Music Sales Limited,
8/9 Frith Street,
London W1D 3JB, UK.

Music Sales Corporation,
257 Park Avenue South,
New York, NY 10010, USA.

Macmillan Distribution Services,
53 Park West Drive,
Derrimut, Vic 3030,
Australia.

To the Music Trade only:
Music Sales Limited,
8/9 Frith Street,
London W1D 3JB, UK.

Every effort has been made to trace the copyright holders of the photographs in this
book but one or two were unreachable. We would be grateful if the photographers
concerned would contact us.

Typeset by Galleon Typesetting, Ipswich.
Printed by Creative Print & Design, Ebbw Vale, Wales.

A catalogue record for this book is available from the British Library.

Visit Omnibus Press on the web at www.omnibuspress.com

Introduction

"But it's crazy, really – no one could change anyone's life. The thing about music is that it reminds people of something deep down in themselves, you know? Something they've lost sometime . . . But I don't think that music really is the thing. And I think it's crazy to look up to musicians. I'm not saying all these people do, but I think that's mad."

– Kevin Rowland, 1993

IT could be argued that Dexys Midnight Runners make more sense now than they ever did in the early Eighties. Striving to be an important group, their dedication and ability to inspire belief went against the ephemeral grain of the times.

Never content to repeat their success, 'Dexys' were one step ahead of the game with defiant tests of loyalty with each record release or fashion change. Defying easy categorisation, anything was plausible and everything was possible. The group embarked upon, and continued to chart, a challenging, opinion-dividing and nonconformist course. Bursting out of the post-Punk late Seventies, they resembled a renegade collective of Birmingham-based outsiders imbued with a firebrand swagger. Sneering at rock'n'roll's stagnancy, Dexys proffered something of passionate substance.

At the band's heart was a true maverick – a gifted wordsmith, co-originator and leader, Kevin Rowland grew into one of the finest white soul singers Britain has produced. On hearing one new composition, fellow Dexys founder member Kevin Archer likened it to "an aural sculpture from a soul bedrock." Together, Rowland and Archer became the vocal epicentre of a furious, horn-driven storm powered by white post-punk anger and black soul spirit – an angry, guitar-wielding equivalent to Sam & Dave. From Memphis to the Midlands.

"Dexys was very much a group and I was very much the leader of it," Rowland explained in 1988. "But I *wasn't* Dexys Midnight Runners. That was always a myth that wasn't true." Addressing the original group's much-championed gang mentality, it was clear from the outset that this was an organically developed collective.

1

Presenting an antidote to rock's cliché-cluttered rulebook, Dexys culti-
vated their own contradictory myth – a clean-living collective who
weren't averse to a moderate level of rock'n'roll excess. With the original
group's legend stemming from ingenious survival instincts, their all-for-
one philosophy was usurped by a three-man songwriting and decision-
making 'nucleus'.

Paradoxically, Rowland's musical perfectionism was informed by a lack
of formal tutoring. With a revolving-door personnel policy, Dexys' frequent acts of reinvention provided some of the strongest, most indelible
images of British pop during the Eighties. While not always popular
among their contemporaries, they resembled a confrontational, spiritual,
regimented brethren. Rustic, romantic misfits, exquisitely tailored bards
. . . indeed, the Young Soul Rebels.

This spirit transferred to their records. A group who twice scaled commercial heights before descending into periods of near obscurity, their
development between 1978 and 1986 offers an incident-strewn, often
quixotic, career path. *Young Soul Rebels'* charts Rowland's early (and
enduring) fascination with the powerful currency of image in pop culture
and Dexys' early development and success, through his suspicions over the
music media and increasingly didactic leadership, to Rowland's short-
lived late Eighties solo career, a controversial studio comeback in 1999, an
aborted Dexys re-formation and their acclaimed renaissance 10 years later
in 2003.

Beginning with *Don't Stand Me Down*'s belated re-evaluation as an
overlooked classic upon its 1997 reissue, the Dexys catalogue has attracted
overdue appraisal. Following 2000's 20th anniversary remastered release of
Searching For The Young Soul Rebels, renewed media interest has been
exemplified by subsequent TV and radio documentaries. However, this
was not particularly influential in my motive for writing this book. Its
starting point was my decision to celebrate the group's acclaimed London
Old Vic Theatre shows from 1981, the high watermark of Dexys' live
career. Rowland has lamented the fact they were never officially recorded.
I resolved to write a testament in their honour, hoping to convey something of its theatrical nuances and powerful, dramatic spirit. If Dexys are to
be defined in time on stage, *this* is what they're like. Working steadily
from this point, the book, an unashamed labour of love on my part, has
involved approximately two years research and writing. Over the years,
some ex-members have argued that their contribution has been effectively
airbrushed out of Dexys history. From the outset, I had hoped this book
might present an opportunity for those persons to share their memories
and offer their own accounts.

I've also offered some insight into the working relationships within Dexys. While everyone has their own view on life as a Midnight Runner, *Young Soul Rebels* attempts to explain how a disparate cast of individuals were united in their dedication, despite a persistent backdrop of financial chaos and encroaching paranoia. Few have stressed that being part of such a dedicated group was ever a particularly easy ride. Yet the former members of Dexys, particularly the original incarnation, enjoyed a spirited sense of camaraderie, mischief and endeavour and, as they admit, no little fun too. Being party to such uniquely passionate music produced its own fulfilment and sense of achievement.

Seeking an insight into the studio process, various commentators were happy to wax lyrical on the significance of the group's underrated and often misunderstood recordings. Their post-Dexys work has been highlighted when appropriate to the main narrative, particularly The Bureau and Kevin Archer's The Blue Ox Babes.

Not all members responded to my requests for input. Thus, absent players' voices have been served by contemporary interviews and documentary contributions. While Kevin Rowland has not contributed to the book, I've drawn upon a wealth of interview material running across the whole of his Dexys career, on through his periods as a solo artist and up to the present day. Considering how the music press have generally seized upon the more unsavoury elements of Rowland's reputation, group members have also spoken of acts of generosity, thoughtfulness and humour, alongside his charisma and charm.

I hope this book offers some rewarding insight into Dexys' magnificent music, and the enigma that remains Kevin Rowland.

Richard White
June 2005

Chapter One

"I'm keeping it simple these days. In a group. Wanted to look good. Wanted to make good music. That's the culture we're from . . . If I'm gonna go on stage or on TV I wanna look good. This is the kind of thing I dreamed about when I was a kid."

– Kevin Rowland, 2003

IT seems that every group is ultimately defined in time somewhere on record. Yet for Kevin Rowland, the grooves that captured Dexys Midnight Runners' gloriously contrary and combustible world on vinyl were often simply not enough. How could they hope to support the full emotional weight and expressive strain of their defiantly individual art? With so much occurring and so much to absorb, the sheer content was often overwhelming. All manner of references could compete for your attention. In an attempt to comprehend exactly *what* it was you'd just heard, the instinctive urge was to re-spin Dexys' recordings. While the wheel of musical rejuvenation had yet to come full circle, an oddly appropriate place to let the needle hit that opening groove and kick off proceedings comes at a juncture offering hope of a creative rebirth. If not a unique proposition, one new, early Nineties composition found Rowland offering a perspective on his past.

In one of the earliest versions of 'My Life In England', his poetic, autobiographical narrative on childhood, Kevin Rowland sang of his return to Wolverhampton from Ireland after living in County Mayo until he was four years old. His family had left the West Midlands shortly after his birth on August 17, 1953.

"I can remember singing songs like, 'I'm a rambler, I'm a gambler, I'm a long way from home,'" he said during BBC Radio Two's Dexys' documentary in 2004. "Those kinda songs. And I remember singing songs at primary school, and it just seemed like an easy thing to do. A very pleasant thing to do, I loved doing it. And people seemed to like it. It was very simple then. Got a bit complicated later."

After being inspired by watching Billy Fury on television as an eight-year-old, Rowland later made an abortive attempt at learning the guitar. Having finished primary school, he relocated to Harrow, north London as a 10-year-old in 1964, joining St. Gregory's Catholic secondary school. He told *Melody Maker* that as a devoted 11-year-old altar boy who regularly attended mass, he'd sat an early entrance exam in the hope of setting himself on the path to his dream vocation as a priest.

Recalling the taunts aimed at his Black Country brogue while confused by his schoolboy colleagues' London dialect, Rowland would swiftly adopt a similar patois. He later frequently pinpointed the physical attention he received from his peers. In the song, thoughts later returned to his birthplace, and what became a teenage passion for Wolverhampton Wanderers FC, paying homage to club legend Derek Dougan. Rowland revealed to music writer Paolo Hewitt in *The Fashion Of Football* that his first awareness of the club came as a six-year-old, on their winning the League title in 1959. Although not yet wholly enamoured of football, he'd considered supporting one of the capital's clubs. Vowing his allegiance to Wolves, he sang of watching his team playing Arsenal, standing on Highbury's North Bank in London. And while boxer Sonny Liston had figured in the song as part of Rowland's childhood dreams of America, he'd also caught sight of the legendary Muhammad Ali after sneaking into Wembley Stadium for the second half of the 1966 World Cup final.

Given the fact that his father was a builder and having decided on manual labour as a more virtuous vocation than office work, the prospect of enrolling at Willesden School of Building in 1967 excited Rowland. Following subsequent expulsion from its strict environment, he finished his academic career at St. James, Burnt Oak.

As a 14-year-old absconder, Rowland relished the delights of London's West End. Visiting record shops in Soho, his friends encouraged staff to play obscure soul records. Rowland later admitted he'd often been in trouble with the police before leaving school, following a spate of court appearances for various criminal acts, including shoplifting and theft, which continued into adolescence. "I suppose my youth was okay but there was a lot of it that wasn't so marvellous and I can honestly say that there's nothing I regret growing out of."

Leaving school at 15, in February 1969, he undertook a job with Dunn's clothes wear company. Fascinated by the sartorial etiquette of a gang of Harrow mods, Rowland's scholarly attention turned to an obsessive education in clothes. Subsequently assuming the pseudonym of King Rollo, he joined a local mixed sex Harrow gang called The Young Kingsbury Team. Buying exquisite clothes and shoes was crucial. Resplendent in Harrington jackets, Ben Shermans and Mohair suits, Rowland revelled in this clothes-obsessed, fast-paced underground movement. In the late Sixties world of colourful expression and hippiedom, he and his sharply dressed adolescent contemporaries thus adopted a reactionary look whose roots could be traced to their middle-aged, conservative American counterparts.

While enjoying a sense of belonging to a movement, its subversive appeal continued to excite Rowland's fascination. His adoration for this Ivy League apparel, incorporating Sta-prest trousers, button-down shirts and brogues, would prove enduring. As a result of a September 1969 *Daily Mirror* interview with a similar teenage gang, the term 'skinhead' was coined. Both Rowland and future Merton Parka and Dexys Midnight Runner Hammond organist Mick Talbot insist it was an inappropriate description for this cult soul and dancehall ethic. It wasn't about football or violence, Talbot maintained in 2003, enthralled with its attendant "seven-inch singles culture", but clubbers with a love of reggae and soul music.

By the time he was 15, he told *Jack* magazine, he'd developed a confidence in his own tastes, eschewing the dictates of fashion. "It's a much misunderstood thing," Rowland told Gary Mulholland. "My generation were the ones dancing to black music." With Jamaican ska becoming popular, a 16-year-old Rowland and his compadres enjoyed looking their best, going to clubs and attending dances where Laurel Aitken, The Ethiopians, Toots & The Maytals, The Pioneers and The Wailers found steady rotation. "You could dance to records but you would never go to see live groups," Rowland later explained.

While white bands held little sway amongst this listening and dancing fodder, Rowland admitted, "It was always at the back of my mind that I'd like to do pop music or design clothes or become a hairdresser, but how could I have told my friends that?" He would later train as a Vidal Sassoon stylist. "I always thought I'd like to get into pop music but when I was 16 I wouldn't have dreamed of telling my mates that, as groups were nowhere as far as they were concerned."

Rowland grew his hair as an overground skinhead explosion ensued in late 1969. Skinheads would proliferate on the football terraces the following summer. His zealous passion for football reached a crescendo during the UEFA Cup final second leg between Wolves and Tottenham Hotspur in 1972. His vehement anger at the opposition fans had "frightened" him. "My life was changing and that was it," he told Hewitt. "I stopped going and I started to change and do my own thing, which ended up being music."

Following varied work as a printer's apprentice, with his dad's own building firm and a stint at C&A, Rowland decamped to Butlins for a summer season's work in Clacton. Later roaming Scotland and finding work in Glasgow and Aviemore, Rowland relished his freedom as a nomadic wanderer. Moving to Liverpool, he told Gavin Martin his existence had veered between extremes. "At first I was living with this group of people who were sort of like hippies. Well, they weren't anything else, dirty and dropping acid and listening to Hendrix all day." Having worked as a boutique shop assistant, he had also been close to marriage.*

On reaching 21, he jacked in employment as a sales rep with a company car and returned to Birmingham, where he took a job in a city centre shop. Rowland still considered that his other childhood dream, of becoming a pop star, was conceivable.

"Despite everything, there'd be the occasional clear moment when I knew I had talent and could be good enough to be a pop singer," he informed Jon Wilde. "I had nothing to lose." He'd later describe his subsequent musical career as a "last-ditch attempt to prove that I wasn't completely worthless." Kevin's elder brother, Pete, was heading a country & western social club group around local Birmingham venues by 1974. With their guitarist handing in a six-month notice, Kevin was told that if he mastered rudimentary guitar he could join the group. He duly did so. There would be no looking back, as he swiftly assumed his brother's lead vocal duties. During an approximate 18-month tenure, Rowland solicited social club crowd approval with inventive stage theatrics. Among the group's covers repertoire was the Jerome Kern *Showboat* standard 'The Way You Look Tonight'. Venturing into Birmingham clubs at the time, Rowland often grew frustrated at watching Northern Soul devotees, resplendent in high waisted, generously flared trousers strutting their stuff. "I don't know what it is about it," he later told *Jamming!* "I used to go and watch them in 1974 when I used to go to clubs, stand there and watch them and I used to get really angry. I just hated it!"

Rowland later emphasised his intuitive flair for making pre-emptive strikes in the sartorial stakes, tapping into prevailing mood swings and trends. "I know what's going to come into fashion," he would explain, "what people will be wearing." A skill, he claims, that was in operation during the period subsequently coined New Romanticism.

"It's probably very true that he did [pre-empt] that. He knows that things go in a cycle," Dexys evangelist and former freelance *Melody Maker/ NME* journalist Paolo Hewitt insists. "And he's always been fascinated by that culture." In his 'high fashion' conceit for a nascent Midnight Runners

---

* In 1991, he'd meet his long-lost daughter Alethea Jane England, conceived during a relationship he'd had whilst living in the city.

image in late 1978, Rowland appeared to draw on certain elements of the ambiguous, androgynous David Bowie/Bryan Ferry school of expression, a hangover from the early to mid-Seventies. "Kevin was very image-conscious. He understood pop music, and he understood the way you use clothes to really subvert things," Hewitt adds. Rowland had clearly been captivated with the colourful sophistication of Seventies glam rock act Roxy Music, being enthusiastic for early classics like 1973's 'Beauty Queen' and ballad 'Just Like You' from the band's *Stranded* album.

Yet this admiration for Ferry's 'stunning' sartorial style soon led him to suspect the motives of the music media. "I started to understand that not all the press were paragons of taste when Bryan Ferry was ridiculed for wearing what I thought were amazing clothes in 1973–74," he informed David Hutcheon. This journalistic assault, including press jibes like 'Byron Ferrari', clearly affected Rowland, who was later fearful of suffering a similar reception. "I think I was afraid of them getting at me on a personal level."

"When Ferry was wearing a tuxedo, Kevin understood instinctively that what he was doing was going anti-rock culture," Hewitt affirms. "And then you look at the *NME* and they really started to take the piss out of him, as they did with Kevin."

In a comprehensive 2001 web interview with *Plan B* magazine's current editor-in-chief Everett True,[*] he stated: "We [Dexys] looked good and because we looked good, people say the image took over. What are you talking about? What's wrong with looking good? It doesn't mean your music isn't any good?" Yet Rowland would draw a discreet veil over this formative point of reference in interviews.

Acknowledging a wavering vocal debt to Ferry, Rowland would also admit his sartorial influence, telling Hutcheon, "We knew that fashion thing was going to be massive and we wanted to be a bit like Roxy Music, a band that would look and sound fantastic."

During the summer of 1976, this dual passion for Ferry and fashion informed the 'art-rock' dalliances of Rowland's next musical endeavour, Lucy & The Lovers. Guitarist Mark Phillips and girlfriend bassist Ghislaine Weston were recruited through advertisements in the *Birmingham Evening Mail*. Their nine-strong personnel was an early sign of the agenda Rowland would adopt two years later. The Lovers included two skimpily attired female vocalists. Informing Mark Ellen in 1982 that The Lovers resembled little more than "a horrible, boring, pretentious arty-farty

[*] Extract from Everett True interview with Kevin Archer and Kevin Rowland published on tangents.co.uk website (2001).

affair," Rowland could often be found on stage in make-up, expansive suit and slicked hair. He'd later wear frilly shirts and a tam-o-shanter for good measure. Yet Rowland later drew parallels between The Lovers' look and a newly emergent agenda accompanying the outbreak of punk. "I started to read about it and noticed the clothes we were wearing were exactly the same," he recalled in 1983. "There were a lot of similarities."

Morphing into a five-piece group, Rowland, Phillips, Weston, backing vocalist Heather Tonge and drummer Lee Burton were suitably re-christened as bristling second-wave punks, The Killjoys in early 1977. Tonge and Burton departed. An additional guitarist, Supanova's Keith Rimmell and more accomplished drummer Bob Peach entered the fray, bringing a notable improvement to their live pedigree. "When The Killjoys started I was really interested in punk," Rowland, a recent witness to the inspiring sight of The Clash at Birmingham's Barbarella's, informed *Jamming!*'s John Tully, who later co-managed the group with used car salesman Dave Corke, who ran The Killjoys' regular home town haunt.

"When punk happened," Hewitt enthused, "it was all or nothing. Someone said to me, 'Do you remember when you told me there were no good records made before 1977?' And I'm sure Kevin had the same opinion as me." The initial flame of fervour slowly subsided. There was little of exception to separate The Killjoys from the innumerable, like-minded groups playing the country's live circuits.

"All that punk stuff – it wasn't like I imagined it was gonna be," Rowland told Radio Two. "It was like I was always dirty, scruffy, carrying the equipment into a gig. By the time you went on stage you'd feel pretty lousy. And it wasn't what I'd wanted it to be like."

Yet something of punk's society-shaking ferment had already been effectively captured on the release of The Sex Pistols' debut single 'Anarchy In The UK' in December 1976. Addressing its ominous times with satirical humour, 'Anarchy' left a deep, indelible mark on its genera-tion. "The Pistols were a good group and they did open it up for every-body," Rowland later told journalist Jim Irvin.[*]

Front man Johnny Rotten's charisma captured Rowland's imagination. For both men, anger was an energetic release. Rowland's came couched in a suitably Cockneyfied, semi-venomous sneer, his sentiments towards prince Rotten immortalised on The Killjoys' two-and-a-half minute debut dispatch, 'Johnny Won't Get To Heaven'. Signing with Lee

---

[*] Extract from Jim Irvin interview with Kevin Archer and Kevin Rowland in 'Regrets? I've Had A Few', originally published in *Mojo*, September 2000 (full version available on www.rocksbackpages.com website).

Wood's independent Cambridge label Raw Records, its release coincided with a time Rowland later described to *Jamming!* as punk's "most intense euphoria" in mid-July. Backed with the churning riff of 'Naïve', the three-chord bluster of 'Johnny . . .' signified all that punk's predominantly limited musicianship would allow. "I'd already written the song – 'it could be me, it could be me . . .'" Rowland revealed in 2004. "I suppose there was some jealousy there, maybe." Firing his opening salvo towards the music press, he proudly eschewed both the *NME* and *Sounds*. The *NME* journalist Gavin Martin later applauded Rowland as Rotten's post-punk, voice of protest successor. *Sounds* announced that record sales for 'Johnny . . .', according to Raw, had reached the 10,000 mark, a major success for a small independent group.

Undertaking their first Radio One session for John Peel on October 18, the band demonstrated an unassuming grip on the art of noise. With 'Naïve' climaxing in a growling, snarled vocal coda and with glistening, razor-wired 'Recognition' and the churning 'Back To Front' also recorded, 'At Night' found Rowland dispensing further food for thought on the music media's questionable powers of influence. While this lyrical strain in The Killjoys' modest *oeuvre* accounted for some of Rowland's preoccupation with the Fourth Estate during the early Eighties, he assured the *NME* in 2000: "But I didn't come into music thinking, 'I'm gonna fuck the press.' I was thinking, 'Great! I'm gonna do interviews!'"

Filmed that autumn, The Killjoys were captured in German director Wolfgang Buld's documentary *Punk In London*. Rowland offered his own interpretation of punk's creative credo as 1978 unfolded. "The original idea of punk was to be different and say what you wanted, when you wanted and how you wanted, and not to copy everyone else." While Rowland admitted to John Hess in February that The Killjoys were strictly bandwagon jumpers riding on punk's coat-tails, a new, more colourful agenda was soon proposed. "The audiences are fed up with the black leather scruffiness that's been the fashion. They want a change – there's going to be one heck of a reaction against punk."

Later boasting of a frequent image overhaul on the group's behalf, The Killjoys were now resplendent in white shirts, replete with blow-dried coiffures and offset by jodhpurs and boxing boots. "Instead of doing fast songs we did slow ones, but we still kept the name The Killjoys," he explained to *Jamming!* five years later, "and that's why the audience hated us." A brief London tour itinerary included dates at The Speakeasy, The Nashville and The 100 Club. "There'd be punks at the front row because they'd heard the record ['Johnny . . .'] and the name," Rowland recalled in 1983, "and we'd come on and do Bobby Darin's 'Dream Lover', Fifties rock'n'roll and country & western!" They would also incorporate covers of Jerry Lee Lewis' 'Great Balls Of Fire' and Buddy Holly's 'Rave On'.

Although a typically tiresome line of enquiry, *Melody Maker* asked why they favoured such a 'retro' musical policy. This early example of Rowland 're-interpreting' bygone material and attempting to connect with its emotional content would find a more successful (and coherent) outlet as the year progressed. Yet it had already provided traces of an irascible, new-wave crooner surfacing from beneath the punk veneer. Recorded on February 13, their second Peel session provided ample evidence. The jagged 'All The Way' featured ringing Buzzcock chords, while the misleading, anachronistically titled 'Spit On Me' was an inverted Fifties rock/doo-wop effort featuring boisterous communal backing harmonies. Even a French chanteuse quality surfaced on the slow-tempo, low-key ballad 'Ghislaine', which featured Weston's amorous Gallic tones.

The session's significance rested on 'Smoke Your Own'. Returning to the thorny subject of the music press, Rowland made reference to punk fanzine *Sniffin' Glue*. Having already questioned pseudo intellectual and philosophical tastes on 'At Night', this lyrical thread was also addressed on the chorus.

By early 1978, 19-year-old Black Country guitarist Kevin Archer's tenure with The Negatives found him yearning for something more substantial. "We wanted it to be a serious group, but it wasn't," Archer told Everett True, "and it was old-fashioned." Meanwhile, Pete Rowland had been scouring clubs at the turn of the year for new groups to manage. "Kevin's brother came to a pub where I was practising with a group," Archer recalled. "Kevin then saw us and liked one or two of the songs." Archer and Rowland struck up a conversation. Following Keith Rimmell's departure, The Killjoys swiftly sought a replacement ahead of an imminent tour. Archer enjoyed his brief tenure with what had become a popular Birmingham outfit, including supporting Nico at the Camden Music Machine and a Raw Records anniversary shindig in Cambridge in May.

With ambitions for landing an album deal and recording contract, the group prepared material for their debut LP; their final session at London's Riverside Studios had produced a new work, 'Definitely Down On The Farm'. Previously aired at the Mayfair Suite in March, *Melody Maker* applauded its moody, Velvet Underground dynamic. Unfortunately, the sole master copy of The Killjoys' swansong vanished. A scheduled London Marquee show was subsequently shelved as press reports in June disclosed news of the group's disbandment. Rowland later admitted to *Uncut* that the group had "revolted". Growing despondent in the wake of his bandmates' departure, ending The Killjoys clearly hadn't been part of the plan. "I would probably still be going now with The Killjoys only the others left," he told *Jamming!*

Old-fashioned musical differences were also given for their demise. "There were a lot of good ideas going about for that band, but it didn't work because there were too many people wanting to do different things." Weston, Phillips and Peach subsequently formed new band, Out Of Nowhere, that summer. Yet The Killjoys experience had proved a vital education. "We learned a valuable lesson there," Rowland conceded to *Jamming!* "We thought, 'We'll make it as The Killjoys, and then do what we want.' We learned the hard way that you have to start out with what you want to do." Insistent that he'd set his sights on a new musical direction and stage presentation as early as January, Rowland asked Archer to join him in a new venture.

Espousing their determination to "swim against the tide", the duo's defiant musical gesture would eventually strike a chord within Britain's disarmingly diverse late Seventies UK music scene. "With punk and everything, it had swept a lot of things away," Rowland told the BBC's *Young Guns* Dexys documentary. "But I knew that people would want to dance again."

Chapter Two

"I FELT that somewhere inside me I could do it, I could be in a group and I could be great," Rowland told Everett True in 2001. "It had been my childhood dream and I'd abandoned it over the years. I felt not very good about myself, and I felt a desperation to do something, to prove myself."

Compelled to react against a post-punk 'subculture' with low aspiration thresholds, a 24-year-old Rowland turned to the healing powers of soul music. "In mid-1978, I started listening to a few old soul records. They sounded so fresh and alive, so punchy and innocent and honest compared to the overproduced groups around. It was inspiring."

Stressing the need to be a purposeful unit with a clear sense of direction, the group would feature a brass section. They would sound great. Most importantly, they would look like no one else. "I thought about the line-up, and the type of stuff we'd play, the clothes we'd wear and everything."

Archer had found the final part of the equation particularly appealing. "At the time, everyone was looking the same. It was a bit post-punk," he told True. "Everyone used to wear punky kind of clothes, black. That's how it started."

"He was getting on a bit in punk terms I guess," teenage fan and later music journalist Peter Paphides observed, "and the point finally came where he wanted to build the type of band that could play the music that he heard in his head. It was time to go for it. He was one of those artists who try and re-create those unique sounds they hear in the real world."

Rowland initially made a strong case for the existence of a foundation building 'blueprint' during the group's formative period. "We planned the whole thing," he insisted to Dermot Stokes in mid-1980. "We accepted that we'd probably be quite successful and we thought out how we'd deal with that and would we do this when we got that and so on. And it's much easier for us now because we made all those plans."

"A lot of planning went into Dexys," Rowland told Jon Wilde in 1999. "But so much of it was accidental and uncertain." A year later, he reiterated how opportunistic the group's formation had been. "We weren't strategic about it, I certainly wasn't," Rowland told Irvin, "but I think we thought we were going to be a successful group, it's gonna be good, we were certainly good enough to make it."

Archer could certainly see it happening. "I got a positive feeling from him. I knew we'd be more successful because the whole thing was a good idea."

During June and July, Rowland and Archer advertised in the *Birmingham Evening Mail* for speculative recruits to join a nine-piece 'new-wave soul band', comprising keyboards, drums, bass, saxophones, trumpet and trombone. The response was encouraging. Eighteen-year-old keyboardist Pete Saunders lived in the middle-class district of Moseley. A teenage heavy rock fan, he had swiftly embraced the British take on American R&B and blues, enthralled with Alexis Korner and John Mayall's Bluesbreakers. Spending two years in a theatre group at Birmingham's Cannon Hill Arts Centre, the pianist was invited to pen material for a musical version of *King Kong*, before performing at the Edinburgh Festival.

He recalls his initial audition. "I got this hippie bloke to drive me out into the Black Country, to Oldbury, and we unloaded this Hammond organ in Kevin's front room. He owned the house, which was quite unusual in those days for a 24-year-old bloke." Rowland placed 'Big Bird' by Atlantic artist Eddie Floyd on the turntable. "I'd never heard it before, and he said, 'Do you like music like this?' and I thought, 'Ooh.' And I said, 'Are you into blues?' I thought, 'That sounds quite like the music I like,' and I played along to the record so that he could see I could play. Then he played 'Tell Me When My Light Turns Green', with the two of them [Rowland and Archer] singing in harmony."

Conceived during the dying embers of The Killjoys' existence, the song's lyrical content provided a clue to its punk origins. Archer had been impressed by an early rendition of the song at Rowland's Oldbury abode early that year. "I just showed it to Kev in my bedroom, the other members of the band didn't see it," Rowland later told author Johnny Rogan. "I showed him on the guitar and it was funny that I already had that soul thing in my head . . ." Rowland and Archer spent endless hours perfecting a startling dual lead vocal approach. The emphasis on sounding unique was as strong as the songs. "We really wanted a vocal style that set us apart," Rowland told Irvin, "and we were aware that all the good groups had a sound that identified them."

Floored by the duo's startling presence, Saunders sensed he was witnessing the new Righteous Brothers at work. "They were a partnership, playing as a team, with electric guitars that weren't plugged in. They were creating the thing together then, and I was really impressed. The two of them were so powerful when they sang."

"Kevin Archer was so vibrant," violinist and future colleague Steve Shaw argues. "He had a similar kind of emotion and anger to Kevin Rowland, but he was very youthful."

Saunders was struck by Rowland's sense of purpose. "Kevin's charisma hit you. There was something special about him – you just knew that what he said was going to happen *would* happen." Having accepted a job in Bristol, Saunders was unable to join immediately. His replica Hammond organ was left in Rowland's house for upwards of three months during the summer. During this hiatus, 18-year-old bassist Pete Williams and proficient, dyed-black-haired rock drummer John Jay, who'd served in the Army in Northern Ireland, came into the fold.

Williams joined in June. Engrossed in the lyrical poetry of David Bowie's *Ziggy Stardust And The Spiders From Mars* album, he was also a fan of punk, funk, reggae, Stevie Wonder, and West Bromwich Albion FC. "It's so difficult to think back to how I thought when I was 18, 19," Williams admitted in 2003 on *It Was Like This*. "I was such a lad, really, a lot younger than my years. I did dream of making it in music. I remember reading Ray Connolly's book *That'll Be The Day* before I saw the film. And it seemed to contain everything I loved at the time – fairs, waltzers. And at the end of that he buys a bass guitar and I remember thinking, 'That'd be great, to live like that.' I did dream, but that's all it was. I hadn't got much confidence in myself as a person."

"When I met him [Williams] at the studio last year [during Dexys' 2003 recording sessions], it was just like when I first met him," recalls Saunders. "He looks the same, he's got that warmth and that humour. But underneath it all, he knows what he's doing. He was self-deprecating in a lot of ways, but there was a rod of iron in the middle of it. He's good to be around. He's got a down-to-earthness, he's clever without being pretentious, and he's got a steadiness which helped make everything else strong, personality-wise and musicianship-wise."

Williams' immersion in music began as a child, later being hit by its power as a teenager. "There was always a piano in my house," he recalled. "My dad was a violinist as a boy, and music's in my family." His uncles had been Fifties era crooners and Williams himself received tuition on the clarinet as a youngster. All of this offered something of a release and a relief from his schooldays. "I was pretty awful at school," he told *It Was Like This*. "Growing up where I did, the school that I went to was mainly factory fodder really." Completely self-taught, Williams purchased his first bass guitar for £15 from a school friend. "There was a friend of mine, Mickey O'Keefe, who played guitar and we used to rehearse at the Catholic Church. If he went to Mass we'd get rehearsals. That's the way it kind of worked, at about 14. And I just loved that."

Having grown up together, teenagers Williams and Archer had combined forces in The Negatives. "I first started singing in a band with Kevin Archer that we had formed. I'd jumped in and played bass in a couple of bands and backed a couple of bands that played social clubs when I was 15, and I enjoyed singing. It was quite difficult with the bass, but the songs I was doing were very simple. And I used to enjoy doing backing vocals in the early days with Kev Archer." Aside from his natural aptitude as a comedian, Rowland later conceded that Williams was a "powerful and underacknowledged" member of the group, with a warm, resonant voice and clear songwriting talent.

Despite the outward impression of a dominant Rowland/Archer songwriting axis among the group's earliest work, alto saxophonist Steve Spooner insists the unacknowledged significance of Williams and Archer's partnership deserves recognition. "A lot of the ideas for those early songs were started before the band, and Pete and Kev Archer were very close," he observes. "I really think that Pete had more influence on those early songs than history dictates. I doubt if Pete would ever say it, but he didn't get the credit he deserved." Unarguably, Rowland was the "major driving force," Williams declared in 2003. "Kevin was the thread. We worked very, very hard in those early days. We really did work hard. But as far as a master plan in the early days, the plan was just to be the best that we could be, as I remember it. And personally, I never had a master plan. I don't plan that far ahead."

"Relative to other people, Kevin had contacts and he had experience," Saunders recalls. "He knew a certain path. It was like, 'We're going to do this, then we're going to do a demo, then we'll get a record deal.' He had been very close to a certain degree of success. He was always very determined, knowing that you basically had one chance to get it as tight and strong as possible. So by the time anyone sees us, it's going to be very impressive."

After placing music press advertisements, Archer recalled a lengthy and discriminatory gestation period spent sifting through 30 or 40 players who, despite their musicianship, lacked the requisite 'feel' and attitude for the mission. "People knew what they were getting into," Rowland affirmed in 1980. "We told them, 'This is what we're gonna do, this is what we're gonna play and this is what we're gonna wear. Are you interested?' A few people joined and then tried to change things. They had to leave."

The humorous essay that accompanied Dexys' 1980 debut album would outline their colourful formation. Yet the search for young soul rebels had also involved spying on suitable brass-blowers in local ensembles. "We used to go round to youth jazz orchestras and things like that and wait outside and look through to see what they were playing," Rowland informed the BBC in 2000. "Two, three, four of us, like a press gang, would kind of go round and look through the windows while they were rehearsing, 'Oh, that one's playing a tenor, that one's, what's that? That looks like an alto, that's a trumpet.' We were like that." It proved a tortuous process.

"It was quite impressive how far people were willing to travel to be turned down," Saunders said, laughing at the memory of bearded brass players from the Isle of Wight. "That was bizarre. Getting these weird and wonderful horn players who had worked with Norrie Paramor and Midland Light Orchestras."

One early summer venture took the quartet of Rowland, Archer, Williams and Saunders to Cannon Hill Park Arts Centre. Playing in a youth wind orchestra, 18-year-old Steve Spooner (later nicknamed 'Babyface') was spotted in the coffee shop following a rehearsal. "These four guys approached me," Spooner recalls, "and they said, 'We're forming a group, do you want to come and have an audition?'" With a pedigree in military and dance band music, he'd journeyed through the Glenn Miller/Syd Lawrence Big Band catalogue in a Birmingham school band, which received mid-Seventies regional TV coverage. A fan of Elvis Costello, he was intrigued by the offer from this aspiring group. "It was a big deal for me. I'd come from a background that had nothing to do with pop music. I'd played sax as a hobby. When it came along, it just took me away. It was incredibly important to me."

An audition was arranged at Rowland's house. Having read the advertisement, the more senior tenor saxophonist Jeff 'JB' Blythe arrived to audition on the same day. He'd been "kidnapped" from cult Sixties UK soul outfit Geno Washington & The Ram Jam Band, a position he had undertaken as a jobbing musician. He would later assume an influential role.

With the group ensconced in Rowland's front room, they undertook a formative rehearsal. Williams sat in on acoustic bass, with Saunders situated in the corner of the room on organ. While Archer strummed an acoustic guitar, percussionist Jay tapped out improvised rhythms on a stool. As the band developed makeshift tunes, Archer hummed the requisite horn lines with Blythe and Spooner working on brass arrangements during an hour-long session. "Then there was a lot of talking," Spooner recalls. "So off we went and both of us [Spooner and Blythe] said yes." They were now a septet. "None of us knew each other from Adam," he insists. "We came from varied backgrounds, I guess by and large working-class backgrounds, and most of us came from that sort of stock."

Archer's and Williams' Black Country, working-class roots aside, Saunders argues their much-vaunted proletarian image was largely a facade. "There was this anti-middle class thing, which was very much of the era, which made me think, 'Great, I'm about as middle class as you can get.'"

Toiling away at Rowland's brother's house in Harborne, they rehearsed as a brass trio during the late summer of 1978 following trumpeter Jeff Kent's recruitment. The night's events at one house party in the district later formed part of the lyrical basis of future 'lost' classic, 'Kevin Rowland's 13th Time'.[*]

After taking umbrage at police officers' warnings about the noise and the arrest of one of his friends, an intoxicated Rowland reached the police station to demand his friend's release. He received a physical reprimand for his earlier verbal protest and a night in the cells. Despite pleading innocent to violent behaviour, his self-conducted court defence was unsuccessful. Meanwhile, the group cast their net a little wider in search of a suitable trombonist. Perusing *Melody Maker*'s 'Musicians Wanted' section in mid-October, one bemusing advertisement piqued 22-year-old Jim Paterson's curiosity. "It said, 'Trumpet and trombone player wanted for new wave soul group.' And I didn't have a clue what that meant, to be honest!" he admitted to Radio Two. "I didn't really have the bottle to answer the ad, but I went to the pub at night and phoned up when I came home at about 11.30 pm," Paterson told Neil Warburton, editor of Dexys fanzine *Keep On Running*. "I spoke to Pete, Kevin's brother, who must have thought I was a total pillock. I think Pete or Kevin phoned back on Saturday and arranged for an audition the following weekend."

Travelling overnight from the village of Portsoy, near Banff, in north-east Scotland, Paterson arrived at Birmingham New Street Station at half-past six one late October morning. Rowland and Saunders met him off the train. Although fatigued and frozen, at their Northfield garage hideout, Paterson's mood soon altered dramatically. "As soon as the band started playing, that was it," he admitted. "I've never felt anything like it. My heart was pumping and I was totally unaware of my tiredness and coldness. It was the best musical experience I had had in my life."

A teenage Paterson had fallen for the garrulous charm of Alice Cooper's 'School's Out'. "When I saw them on *Top Of The Pops*," he told

---

[*] With his twelve previous convictions in mind, Rowland recounted in the liner notes to *Don't Stand Me Down* in 2002 that it was "nothing short of miraculous" he had never been imprisoned.

Warburton, "I was 16, at that age when you are discovering a lot of things that are probably going to change your life forever. I loved the theatrics of it and the rebellious side of it. It was the right song at the right time of my life." "One day," he informed his parents, "you'll see me on that show." This six-foot-plus skinhead Scotsman's innate musical ability was subsequently shrouded in the group's (particularly Rowland's) determination to be perceived as non-musicians.

While personality and attitude were considered important, Blythe's and Paterson's experience proved invaluable. "Jeff and Jim were really good players. They were eighth or ninth grade. Then me, Kevin and Pete Williams weren't so proficient," Archer told *Record Collector*. "There were varying degrees, but everyone accommodated everyone else."

"Kevin Archer was a hell of a lot better guitarist than he used to like to pretend," Saunders insists. "It wasn't fashionable to appear to know what you were doing then. Me, Pete [Williams] and Kevin Archer were of a similar ability. The horn section were the best trained musicians."

Initially envisaged as a standard four-piece brass section, Rowland and Archer had little idea how a frontline horn assault would operate. "All they knew was from records they'd heard at the time," Spooner insists, "and your standard brass section tended to be a trumpet playing the high melodies, trombone as the bass and the saxes droning in the middle."

Having played in the BBC Midlands Orchestra, Kent's unerringly accurate rendition of the *Grandstand* theme tune was a source of irritation to Rowland. "Jeff was a nice enough bloke, but he was far too sensible, he was like a regular pro type of musician," Saunders admits. "He was there until just before we started to do well."

The reasons for Kent's departure are unclear. Whether honouring previous commitments or through a dispute, he eventually flew the coop. His place in the group's history was all but erased by early 1980. "No one played it [trumpet] hard enough," Rowland told *Record Mirror*. "We auditioned over 18 players, but we just couldn't find anyone to play it brash enough."

Dexys decided on a distinctive, three-pronged brass attack. Having graduated in 1977, Paterson's music college education in Leeds brought a strong songwriting sensibility and jazz-orientated improvisation to proceedings. When Paterson soloed, people listened. "It was a new experience for me. I'd only done classical, jazz and brass band stuff before," he told *Keep On Running* in 1997. "It wasn't so much the music as the different lifestyle."

A professional, Blythe had also graduated through the music college system, while Spooner regarded himself as a dedicated, proficient musician.

"Kev Archer had got tunes in his head that he could whistle out," Spooner insists, "but we kind of developed them between ourselves. It was much more of a group effort, because it was such a new sound. Nobody else had ever heard it. Jeff would get the basic brass riff, and then scribble down on paper 'alto to do third-fifths' on that, and 'trombone can do this'. And the two of us would say, 'Maybe this would sound better?' 'Cos we would be playing almost in unison."

"A big part of the sound was Jeff Blythe's arrangements," Saunders emphasised. "And you got a lot of nastier-sounding jazz harmonies going on. Jeff knew his soul music, but he also brought this jazz knowledge to proceedings."

Blythe outlined the group's vital brass chemistry to *Hot Press*. "I play sax because it's the instrument I can put most feeling into – just one of those things, it clicks. And I've never met anyone who could put as much feeling into the trombone as Jimmy."

"Everyone had their place," Saunders confirms. "The last thing you needed was someone who wanted to be Charlie Parker. You needed someone like Steve to hold it down and move in the right way." Their sound later raised a few eyebrows in the studio.

"The tuning was part and parcel of the sound," says former rock journalist, mid-Seventies Olympic Runner pianist, falsetto vocalist and producer, Pete Wingfield. "It actually made it more reggae-fied. The trombone was way higher in the mix, which is a reggae thing. Not that they were playing reggae, but that treatment made it rootsy, and it sounded great. It gave it its own thing."

However the horns weren't given free rein. Moments of individual brilliance raised the temperature, but lengthy solos were prohibited as the group honed a much sought-after, unified sound, with the brass as the fulcrum of the group operation. "That sound was starting to get out," Spooner insisted. But there was certainly no temptation to become the in-house property of producers. "Kevin didn't need to say, 'You're not doing that.' We wouldn't have done it."

"The real attraction for me," future Dexys organist Mick Talbot told the BBC, "was that they were a seven or eight-piece soul band. They weren't a sort of four or five-piece band with session men twice their age playing horns."

"They were out on their own, really," Wingfield insists. "There wasn't a great swathe of bands doing the same thing. It was a reaction to all the guitar groups around. It was a post-punk thing." In mid-1980, Blythe would rave to journalists about youngsters having more interest in playing saxophone than becoming guitar heroes.

Chapter Three

UNABLE to relate to Birmingham's rock-centric, gig-going strong-hold, Rowland and Archer both confessed to a genuine love of disco and funk in the late Seventies. Aside from James Brown, choice of material included The Commodores, Rufus and assorted 'heavy funk'. The Sly Stone-influenced Ohio Players, New Jersey's proto-disco Kool & The Gang, the infectious funk of The Fat Back Band, earthy, wah-wah infused Hamilton Bohannon cuts and Barry White were later offered as the group's most inspiring funk/disco fodder.

"All of us liked disco music when it was powerful," Archer told *Hot Press* in 1980. "It's bland now, but I used to go to discos when I was 15 rather than rock concerts, and the music was great. Great *feel*, y'know? And that's what we're all about."

While Rowland had happily donned a suit at discos during punk, they thankfully passed up on covering the likes of 'YMCA' and 'Disco Duck'. Tiring of The Sex Pistols' nihilism, Public Image Ltd's 'Death Disco' found John Lydon's collective melding disco, dub and experimental guitar in reaction to punk's restrictive mandate. The duality of groups who had been excited by the rise of both disco and punk was not uncommon, Jim Irvin recalls. "The Sex Pistols had been singing about 'no future'. I think that was a prevalent attitude at the time with kids who had a feeling of futility, both politically and socially. Yet at the same time there were records like [Chic's June 1979 classic] 'Good Times'. That dual aspect was a pervasive thing."

A group offering more emotional content than a then obligatory 'fuck you' was a brave musical move. "I think Dexys represented that quite well in a way, because they were about that cross between a punky atti-tude and a soul influence." Establishing a horn-driven sound that boasted what Williams called "the aggression and the immediacy" of punk was crucial.

"We used to go on stage with pure aggression in the early days, right on the arse end of punk rock and everybody, the brass, was just full on," he reflected in 2003. When interviewed for *It Was Like This* Talbot claimed the group infused a "punk spirit" into their "hard-hitting soul revue".

"We played soul like a punk band," Spooner describes. "Soul punk does just sound an awful term, but there it is. The two Kev's had played in The Killjoys. Pete was well into punk. There was definitely a punk influence there."

"It had the raw emotion of soul, from the heart. It was self-expression, with Kevin testifying," fan and later *Melody Maker/Sounds* journalist Chris Roberts insists, "and yet it had the provocativeness of punk. It was stroppy and feisty and fiery. Dexys pointed towards a lot of classic black music. Kevin had the punk background, but he was also listening to a lot of soul vinyl."

Later proving to be a sonically ambitious musical unit, teenage fan Kevin Adams believed the group were focused on channelling punk's ferocity into a brass-driven soul tradition. Paolo Hewitt disagrees. "I think it was more of a Northern Soul thing. A big four-four beat, great horn riffs. You can't play punk with soul, there's no such thing as soul punk. You're looking to make people dance, to make them happy."

"I think even some of the group thought, 'This is a bit old-fashioned,' y'know. 'Haven't you heard the new Vibrators album?'" Archer told the *NME* in 2000. "When we started to play, one or two of them really tuned in."

"I can remember going on a record buying spree and buying 'Motor Bikin' by The Vibrators.* I didn't know about soul music until I went for my audition," Saunders recalls.

As Rowland admits, the group embarked on a voyage of rediscovery. Mining a rich seam of authentic works, they delved into the bountiful treasure chest of Sixties soul music. Records boasting vibrancy, honesty and innocence were sought for inspiration. The school of musical education included James Brown, Otis Redding, Aretha Franklin and Sam & Dave. "The Stax and Atlantic singles made sense to me," Irvin confirms. "I'd always liked things like The Isley Brothers and I detected something of that in there."

"[Dexys' sound] was more of a Stax sound with those horns. It was like Otis Redding records, that sort of warm sound, leading the melody," Hewitt insists.

"It was my kind of thing," Wingfield enthused. "I was a big fan, as they all were, of Stax and Atlantic stuff, and they were keeping the faith. It was a pleasure to hear."

Also, several Northern Soul and British R&B curios, including works from Johnny Johnson & The Bandwagon, UK R&B outfits Zoot Money

---

* Actually, 'Motor Bikin' was a Top 10 chart hit for Vibrators' RAK label mate Chris Spedding in 1975.

& The Big Roll Band, Geno Washington & The Ram Jam Band and Cliff Bennett & The Rebel Rousers were added for good measure. Archer assumed lead vocal duties on the latter's 1964 Top 10 UK single 'One Way Love'. The typically Americanised vocal phrasing of this British R&B cut was ripped up, while the original's fruity, squalling horn sound gave way to a clamorous brass pulse. "Often we'd talk about records and discuss which ones we'd do. Kevin would say, 'We should do this, like [Zoot Money's] 'Big Time Operator' or [The Bandwagon's] 'Breaking Down The Walls Of Heartache'," Saunders recalls. "I think it was songs that his brother knew that were suggested to him."

Cliff Nobles & Company's instrumental dance-craze 'The Horse' was tackled with barnstorming aplomb. Opening the group's sets, the 1968 US number two hit was a percussive-powered, horn-charged tirade, while their take on Aretha Franklin's version of Otis Redding's 'Respect' remained a live favourite throughout Dexys' career, including one of Rowland's fiery on-stage monologues dealing with soul power and self-respect. Among these interpretations came a 'definitive' reading of Sam & Dave's classic 1966 hit, 'Hold On, I'm Comin'. It's tough-edged percussion and swarthy sax momentum was frequently employed in a tumultuous finale. "It wasn't a well-known song when we were doing it," Saunders recounts. "There weren't soul bands around. People would say, 'Oh, I love that song you wrote called 'Hold On, I'm Comin'."

"Every time I'd tell people, I'd mention Sam and Dave, and they didn't know who it was, 'cos they were so into punk. It was confusing for them," Archer remembered in an *NME* interview.

The group later took inspiration from The Bar Kays' 1967 Atlantic cut, 'Soul Finger'. For Rowland, 'Seven Days Too Long' evoked memories of truant teenage capers. His first exposure to this Chuck Wood floor-filler had come in a Soho record store in 1968. "[It] was a Northern Soul classic. Everyone in the group had heard it so it was a natural choice for us to cover it," said Archer in the liner notes to the (2000) CD reissue of *Searching For The Young Soul Rebels*.

Zoot Money's 1966 single 'Big Time Operator' found a place in the group's set. "If you still haven't heard of Zoot Money, consider this an education," Rowland informed the audience on stage. Yet locating this source material proved expensive. Money's cult classic cost £15 from a record shop in 1978. The group would also scour Oxfam shops for Marvin Gaye records. "One of the first albums I had when I was a kid was a copy of an Atlantic sampler called *Black Soul Volume 3*, with things like Booker T's 'Green Onions' and Carla Thomas, one of the few places that you could get those singles all together at that time," Jim Irvin recalled.

"You couldn't just go to Woolworths and buy a soul compilation," Saunders confirms. "It was hard to get hold of them."

Throughout the Seventies, very little black American soul music surfaced on daytime radio. Playlists were rarely retrospective, the focus being on new records. Now regarded as standard fodder, Dexys took the radical step of covering scarce black soul archetypes. "Kevin was part of that tradition which started in the late Fifties, and early Sixties, of white guys who absolutely adored black music and wanted to reflect that within their own craft," Hewitt points out. "In all his music, when there is a black element to it, he is at his happiest."

Boasting a warm energetic force, Dexys shows were thrilling, demonstrative affairs. And they were fired by a burning preoccupation to communicate their own powerful brand of redemptive soul. As the musical message spread, the crowd were encouraged to feel the power. "There was a 'we're on a mission from God' feel," Saunders affirms. "The music comes from gospel, that's its roots. It makes you think about a higher plane, and you believe in it. You find yourself aspiring to something and wishing to inspire something, even though it's fairly nebulous."

Irvin compared the live experience to a "bunch of suburban Birmingham kids pretending they were Al Green."

"I'd like to see the charts filled with soul, loads of feeling everywhere," Rowland later exclaimed.

"You're talking about 18-, 20-year-olds, for whom the Sixties is something that they've heard about," Saunders adds. "Only certain people in Britain listened to that sort of music." Damascene conversions swiftly occurred for the group's youngest members.

"Instantly, that music inspired me," Spooner admitted. "I knew Kevin had loved it, Jeff certainly had a liking for it. But for most of us, it was fairly new music. I was 18. We were all kids. At that age you're into your own music, aren't you? You're exploring, but you haven't had the years to listen to the music that's around."

"The horn players loved it," Saunders concurs. "The soul thing for them was a way of being in something like a pop band, it's got that feeling." Billy Preston, Booker T & The MGs and old R&B artists like Jimmy McGriff were choice listening, as well as Ray Charles, a hero to Saunders' successor, Mick Talbot, who considered Brother Ray "one of the godfathers of soul music."

"It was a pretty new discovery, which I instantly fell in love with," Spooner unashamedly admits. "I'd heard these songs over the years, but sitting down and listening *hard*, it wasn't like hearing the brass section out front. It wasn't all sax solos and Commodores-type brass section."

"We learnt about the sparsity of soul music," said Saunders. "It's very disciplined music. The only person who lets go is the singer. Everything is geared towards discipline. We played to get the message over, and it made it very powerful."

Yet any assessment of Dexys' stance based strictly on the Atlantic/Sixties soul template would be wide of the mark. Talbot applauded the integrity and fierce individuality of their output. "It was very sort of sincere in its appreciation of American R&B, but it was its own thing," he told the BBC. "And it felt for real. It didn't feel like a sort of pastiche."

"That driving bass made it very distinctive," Saunders reiterates, "and the fact that Kevin is not trying to sing like a black American."

"We weren't trying to be authentic," said Rowland. "We were trying to get to the spirit." Undeniably real, their unique approach set them apart. "The important point is that it was radical to do what we did in 1978," Rowland told *Jack* in 2003. "We looked back to the Sixties and reinterpreted it. People thought we were a joke. We knew better."

Regardless of musical or personal background, dedication and discipline helped engineer a genuine group unity. The requisite attitude and empathy was crucial. "It was very strict. It was crucial at the time, because we had to get people believing in it," Archer informed Keith Cameron. "The idea was to keep all of us the same."

"It was pretty disciplined right from the start, but this wasn't Kevin Rowland deciding, 'I'm gonna discipline everybody,'" Spooner insists.

"The country was very different in those days. There was a greater sense of people being committed to causes," Saunders emphasised. He argues that their fraternal social bond wasn't as strong. "We did rehearsals and we'd go back home. We didn't really coalesce. We didn't go out drinking with each other because we didn't have any money, and we lived in different parts of Birmingham. We had these band nights out which usually ended up being a bit unfortunate. There wasn't a lot of fun."

"We all sat around and took the issue seriously," Spooner recalled. "We said, 'If we're gonna do it, let's do it properly.'" A strict nine-to-five rehearsal schedule was crucial. With some of the group on the dole, those in employment handed in their notice with immediate effect.

"It was fairly instinctive really. I just think that they worked hard. They did a lot of rehearsing," Talbot observed during *It Was Like This*. For the first six months, Dexys drilled themselves into an unbeatable unit, honing ideas in an industrious fashion. Whether contending with an irate neighbour at Rowland's brother's house in Harborne or a freezing cold Northfield garage, with only a tiny electric heater, Dexys' *modus operandi* was workmanlike.

"We met up, got in the garage," Spooner recalls, "and away we went."

With 'Tell Me When My Light Turns Green' swiftly introduced, the newly rechristened Killjoys track 'Definitely Not Down On The Farm' was part of the group's early live repertoire. (It was demoed in 1981 under the new title, 'Never Never'.) "That was one of the few songs we rejected," Spooner admits. "There was an initial batch of, perhaps, 15 songs and that was it. It wasn't like there were prolific songwriters there." Over a menacing post-punk bass run and watertight percussion, Archer's dramatic "never, never" refrain, set against alternately blaring, brooding brass, supported Rowland's unresolved attempts to assuage confusion. Its individualist sentiments later resurfaced on the 1981 track 'Liars A To E'.

"Seeds of ideas for songs were 'pre-group', if you like, from just talking about it. And within a week we were actually playing tunes," Spooner recalls. 'Hold On I'm Comin' was one of the earliest cover versions attempted. While rehearsing in Northfield with the group in "high spirits", the Rowland-credited 'Burn It Down' was also conceived.

"When Kevin first came up with this song," Archer later commented in the reissue liner notes for *Searching For The Young Soul Rebels*, "it felt good to play from the start." Its tight, rhythmic unity underwent meticulous development during the process of a wholehearted group endeavour. "Not one person, not Pete, not Jeff, came in and said, 'I've got this song, and this is it.' It was all just vague ideas which developed within the group." Outlining their songwriting process in mid-1980, it appeared a slow, thorough and incredibly selective procedure.

"We don't use any songs or any ideas that people come up with, we have to mull them over and live with them for a long time, see what's really gonna work," Blythe told Dermot Stokes. "It's one of the reasons we don't write a great deal of songs."

"We've got to think it's great before we show it to the rest," Rowland insisted.

Archer recalled their approach as "a rigorous and painstakingly hard process. Timing and assertiveness were high on the list of priorities," he outlined in 2000.

"Rehearsals meant lots of cigarettes to keep warm. It was hard work, but it was great," Saunders reflects. "They were fun enough to go to. We were working on new songs, working on arrangements. It was very straightforward, and it was very co-operative." A very definite, organic process unfolded.

"Imagine a few months of that; you become this *thing*," says Spooner. "Kevin had his own agenda and was the leader of the band, but it was a group effort."

"We were so insular and we worked so hard. We locked ourselves in garages and we'd squat in certain places in those days, and all we'd got was each other," Williams recalled in 2003. "All my other friends had girl-friends and were kind of getting cars, and I'd be hanging around with a bunch of blokes who were a bit older than me, and working on music. And that kind of engendered a belief in ourselves."

Running off leads and ripping into electricity supplies, abandoned warehouses, derelict squats and disused buildings (including a listed Weights and Measures building) were later sequestered. "We got moved on three times from three different places by the police," Archer told *Melody Maker* in 1980. "They knew it was us every time, but we used to give them different group names and they'd stand there bewildered saying, 'I'm sure it was you we saw the other day.' It was great.' "

With their formative musical forays under way, a brainstorming session was undertaken to christen the collective. Each member was asked for a handful of suggestions before meeting one evening in a Birmingham wine bar. No one was particularly enamoured with what they heard. After Rowland had already introduced 'dexys' to the fray (in reference to a favourite mod/Northern soul scene pep pill, Dexedrine), John Jay then purportedly offered the idea of 'midnight runner'. While some of the group had never heard of Dexedrine, Rowland insisted that they had simply settled on a strong sounding name. It later made for fascinating viewing on *Tiswas*. Host Sally James questioned Rowland on the group's unusual moniker one summer Saturday in 1980. "Do you know what dexys are?" he deadpanned.

"Well . . . yes," James replied.

"Well then . . ." Rowland retorted.

Resolute in their belief that there was no competition, Dexys later adopted what Rowland coined a "siege mentality" towards their contem-poraries, distancing themselves from any particular musical clique. "We just carved our own way," Rowland ventured to *Hot Press'* Dermot Stokes in July 1980. "We wanted to go out on a limb because we knew the whole scene in England was so incestuous, so stylised. There's so many rules, unwritten rules you have to obey." A particular antipathy was directed towards the supposedly middle-class outfits who constituted Birmingham's student-led, artistic Moseley scene (later described as the city's "wannabe Greenwich Village"). "There was a scene of groups centred round Moseley and none of us lived there except for our keyboard player Pete Saunders, who knew and associated with those types," Rowland recalled to True in 2000.

"There was a band called Fashion, who were the first band from

Birmingham to get anywhere at all. And down the road, UB40 were just getting going," Saunders recounts. "They were far more working class than Dexys were, they were really nice guys. And there were The Au Pairs, and a group called Rudy & The Rationals, who were to become The Beat. There was a lot going on."

Dexys briefly employed the services of a drummer whose girlfriend played in The Au Pairs. The association was swiftly curtailed following a fracas at a Birmingham party celebrating the release of The Au Pairs' debut single. Rowland eventually grew to regret this exclusionist strategy. "Now, I feel I missed out on an awful lot, because they were my peers – someone I could relate to. And because I didn't mix with them, I ended up alone," he informed Everett True. "It was a strength and a weakness."

"I guess we believed that we were gonna be the best band in Birmingham," Williams stated in 2003, "and then when we started playing London, we wouldn't take any shit off anybody, and we did supports and the 2-Tone [November/December 1979] tour and we just wanted to blow the other bands out of the water really. Just be as direct and play as honestly and as hard as we could."

"No one liked us. Even when we played live in Birmingham," Saunders emphasises. "It wasn't the sort of band that people got behind and had a following. I think that bonded us, 'No one liked us, everyone hates us.' Kevin helped reinforce that spirit of alienation. He couldn't really understand the idea of fraternisation with other musicians."

"We just seem to annoy a lot of people," Paterson noted in 1980. "I think it may be because we take the music seriously when they expect us to be jumping up and down and having a laugh." He later told Neil Warburton: "It did feel like being on some sort of crusade, being part of something new and refreshing and exciting, being part of a gang of people that actually meant something."

"It was more than a band. A band would not be a word to describe it adequately," Blythe told the BBC. "A tribe would be a better word, a small tribe." And while Rowland has maintained that former Clash manager Bernie Rhodes later encouraged Dexys to foster a gang mentality for press purposes, that ethic was already in place.

"We weren't just a bunch of thugs," Archer informed True, "we had intelligence and we came through all that. They saw we weren't just yobs or whatever. People saw us as a real group."

And one that evolved into a tight union, as Spooner states. "We were spending a hell of a lot of time together, influencing each other within a short space of time. Before we'd even played a gig, we were a solid unit."

Chapter Four

FOLLOWING four months' worth of rehearsals and after a week spent undertaking a nine-man interior paint job on a run-down house in Wolverhampton, Dexys Midnight Runners played their first show as a nine-piece group at Dudley pub, The Hen & Chickens in December 1978. Rowland remembered a distinct sense of 'anti-climax' in 1999. "We all thought it was going to be amazing. I think the audience was baffled."

Following the gig, the group traversed icy conditions to get back home. "I remember I wore mirror shades and I realised that I couldn't see anything," Saunders laughs. "And I remember 'Ain't No Stoppin' Us Now' on the jukebox, which I liked. Having gotten into soul because of Dexys, I was getting more and more into disco. I was part of this whole non-rock world of groovy music, which I'd fallen completely in love with."

A witness to their early live shows in various Birmingham pubs in early 1979, fan Kevin Adams was suitably drawn to their musical commitment and intensity. "I remember the first night I saw Dexys play live, they just blew me away," he admitted to journalist Ted Kessler. "When they started to play, the music had so much energy – but with a brass section!"

"It wasn't like we were doing a gig every week," Saunders ruminated. "There wasn't that much going on. But he [Rowland] knew he had to get us into a state where we were good enough to play in front of the right sort of people. And we did loads of hopeless gigs. We never got any money for the gigs we did in Dexys. It was quite a revelation to have done small gigs with other bands later and got paid."

The paint job stint subsequently funded Dexys' first point of entry into the studio. Their earliest demos were recorded at Outlaw, a badly whitewashed, derelict building situated in a dubious road in Birmingham's Five Ways district. Three original compositions were committed to tape in December, including 'Tell Me When My Light Turns Green' and 'Don't Come Any Closer', later rechristened as 'I'm Just Looking'. Even at such a formative stage, both songs boasted finalised lyrics. More compact and sprightly in comparison to its album counterpart, Jeff Kent's clarion-like trumpet headed a three-minute rendition of 'Tell Me'. Evincing an early emphasis on rhythm and percussion, the characteristic brass was found forcing its way to the front. Galvanised by some urgent bass and perfunctory keyboard work, the defining power of Rowland and Archer's stylised vocals were still in an intriguing state of development.

'Don't Come Any Closer' suggested some of the dramatic nuances and dark inflections that later surfaced on their debut single. Given the earliest possible insight into the confrontational, rather than whispered, introduction, this was an impressive Rowland vocal performance. Despite its unusually bright horn sound, some superfluous, slightly heavy-handed drumming hampered the track. The atmospheric power of Saunders' haunting, smoked-coal organ sound was yet to come to fruition.

The session included another of Dexys' earliest compositions, the unreleased original 'It's Up To You' on which Archer undertook lead vocals. With largely indecipherable lyrics centring on a resolve to grab the initiative and self-improvement, it was an oddly fussy marriage of over-employed snapshot drum-rolls and sassy, relentless horns with an off-kilter trombone solo. Failing to pass quality control, this was one Dexys proto-type that wasn't pursued further.

In the early process of honing arrangements and refining a com-plementary sound, their three-track demo was a promising effort. Instantly familiar, the musical formula appeared to be falling into place. Demo tapes were then hawked around London's record companies as most of the group undertook their first visit to the heartland of the industry. Cherished by almost all concerned as a move born out of necessity and no little hard-ship, Dexys' train-bunking excursions now became the stuff of legend. One of their later touring accomplices recalled the austerity of life on the road. "It seems odd now, because rock music has returned to excess, but in the early Eighties it was different," Specials maestro Jerry Dammers told *Mojo* in 2001. "I remember Bad Manners staying in a hotel where the carpet in the lobby was made out of remnants. I got a train once with Dexys Midnight Runners and they all had to bunk the fare."

"There was no money, we were all signing on the dole," Saunders recalled. "But we had our very first rehearsal at Kevin's house that he had a mortgage on, which he *owned*. And we're only young lads. There's always a purity in poverty. If you haven't got anything, it's very easy to stay pure and good. It was a time when people had very few distractions and we were very poor. And it was like we were willing to sacrifice everything for this thing. We *really* did."

In typically precision-tooled fashion, Dexys' fare-dodging tactics soon improved as their escapades gathered steam. Splitting in half, they would operate with military precision. Due to the dilapidated state of British Rail services, public toilets were frequently rendered unusable. One of the entourage proceeded to remove an 'out of order' sticker for later use.

With calculated timing, one group of four suspects positioned themselves around the last seat in the carriage, next to the compartment doors as the ticket inspector approached. Before he'd caught sight of them, three of the group would swiftly disappear from view. Armed with screwdrivers, they'd undo a toilet door handle, plaster an 'out of order' notice on the door, secrete themselves silently inside the cubicle and wait for the train guard to pass. The other member would offer to hand the inspector his ticket before barging past the guard to join his cohorts.

Dexys continued to travel within their means. Once press coverage was initiated, they weren't averse to playing up to their image. "If I'm honest, I think we did it once or twice around the time of 'Geno'," Spooner admits. "But it was something we had to do in the early days. It was essential and it was great."

Williams told Carrie Shearer that the excitement surrounding the group has been sorely underplayed. "One of the things that never really comes across in anything I've seen about Dexys Midnight Runners is the sheer fun that we had in the early days. For me, at 18 when I joined, it was all about doing stuff together."

Publicity photographs and subsequent videos gave an accurate depiction of life as a Midnight Runner, often found hopping train station ticket barriers with guards in hot pursuit. For those unfortunate enough to get caught, transport police interrogation frequently ensued. A sense of inevitability coalesced around the group. "There was a feeling that nothing really was going to stand in our way," Williams told the BBC. "Distance was no object. None of us owned a car or anything like that, and we were going up and down to London, chasing gigs or chasing record companies, and we used to bunk the trains everywhere." A nervous, adrenalised excitement accompanied them en route to the capital.

Dexys' first full-length *Melody Maker* feature in April 1980 illustrated their travelling habits in full detail aboard their first nationwide headlining tour. "I got on this train, and I found them sitting in this carriage," Paolo Hewitt recalls, en route to Shrewsbury. "They were all sitting there and I said, 'Hi, I'm Paolo, I'm from the *Melody Maker*.' They wouldn't talk to me on the train. I tried talking to Kevin, but I just ended up getting my book out and read it until we got there. We got off the train, I got a ticket and I said, 'Look, there's the exit over there.' And they said, 'Keep walking, keep walking,' and they were looking for the lift. And they couldn't find it so they just jumped over the wall, and I was left standing there!"

Hewitt filed what was deemed a misrepresentative account of the group and its ingenious strategy. "You made us look like villains," he was told. In their own inimitable fashion, cost-cutting advertising methods were also employed, Williams recalls, in promoting forthcoming home town gigs. His artistic handiwork responsible for one of their earliest flyers, the lanky Paterson could frequently be found splattered in strong, Solvite adhesive as group members clambered on his shoulders, gamely pasting posters upon the ceilings of the city centre's underpasses.

Mischievously booked to gig alongside a defunct Killjoys on a pre-Christmas 1978 city club bill, Dexys had also been scheduled to play both Barbarella's and Aston University shows the following March. With the latter venue subsequently used as a Dexys rehearsal space, their show was subject to a last-minute cancellation. The group staged a sit-in, despite threats of eviction from the rugby team. A money-raising venture at this seat of learning paid dividends as the light-fingered mob roamed the campus corridors, Rowland told Everett True. "They had these language classes where you get these headphones, with one ear-piece and microphone at the front. We went in and picked up as many as we could, came out with about 30."

"People did sometimes comment on the rigidity, but there was also quite a lot of fun as well," Rowland admitted to the BBC of their shop-lifting expeditions. "Some of the people had never done that before in their lives, whereas I was more of an expert at it!"

"You couldn't just go into a shop without something being stolen. Everything was an incident," Saunders insists, later becoming compulsive in his shoplifting habits. "It wasn't like we all did it. I felt I'd really let myself down if I walked out without something. It got so stupid." Purloining vital supplies, eating their way around a supermarket or absent-mindedly fleeing restaurants without paying was not uncommon. Invoices were often sent to the management offices. The group were later introduced to the middle-class Birmingham Arts Centre, who offered to record demo tapes free of charge in a local community initiative. Dexys responded to their kindness by stealing a large tape recorder, Rowland admitted.

The group later had an idea for a visual project. "We wanted to do a backdrop for a sky at night with stars in it . . . So they helped us paint it, I suppose they were trying to be helpful really. I suppose I was a little bit resentful about not knowing about this place. We had anger about that, and we'd nick stuff."

"We used to nick the cake!" Rowland also told True. "Funny thing was, these were all very posh, middle-class people wearing dungarees and vegetarians and stuff like that, in this vegetarian café," recalling Williams' attempt to secure a job there.

Another infrequent money-making venture involved various group members being paid as humpers, unloading sound equipment from a van into Birmingham's Barbarella's club and (theoretically) back again after a gig. Often bidding farewell to the roadie before stashing their fresh cache of sound equipment somewhere discreet, they'd sell it on the following day to unsuspecting music shop proprietors. A guitar acquired from the Black Country front man of one household Seventies British glam-rock act was sold on across the Channel as Dexys undertook their bunking feat *par excellence*. Approached after a home town show by one French promoter to play a summer jazz festival, the group succeeded in making a return journey from New Street Station to the small town of Melun-sur-Seine, 20 miles south of Paris, for under £20 by boat and rail. Bunking across the capital via Le Metro, they then jumped the overland train.

"It was like playing in a town square, playing this little festival. All we got to eat were chips," Saunders laughed. With Smethwick-based drummer Trevor 'Tricky' Hadley in tow, Dexys were housed and fed. "It was never much fun. We were all very poor and extremely frustrated," Saunders insists. "Most bands I've been in, usually you get sex along the way. In Dexys, there was nothing. There was something very unsexy about us."

At least the money-making scheme that funded their venture was a triumph. "We had to bunk down to London, and we'd got our instruments with us, no PA systems, and we just literally went over there and we busked outside the tubes," Spooner recounts. Passers-by stared in mild bemusement as the group showcased their modest repertoire, making a handsome profit from their impromptu set.

"They're used to seeing someone with a guitar, and there's eight of us banging things and blowing things. That's where the 20 quid came from. We'd raised the ferry money, got over there and bunked the French trains." The group figured that it sure beat travelling on British Rail. "Getting to places and not paying," Williams recalled on *It Was Like This*. "The cheek of us was immense."

Appropriately, taped announcements between songs at their earliest dates (including one school disco) took the form of train noises and a station tannoy delivering news on departing and arriving songs. "The band waiting on this platform is Dexys Midnight Runners," audiences were informed. When the group inducted 'Geno' into the set, a tape of chanting crowd noise preceded the song. Apart from playing other one-offs like a Sheffield teachers' training college, Dexys' live appearances were sporadic. After becoming regulars at Birmingham's Cedar Club Ballroom, they established a Friday night residency at Mr Sams in Needless Alley, off

New Street in the middle of town. An advertisement for a mid-May Birmingham Imperial Hotel show in 1979 bore a black-and-white illustration of a sax-wielding Blythe, the slogan 'Straight To Your Heart' emblazoned across the xeroxed sheet. Dexys had "built up a buzz," according to Rowland. "People were coming and it was good."

Meanwhile, a growing retinue of 'mod' kids populated regular Saturday lunchtime shows at the Midland Hotel. "At some of those early gigs we did, most of the people didn't know what the fuck we were doing there, or said, 'Where is the guitarist?' They weren't very successful," Saunders admits. "It wasn't like watching a soul covers band that was quite dancey. It wasn't until the mod thing started happening that it began to change."

Without unanimous group approval, Dexys had assumed a wild, colourfully improvised 'underground' look. Various elements of The Killjoys' final incarnation had informed their image, one that Rowland later considered a precursor to the flamboyant styling at the visual vanguard of much of early Eighties' pop. "They'd got through the punk thing," Hewitt maintains, "and he'd thought, 'There's gonna be a reaction to this, people are gonna want to look good.'"

A Nottingham Trent fashion student, who also made clothing purchases on the group's behalf, was commissioned to devise something suitable under Rowland's auspices. His Vidal Sassoon-honed hairdressing skills were also put to good use. "Kevin used to experiment with us quite gladly, and we were quite happy to have outlandish haircuts," Williams admitted in 2003. The focus was firmly on an eclectic blend of extreme, individual styles.

"There were various personalities in the band and the look kind of reflected people's characters," Williams recalls. He adopted a "kind of Babe Ruth look," garbed in baseball cap, braces, dickie bow, and white shirt. Among the ranks were a white-coated lab technician, a space cadet, and a Cossack. Saunders recalled Rowland buying him a fencing shirt. While Spooner and Paterson dressed as relatively straight-edged Sixties mods, be-jodhpured sax player Blythe wore an asymmetric haircut (later reminiscent of The Human League's Phil Oakey), resembling an ocean-liner waiter in white jacket, 'El Presidente' sash and shades. A satin-pantalooned, cropped-haired Archer wore long strands of hair, boxing boots and short, tight-fitting jackets.

As for Rowland . . . "I had my hair like Stevie Wonder on *Talking Book* on the top," he told *Mojo*, "like a veil criss-cross across my face and wild at the back."

He could also be found in eye-catching pink satin-tailed regalia, with greased quiff and make-up. "It was bad taste, by even New Romantic standards," Saunders laughed. "Kevin was really enthusiastic about it. He had a way of making you think that this is going to get us somewhere. As much as Kev spouts on about that, if you read in between his words, he'd love to claim credit for the whole New Romantic look."

Spooner feels it is an undeserved plaudit. "We're talking about 1979 Birmingham here, all sorts of people were walking about dressing up."

Rowland told *Sounds* the following January that they attracted a mixed sex crowd of local Romantics to their shows, sporting a garish choice of attire. "One of the first big gigs we did [headlining at Birmingham's Romulus with Joy Division in August], Boy George turned up, dressed up to the nines," Spooner recounts. "He looked like Boy George, but with the make-up slapped on. There were people in all sorts of fluttery clothes in those days."

Initially mesmerised by the confrontational image as much as their sound, Kevin Adams told Ted Kessler, "They were certainly dressed very strangely for the time in baggy satin trousers with boxing boots while everybody else seemed to be wearing tight fitting jeans with leather jackets."

The high wire, all-frills act played legendary Liverpool club Eric's in the summer of 1979, marking organist Mick Talbot's first encounter with the group. Along with his brother, Talbot was part of the mod-derived Merton Parkas. Dexys offered support that night. As Talbot watched them soundcheck, the music left an indelible mark. "Being a soul fan, [it was] the fact that they had a three-piece horn section. Of that time, in the late Seventies, a lot of pop or new-wave bands would kind of use a horn section as a production gimmick on one single, and they'd be geezers with greying beards shunted away in the background. It really impressed me that there were eight people on stage and they were all sort of late teens, or early 20-year-olds and there was a real collective gang thing about it. It wasn't just session players tacked on the end, and it had a real nice spirit to it."

Among a growing home town brigade of bewildered admirers drawn to this bizarre live experience were The Specials. A thrilling multi-racial ska/reggae collective headed by Jerry Dammers, they boasted a frenetic, punk-like energy that infused their vibrant material. Having been introduced to former Clash manager Bernie Rhodes, Dexys had watched Dammers' group and enjoyed the experience. Their exposure to The Specials was crucial. "It was music that was not a million miles away from what we were doing, and people were into it," says Saunders. "We saw that they knew how to perform. When we started watching The Specials, we realised we might have a chance."

Chapter Five

FORMERLY The Coventry Automatics, The Special AKA's concept was born on The Clash's 'Out On Parole' tour in the summer of 1978. Jerry Dammers secured his group a support slot following a meeting with Bernie Rhodes, who was subsequently asked to oversee their affairs. Broadening his managerial scope, Rhodes' pool of artists included Vic Godard of Subway Sect and soul outfit The Black Arabs. While encouraging Dammers' men to devise a complimentary look for their sound, their leader brushed off suggestions that Rhodes had masterminded the 2-Tone rude boy image. Rhodes would attempt something of a punkier persuasion with Dexys the following spring. "He tried to get Jeff Blythe to wear an *Anarchist Cookbook* T-shirt with a photo of Jerry Lee Lewis and directions of how to make a bomb," Rowland told Johnny Rogan.

The Specials were packed off to Paris for their rites of passage after Rhodes left them stranded at Dover with their equipment and a map. They hitched from Calais before roaming the capital's boulevards, in search of their designated venue. Encountering genuine gangsters in the hotel lobby threatening to steal their equipment, the incident was enshrined on their aptly titled debut single, 'Gangsters', featuring a humorous sideswipe at Rhodes' self-acknowledged tendency towards 'complete control'. Marking the end of his short-lived tenure, the group returned to Coventry to fuse their sound and vision. Having been established as an ambitious independent operation, the 2-Tone label's overground ascent was initiated once 'Gangsters' went into the Top 10 in July '79. Dammers had already hankered after Dexys' unified brass sound before The Specials recorded their tight, adrenalised eponymous debut LP at London's TW studios in June, with producer and champion Elvis Costello. (He'd later vote 'Dance Stance' one of his favourite releases of 1980.)

"We were using brass before The Specials and when they saw us they asked if they could borrow ours," Rowland insisted.

"We didn't let them. We wouldn't have done that, no fucking way," Spooner argued. "We'd have said no way ourselves. We thought we were *it*." Dammers then visited Dexys in Birmingham, determined to capture their signature and get them on tour. Rowland dismissed the label as a good time, revival-driven bandwagon that briefly included Madness alongside The Beat, The Bodysnatchers and The Selecter in its throng.

"To most people turning down The Specials' offer was madness," Rowland informed *Record Mirror* in early 1980. "I thought a lot about it, but I just knew it wasn't right."

Dexys also vetoed the idea of wearing tonic suits to enrapture the crowd. "Whereas before there were bemused punk and rock fans, the fact that there was a mod thing happening, suddenly, the idea of a band with a horn section meant people started turning up in suits," Saunders recalls. "Jerry Dammers and [Specials frontman] Terry Hall were two of the most decent people you've ever had an involvement with in the music industry. The lengths they went to to get us on that 2-Tone tour. They tried so hard . . ." The ensuing dialogue during the summer ran along similar lines to this:

> The Specials: "*We want you to be on the hippest record label in the country at the moment.*"
> Dexys: "*We don't want to be on another band's record label.*"
> With talk of expenses being paid, the hottest band in the country attempted another ploy: "*You are a really fantastic band. Come on the tour.*"
> "*No.*"
> The Specials made a further proposition: "*How about you lend us your horn section and you go on the tour for nothing?*"
> "*No.*"
> And another . . . "*How about we put your record out and you come on tour?*"
> "*No.*"
> "*Alright. What if you just come on tour, and we'll pay you?*"
> "*Okay.*"

"It was just part and parcel of that attitude, 'We're the best and everybody else is shit,'" Spooner asserted. "It was a young, cocky attitude. Of course, when you look back, The Specials were one of the best groups the UK has ever seen."

Continuing to venture into small club and pub gigs, including supporting Toyah Wilcox, Dexys made their London debut at The Windsor Castle on Harrow Road. Their second, unforgettable foray onto the capital's gig circuit came at the reopened Camden Electric Ballroom, north London, on July 21. However, John Jay had decided to leave. "He was a bit jittery sometimes," Saunders remembers of the ex-Army drummer, "and I think he'd seen some things he shouldn't have seen."

By his own admission, guilty of sowing the "seeds of disloyalty", Saunders had decided to join a social club group relocating to Abu Dhabi to play hotel lounges. He'd been offered good money for shows in the North East in the interim, unaware that Rhodes had secured a slot at the Ballroom. "I thought, 'Fuck, I've gotta do it. I can't miss out, they're gonna break.' And so I went back, got in the van and John Jay was there, sat in the back of this transit van. He said, 'I didn't want to come!' He was made an offer he couldn't refuse." Initially advertised as a 2-Tone evening featuring The Selecter, Madness and The Specials, Dexys (who later took great delight in gaining entry to Camden's Music Machine as Specials impersonators), took the stage at a Rough Trade showcase under the guise of Subway Sect, despite not having been booked to play.

With Vic Godard's group withdrawn from the event, Rhodes encouraged Dexys, still without a record deal, to play. The stage was set. The dread-filled atmosphere, partly relieved as the group opened proceedings with their voluble brass assault, perturbed one reviewer. Yet *Sounds* were clearly impressed with Rhodes' "latest demons". "Halfway through the gig," Saunders recounts, "someone from Birmingham said, 'I know you, you're Dexys Midnight Runners.' They'd recognised the painting on the front of my organ." Rhodes was called to reassure Rough Trade that he was promoting another band in Subway Sect's absence. Dexys were well received. "People had come to see Kleenex and The Raincoats. We could play in time, and we had tunes."

Appearing on stage to announce that Dexys' half-hour show time was finished, the stage manager was unceremoniously kicked off. The music went flat. The PA system was switched off. Rowland then urged the horn players and drummer to keep going. After Rhodes got the PA switched back on, the group played out an encore before John Jay's drum kit was chucked off the stage. The sparks had certainly flown. A home town Romulus gig on August 8, supported by Joy Division, was an audacious piece of opportunism on the promoter's behalf, given the contrast between the Runners and singer Ian Curtis and co. Rowland later described the polarity between the bands as "worlds apart".

"They were very much a fledgling group at the time, they hadn't done much," Spooner recalls. "And they had come down from Manchester to support us. There wouldn't have been any friendly chat because they were just the support group." Although impressed by Dexys' *joie de vivre* and applauding their urge to develop an identity, reviewer Martin Culverwell, noting their debt to Roxy Music, didn't rate Dexys' chances of survival very highly.

A young, reggae-fied UB40, who as a middle-class Moseley band appeared to typify most of what Dexys stood against, also supported them on a handful of summer Romulus bills. While Rowland's voice and a disciplined brass section caught *Sounds'* ear, they feared Dexys had, rather perilously, tied their fate to the ensuing mod revival on a transitory wave of Sixties nostalgia. Dexys' desire to avoid becoming stereotyped and shunning 2-Tone's advances were also acknowledged. "It [joining 2-Tone] could destroy us, so it seemed the natural thing to wait a bit longer for another deal," Rowland reasoned in 1980 as the group's six-month pursuit of a recording deal came to an end.

A distribution deal was struck during the summer with Bernie Rhodes' Oddball Records company. Credited under the alias of Foote & Mouth, the group recorded their debut single at Chalk Farm studios in Camden Town with Rhodes and engineer, Mickey Foote. At Rhodes' behest, the pyrrhic spirit of the song's original title, 'Burn It Down', was traded for 'Dance Stance', encapsulating something of the burgeoning 2-Tone's energetic, agenda-setting fervour. "Bernie had cooked up a recording deal for us and we came down to London in the summer, and recorded at a studio next door to the Monarch," Saunders recalls. "We didn't know what was going to happen. We heard it was coming out on Oddball, and then we heard that dreadful mix, and we couldn't believe how bad the mix was." 'Dance Stance' and its B-side 'I'm Just Looking' were later licensed to EMI.

Having overseen the early Killjoys' career, used car salesman and promoter Dave Corke assumed the mantle as Dexys' first manager, with Rowland attracted to his Arthur Daley-like persona. "Dave Corke knew Bernie Rhodes, he'd had some dealings with him, and he was a promoter around town before the group formed," Spooner recalls.

"Dave's involvement wasn't that early on," Saunders corrects. "There was one gig in Derby where he came up with this ludicrous flat-bed truck. He seemed to specialise in second-hand East German vehicles. Kevin would be driving to a gig in a Wartburg or Muscovite car that didn't really go!" Corke's association with Rhodes stretched back to the controversy-laden 1976 'Anarchy In The UK' punk tour. As Dexys garnered their very earliest press attention, Rhodes gradually assumed greater managerial duties from Corke, who still remained in the frame.

"We'd got to the stage," says Spooner, "where things were starting to kick off, and we decided that Dave wasn't quite up to the size of it. And then Bernie comes in."

"We thought it would be a good idea to get involved with him," Rowland informed the *NME* in 1980, telling Johnny Rogan two decades later that Rhodes' main coup was securing the EMI deal.

Telling the *NME* that they had signed for a £10,000 advance, Rowland insisted, perhaps tongue-in-cheek, that the company's non-image had been crucial in their decision. But with EMI adamant about seeing evidence of a subsequent spending plan, Rowland soon understood the financial conundrum that a poor deal presented to the group. "I think Kevin had a sneaky admiration for Bernie," Paolo Hewitt insists. "I don't know what happened with Bernie Rhodes. I think it was like meeting like. I think Kevin was totally tapped into that thing anyway."

"There's a lot of good in him [Rhodes]. He's a very creative man," Rowland admitted in 1980. "We wouldn't slag him off like other bands have."

Partly through his work on The Clash's recent sprawling celluloid exploit *Rude Boy* (1980), director Jack Hazan struck up a relationship with Rowland, cemented in 1985 with Hazan's undertaking of Dexys' three magnificent promotional films. Alongside record artwork, essays and promotional advertisements, they were vital outlets for Dexys' non-musical communiqués. "Kevin came to me out of the blue because I'd done *Rude Boy* with The Clash," Hazan told Daryl Easlea in *Record Collector*.* "Bernie Rhodes had been the manager of The Clash and then took over Kevin's career. I started talking to him about Bernie and how important it was to get the right attitude and design into promos."

"I could see Kevin having heard things in the past as a Clash fan and been influenced by all that," Spooner concludes.

Yet considering his brief tenure and Dexys' determined, self-sufficient outlook, Rhodes' impact should not be overstated. "He certainly had no influence over the music," Spooner asserts. "He didn't say you should go in this direction or that direction. I always thought that 'character' was the word. I think he was just looking for the next band to manage, and the association didn't last long, probably three or four months." It wasn't as though Dexys had suddenly happened once Rhodes arrived on the scene.

"The biggest thing that happened was us going on The Specials tour, almost despite having an involvement with him," Saunders suggests. "You can imagine what Jerry Dammers must have thought. They'd just put out 'Gangsters', inspired by Bernie Rhodes. Jerry was the one who made it happen, not Bernie."

* Unpublished extract from Daryl Easlea interview 'Don't Let Me Be Misunderstood' (full version available on rocksbackpages.com website). Original article published in *Record Collector*, 2002.

In similar fashion to The Specials, a hungry and poverty-stricken Dexys had relocated to London, also making use of Rhodes' Rehearsals space in Camden. With most of the group signing on in Birmingham, they briefly made Rehearsals their HQ. Conditions were spartan. "We moved ourselves down for a few weeks or so. I can remember we slept in there," Spooner recalls with a shudder. "It was a little rehearsal studio in an old warehouse, full of all sorts of shit. We made our bedding out of boxes of old Clash combat trousers, all ready to be sold on to the shops."

"At one stage, they used to make bondage trousers there. We found all these bits of clothes and buckles," Saunders recalls. "So you suddenly realise that this whole punk thing had been manufactured here." Old demo tapes of Joe Strummer's pre-Clash outfit, The 101'ers, were also unearthed. Mickey Foote employed Paterson's non-musical expertise on one occasion in laying fibreglass insulation on some roof space. The trombonist ended up covered in cuts. Rhodes' next move was to bring in new drummer, Subway Sect's Bobby 'Junior' Ward, following Jay's departure. The taut, Bethnal Green-based percussionist was likened to an East End, Ray Winstone-esque character. His drum stool incumbency lasted for around four months, but his part in the group's story was preserved on their debut single.

With The Specials busy making chart headway, Dexys agreed to support them at a Factory club show in Manchester. An almost calamitous decision, their foray onto the Hulme stage proved oddly pivotal. Experiencing a hostile encounter of the closest kind with the skinhead constituency in the Manchester audience, Williams recalled the decidedly unwelcoming committee of a "sea of boneheads" storming their dressing room.

"When the first group started we used to get all these Madness and Specials fans and they'd be there Seig Heil-ing and shouting for 'Geno', and it was so fuckin' useless, I'd just end up arguing with them," Rowland recalled.

Taking one look at the group, they judged Dexys to be fair game. "They came into the dressing room and tried to smash the washbasin with a bottle," Saunders recounts. "And then the bloke tried it again, and he's left with no glass. It's like a military situation, where loss of face by the commander can actually turn it from being really dangerous to not feeling quite so scared any more."

Aware of the animosity they faced, Dexys discussed the implications involved in tying their colours to the mast of 2-Tone's nationwide tour in the early winter of 1979. "We knew we couldn't do the tour in those outfits," Rowland said. The velvet, the pantaloons, the jodhpurs *et al* were, to most of the group's relief, swiftly dispensed with – a 'compromise' Rowland now regrets. "It had been quite an identity for us, and we did have this self-belief that we would come through," he later told Jim Irvin. "I often wonder if we'd held out what would have happened to us when the New Romantics came along."

Chapter Six

DENYING any sartorial statement of his own, Rowland insists it was Paterson's appearance in a freezing rehearsal room, wearing a polo neck and wool hat that provided the catalyst for Dexys' transformation from colourful individualists to austere uniformity. Others claim that the image was actually Rhodes' idea. Various cinematic associations were made, including the rugged outlook of Michael Cimino's *The Deer Hunter* and, significantly, the American stevedore chic of the New Jersey docks, the setting for Elia Kazan's Oscar-winning 1954 masterpiece, *On The Waterfront.* "They'd have these kind of checked, lumberjack-style jackets on and polo-necks and woolly hats on," Rowland told the BBC. "I'd always thought they looked good. That's what it was really."

"As soon as I saw it, I remember having a chat with Kevin about *On The Waterfront*, that's what it made me think about," Mick Talbot recalled on *It Was Like This* in 2003. "The longshoremen in America. That's the sort of look that I gleaned from it." Comparisons were also made to the Italiano mobster look, suggestive of the shady, New York underworld culture of Martin Scorsese's Little Italy-based *Mean Streets.* De Niro's character Johnny Boy caught Rowland's eye.*

A group outing to Islington Green was undertaken to watch the film. "We went to a pizza place across the road," Saunders recounts. "It used to be a big Italian area. I was about to have a 'what's a mook?' experience in the film, and there was a fight going on in the middle of this café!"

While a trilby-wearing Rowland briefly assumed the identity of Carlo Rolan, Archer had already adopted the distinctly downtown alias of Al during Killjoy days. "It was a very spiffy look, very Italian with the little 'taches and that hot sweaty thing that surrounded the music at that time," Rowland described. Denying *Mean Streets'* sartorial influence in 2003, he insisted he'd simply enjoyed suggesting references. Dexys walked Birmingham's very own mean streets carrying cumbersome holdalls, drawing comparisons to the sewn-badge Gola and Adidas bags native to the rare soul scene.

* The two men even share the same birthday.

44

"All right, we had kitbags," Rowland grudgingly conceded to *Jamming!*, "but they [Northern Soul devotees] never had woolly hats, donkey jackets, fuckin' leather jackets or little 'taches!" Attempts to shoehorn Dexys into a Northern Soul tradition failed miserably. "I just couldn't believe it – someone said we were Northern Soul merged with a little bit of coal miners," an incredulous Rowland recalled. "It's really simple and clear cut. How the fuck can they get it so ridiculously wrong?"

Dexys braved Leith's bitter dockside chill when photographed in Scotland on tour in January 1980 against a backdrop of cargo ships and cranes. *Record Mirror* noted their resemblance to a Navy-like clan of *Last Detail*-era Jack Nicholson clones. "Did we have the image of a lean mean fighting machine? I thought we looked more romantic or spiritual," Rowland suggested to Irvin. Yet, as he also confessed, a state of "near chaos" was never far from the surface. Rowland and Archer decided to initiate Rhodes' and Corke's idea of a three-man songwriting nucleus at the end of 1979. Rowland was adamant that he took little pleasure from this venture. "In a way, I regret the nucleus, I think it did cause a bit of a divide," he told Jim Irvin. "We still did try and include everybody in decisions but on a financial side it caused divisions, even though we never made any money." Rowland felt its existence was initially irrelevant. "It was a gang feel at first, it didn't make any difference, but by the time it fell apart, I owed lots to the publishing company."

The three-man nucleus of Rowland, Archer and Blythe were contracted to EMI, undertaking most of the decision-making and songwriting responsibilities with an entitlement to publishing royalties. "Those who were writing the songs were getting the lion's share anyway through publishing royalties," Spooner reasoned, "so what harm would it have done to share out the rest [mechanical royalties] amongst us?"

"Quite early on, and before the release of 'Dance Stance'," Williams told the BBC, "Kevin broached the idea of forming a nucleus. From what I understand, that's why there was only ever three people signed to EMI."

"The nucleus thing was done so that the five of us didn't know what was going on," Spooner concludes. "All the Dexys money basically got split between the three of them."

"I can remember Kevin talking about it at one stage," says Saunders, "and the idea was he needed to make decisions as a three-piece. And there is some truth in that. You see a lot of bands not getting anywhere at all because they spend all their time discussing things. Democracy doesn't usually work with bands. That three-man deal was done when it ['Dance Stance'] got to Number 40, and then EMI signed them."

In Dexys' BBC documentary, Archer said that the nucleus was originally intended to grow to incorporate other members, once ideas and contributions were accepted. "It was a terrible thing," Spooner declares. "We all put our heart and soul and life into that, and we all deserved remuneration. It was the principle: eight men deserved an equal share of the mechanical side of things. I never saw a penny from Dexys."

In the liner notes to the reissue of *Searching For The Young Soul Rebels*, Archer admitted that maintaining a nucleus at the group's core had not been easy. He claimed Paterson had declined the "added pressure" of a place in the inner circle. "I don't know why EMI just signed up three people," Paterson questioned the same year. A sense of division was palpable despite the confusion. "I don't know how it managed to get to that stage. All I do know is that it was very confusing at the time. It felt like there was already a split happening."

Meanwhile, the nationwide assault of the UK's hottest independent label was realised once Madness, The Selecter and The Specials all appeared on *Top Of The Pops* on November 7. Dexys' brief participation with 2-Tone would prove part of a learning curve. They joined up two-thirds of the way through the tour on November 15, two days after Madness departed on their own headlining venture. For Rowland, Dexys were, albeit briefly, part of someone else's musical manifesto. "If I had my time again I'd vote not to do it and stay as we were. I was weak and went along with aligning us to something which we weren't."

Archer felt Dexys had given "all the wrong signals" to their audience. For the rest of the group, the tour was exactly the *right* thing to do.

"What an eye-opener for all of us, Kevin included," Spooner enthuses. "We'd done a few gigs by then, but we hadn't gone on tour, we hadn't played to audiences. We'd played to pubs. I look back and think how natural we were. Yet The Specials were such a fantastic group. And The Selecter were pretty hot in their day too."

"They [The Selecter] would jam on stage to make sure we never got a soundcheck," Saunders unhappily recalls. "The Specials would get their soundcheck done in an hour, but The Selecter wouldn't let us use their equipment. It was all the more satisfying the couple of times we really blew them off the stage." It proved a frenzied concert initiation. A communal electricity seared through the crowds, bodies frequently piling onto buckling stages.

"The Specials' gigs and 2-Tone gigs were the wildest this country has ever seen," Jerry Dammers told *Mojo* in 2001.

"They were just absolutely fuckin' incredible. The Specials were the best live band I've ever seen," Saunders gushes. "I saw them 30 times on tour and every night I'd make sure I saw them, they were *that* good."

"The places were always heaving. There was terrible violence with the politics in those days, but people were buzzing, dancing," Spooner insists. "Just *fantastic* gigs."

"There was quite a lot of trouble because that British Movement thing was always in the background," Saunders recalls. "Kevin made a real point of letting people know we had nothing to do with that."

"I really wish there hadn't been any [aggravation at the shows]," Dammers told *Mojo*. "The great majority were trouble free, but there were a few where a minority thought they were supposed to have a scrap." Trouble had brewed between one of the Dexys camp and Beat manager John Moston, while there was also an altercation with The Specials' road crew. Thankfully, Dammers and co were preparing the ground for Dexys' brand of new-wave soul music.

The Specials were getting the gospel over, Saunders argues. "They didn't want to just play ska as it should be played. It was more of a complimentary music."

As exemplary hosts, The Specials' tour bus frequently returned the group home to Birmingham. Dexys were usually given two hotel rooms on tour – one for the soundman, the other for the eight-man group. To show their gratitude, Dexys charged hotel food to The Specials' tour bill while maintaining a distance from their touring accomplices. "I used to know Roddy [Radiation, Specials' guitarist] and Horace [Panter, bassist]," Saunders recalls. "We weren't allowed to fraternise. Here you are, you're on the hottest tour in the country, and everyone else is having fun except you." Dexys earned a fascinating reception.

"I can remember people's faces," Spooner recalls, "like there was a wind blowing them back, literally standing back going, 'Wow, what's this!' Nobody had heard anything like us. We were full on. It was an assault. There was no competition. We were *it*." Dexys witnessed the extent of 2-Tone's popularity at first hand while on a tour bus in Wimbledon. Streets were packed with Specials fans waiting to mob the group at a record signing session. By February 1980, Dammers insisted 2-Tone had become a "monster".

The tour led them through more than a dozen dates, beginning in Carlisle and ending just over a fortnight later. Transmuting from an idealistic garage band into a powerful working unit, this was essentially the making of Dexys as a live force. Playing night after night, they started to deliver on stage. "It was useful for experience," Archer admitted to Irvin. "Being on stage in front of 3,000 people on that Specials tour, at first we were so nervous you wouldn't believe it. They [The Specials] were bouncing around, and that energy really shook us up. We thought,

'Bloody hell, we've got to perform, we've got to play, we've got to develop this intensity.' Kevin wasn't a fan, but he could see they were effective."

Overcoming any early trepidation, Rowland started to hone his stagecraft. "The first two nights [at Carlisle and Leeds] I didn't know what to do with my hands," he told the same journalist. "I'd just given up smoking and started going down the gym and I'd done loads of weights and I thought, 'This is good, I've got all these muscles.' But when I went to perform I found my legs were really stiff." The Leeds crowd were treated to Rowland's lyrical (Saunders co-penned) broadside at the Pennine populace in the bewilderingly titled 'Thankfully, Not Living In Yorkshire It Doesn't Apply'. The organist began work on the song while employed in a shop selling dope accoutrements on the old Kensington market.

"I wrote it in my head on the tube on the way back home each day, and it came together. Kevin said, 'I can do something with that.' And he came up with the world's strangest lyric, about his dislike for Yorkshire people, how they think they've got a monopoly on that sense of down-to-earthness." The song's pummelling urgency became a genuine crowd pleaser. Meanwhile, Dexys frequently ventured into the back of the audiences to initiate clamorous requests for 'Geno'. Before long, more than a hundred people had enlisted in a football terrace chant.

The group went down a storm at a show in Malvern. With the venue's management encouraging the group to end their set, Dammers insisted Dexys enjoy their moment. They'd earned their encore. "It's better for everyone if they do it, it's a good gig," he raved.

In 1996, *Q* acclaimed the Liverpool Royal Mountford Hall show on November 21, 1979 as one of the UK's 100 greatest ever gigs. Following their first major Irish shows in Belfast and Dublin, Dexys played the Lyceum on November 25. Anticipation was heightened as the tour reached the capital. "That was the apogee of 2-Tone for me," Specials' bassist Panter told *Mojo*. "Coventry was an industrial motor city, lots of unemployment. Without being melodramatic, it raised people's spirits here a bit." *Melody Maker*'s Simon Frith sensed Dexys were at odds with the movement's spontaneous vibrancy; a functional support act for the main event. However, their stock continued to rise. A witness to their Lewisham Odeon show, one of the last on the tour, *Sounds*' Garry Bushell applauded the self-belief and gusto of their brass-driven offerings. Yet he also levelled revivalism charges at the group. The same paper sought an interview with Dexys at a Manchester gig on December 10.

Granada TV boss Tony Wilson had also been keen for the group to appear on the station's *World Of Pop* regional magazine. "I remember being commissioned to interview them, and went to Pips Disco to meet them," recalls freelance journalist Mick Middles. "I sat and waited all night and they didn't turn up. Someone said their van had broken down. As far as I could tell, no one in Pips even knew they were supposed to be on, so they weren't missed."

Two days later, the group played to a handful of bored rock punters in Newtown, Wales. More notably, it became Saunders' last Dexys gig for five months. Driving from Norwich, he'd run out of petrol just outside town. Rescued by the group in their transit van, they dropped him back at his car after the show, where he spent a frozen night on a petrol station forecourt. Passing out after returning home, Saunders was suffering from hypothermia, nervous exhaustion and a raging temperature. Taken to hospital, he was kept under observation and ordered to rest. Subsisting on a student grant without travel expenses had dulled Saunders' enthusiasm. He'd also grown tired of Corke. Making no point of actually leaving or making an effort to maintain contact, he didn't receive any reply.

After enthralling audiences outside Birmingham and having aroused national media interest, Dexys' brief place on the 2-Tone tour was a pivotal moment. And if The Specials could break into the higher echelons of the charts with 'A Message To You Rudy' (in October), then why not Dexys too?

Issued in late November, midway through the 2-Tone tour, 'Dance Stance' introduced the world to an eight-piece collective of startling poise and sense of purpose. An act of catharsis, 'Dance Stance' was Rowland's response to the prevailing attitudes towards Ireland and the Irish in the late Seventies. "Irish jokes made me sick. A lot of people believe all that stuff," Rowland admonished.

"It wasn't like a political manifesto, but Kevin had a very strong anti-racist streak," Saunders argues. "He was very conscious that what people had said 30 years ago about black people was being said about Irish people coming here."

Intent on silencing the ignorant culprits, Rowland issued his warning. A powerful litany of Irish authors and playwrights were employed to make his point. Yet his sole exposure to these literary luminaries consisted of Brendan Behan's classic memoir *Borstal Boy*. Picking up a Behan biography, Rowland had discovered a list of authors inside the book's flyleaf.

Illustrations of Eugene O'Neill's *The Hairy Ape* and George Bernard Shaw's *Pygmalion* adorned promotional adverts for the single, while Sean O'Casey's *Juno And The Paycock* appeared on subsequent adverts for 'Geno'. Having been absent from university on tour for much of his first term, English student Saunders submitted a copy of the group's debut single instead of an essay to his 'progressive' female Irish lecturer. "Listening to 'Dance Stance', it was educating me," Dexys fan Eddie Cooney recalled. "I never told another racist joke of any kind . . . who says music can't change things?" With the beginnings of The Troubles and IRA terrorist campaigns, an undercurrent of anti-Irish resentment was inflamed among the British inner cities of the mid-to-late Seventies. "I was working in a shop in Birmingham in '74. Listen, it was terrible what had happened there, y'know, it was awful, those pub bombings," Rowland informed Radio Two in 2004. "There were scares all the time and we'd all have to go outside the Birmingham Shopping Centre near where it happened."

The menacing air of injustice was gilded by Rowland's finger-pointing lyrics. Its dense, smouldering horns (with an opening brass riff reminiscent of Bob & Earl's 'Harlem Shuffle') emanated a seething antipathy to match. Against an insistent bass figure, demarcation lines were drawn. If Rowland's anguished vocal had not actively politicised the debate, he'd provided stirring food for thought.

The flipside, 'I'm Just Looking', incorporated Rowland's frustrations at the failure of a workshop showdown to materialise, later admitting his former factory colleagues' lack of self-assertion was "alarming". After leaving school, Rowland immersed himself in left-wing politics. "I grew up working class and I'd been a socialist," he informed *Sounds* at the time. "The song is more or less saying I've given up on that . . . well not entirely."

Against a backdrop of union-versus-management industrial conflict, Prime Minister Margaret Thatcher and her Conservative government were preparing the ground for the Eighties meltdown of British industry. "It was a very different world," Saunders recalls. "It was hard to get hold of credit or a mortgage. People were still working class, but proud of what they were." A darkly poignant, Hammond-led entreaty was underscored by Blythe's exquisite brass arrangement. Rowland added a bleak, un-settling lyrical contribution. The reference to a white equivalent of New York's Harlem ghetto supposedly referred to Birmingham's Handsworth district, while the song's subject was reputedly a former Killjoys associate.

Saunders felt 'I'm Just Looking' resembled pianist Alan Price's Animals work. "It sounds quite British, it doesn't sound like an old American song. What made it work was Kevin going for it 100 per cent. He sang it like he really meant it."

At Bernard Rhodes' behest, the song's intimidating introduction became an unnerving heavy whisper. "I think Bernie made [Rowland]

50

paranoid about his voice," Paolo Hewitt insists. "But he became such a great singer over the years." Rhodes encouraged Rowland to look to Elvis Presley and Frank Sinatra's examples in undertaking a unique stylised approach. The Chairmen Of The Board's Norman 'General' Johnson's wavering yelp had been a template for developing a vocal identity.

"There was an ambiguity and forcefulness with Kevin's singing, but it wasn't a masculine voice," says Saunders. "There was vulnerability and a warmth which you don't get now." Failing to capture the group's musicality, Rowland felt Rhodes' and Foote's echo-laden production had reduced the group's sonic brass immediacy to a muted clarion call.

"For a first effort, it was pretty bloody good," Spooner opines. "It wasn't until Pete Wingfield came on board that we looked back and said, 'Well, it was a bit wimpy, wasn't it?'"

"As soon as we did the single, Bernie Rhodes was out of the picture really," Rowland told *Record Collector* in 2000. "The management is there to get our point of view across, not to be a Svengali!" Rowland had railed to the *NME* back in the summer of 1980. Strong misgivings on the financial front and Rhodes' tendency to want 'complete control' have been cited as major factors in his eventual dismissal.

'Dance Stance' peaked at number 40. Rowland admitted in January 1980 it would have been a "guaranteed smash" had they put pen to paper with 2-Tone. The *NME*'s Nick Kent felt Dexys worthy of every bit of praise heading their way. Gavin Martin called it a classic, while it took The Clash's finest moment, 'London Calling', to deprive 'Dance Stance' of *Sounds'* Single of the Week accolade.

With it's pride in the face of prejudice tempered by a recognition of failure, 'Dance Stance'/'I'm Just Looking' was a dramatic piece of confrontation on vinyl. "I always thought it was very confrontational," Hewitt insists. "He [Rowland] used to go out on stage and make his mark. I remember them doing 'I'm Just Looking' and Kevin saying, 'I want quiet,' and hushing the crowd. And there was a lot of shouting, 'You what? You want to fuckin' 'ave it?'"

In getting straight to the heart of the matter, Dexys had delivered a fierce opening statement of intent at the turn of the Eighties.

Chapter Seven

ORIGINALLY entitled the 'Feeling The Power' tour and culled from one of his choice on-stage phrases, Dexys' mammoth two-month, 44-date UK jaunt would provide some of Rowland's best memories during an incident-strewn career. "You know what was good for me?" he reminisced to Everett True in 2000. "Before *Searching For The Young Soul Rebels* was the 'Straight To The Heart' tour, playing all those universities and all things like that. Going in there and people hardly knew us, but by the end of the evening we'd won them over."

The lengthy sojourn was prefaced by a Dudley JB's show on December 21 before a classic Camden Electric Ballroom performance six days later. Supported by The Purple Hearts and The Nips, a 10-song, soul-punk tumult ensued. "It was always a really good balanced set actually," Saunders insists. "'Tell Me When My Light Turns Green' sounds like an odd sort of song nowadays, but it was good to play a bright, breezy thing early on in the set. There was 'Respect', 'Big Time Operator' and 'Thankfully . . .' grooved much more than on the record." Opening with 'The Horse' and climaxing with an incredible rendition of 'Hold On, I'm Comin''', their rabble-rousing punch was delivered at a relentless pace, complete with scabrous horns and new drummer Andy Growcott's belligerent percussion.

Sixteen-year-old keyboardist Andy Leek had also been inducted as Pete Saunders' replacement. Leek told *Keep On Running*: "A guy named Roy Williams, who used to manage this club in Wolverhampton, phoned me up and said there was a group called Dexys who needed a keyboard player. He didn't tell me anything about them or anything. I went along to an audition and they asked me to join and that was it." Leek had played in a Telford group with Black Countryman Growcott. Following Bobby Ward's departure, Dexys rehearsed both men in December.

"Stoker was like the drummer Animal out of *The Muppets*," Spooner recalled. Growcott got his nickname through his rhythm propelling exploits, part of what Archer called the group's "locomotive crew". "He became a forceful character as time went on, and I know Kevin got annoyed with him and it didn't seem to bother him. He was a big personality. And when he finally joined he fitted in instantly, as a person and musically," Spooner added.

Saunders insists Growcott's fearless strength was essential. "He would say what he thought and he wasn't frightened of anyone, and he knew he was good. He had the force of a rock drummer, but he could be quite funky, groovy. We worked through various drummers, who either wanted to be a John Bonham, or a jazz drummer or a clever funk drummer." Playing with certainty, Growcott invested authority in the group's music. His photogenic looks also became the iconic focus of the group, his features adorning subsequent posters and promotional adverts. Combined with Williams' nimble, driving baselines, Dexys boasted a fearsomely accomplished rhythmic foundation.

After winding down from the Electric Ballroom gig, the *NME*'s Roy Carr interviewed the band. Heralded under the headline 'Funky Butt Fassst!' in reference to The Ram Jam Band, the paper's perspective did little to solicit Rowland's approval. "I was a bit pissed off that the very first interview in the music press, which was the *NME*, didn't afford us much credibility," Rowland told Johnny Rogan. "We'd just done the 2-Tone tour. They sent Roy Carr along, because he'd been around in the Sixties and that was the whole angle of the article." He had a point. "We were seen as this revival group, which I didn't like," Rowland further reflected in 2000. "I just felt they weren't really taking us very seriously. We were just being awkward really. Well, I was anyway."

Rowland informed Carr that retaining a distance was the price they were happy to pay in maintaining their integrity. "Despite what you might have heard," Rowland told the Electric Ballroom crowd as the Seventies heaved its final breath, "despite our cold exterior, our hearts really are full of soul."

With 'Dance Stance' bubbling under at number 78, a London Marquee gig on January 6 drew a 500-strong Sunday night crowd enticed by Dexys' contemporary brass barrage. With The Clash having sold out at Aylesbury Friars a fortnight earlier, Dexys' nationwide jaunt opened at the same venue on January 19. An almost missionary zeal characterised the lengthy wintry tour between January and March. Warming to the task of converting audiences, Archer would hush agitated crowds into obedient silence. On other occasions, Dexys would line the front of the stage, attempting to placate the restless by transmitting the 'soul power' in frowning silence. It was an incredible sight.

Six days later, they won over *Melody Maker* journalist Paolo Hewitt. "I first saw them at what was then the Music Machine at Camden. I know it was a cliché, but they did knock you off your feet," he told Radio Two. Hewitt had gone to watch Shane McGowan's band The Nips, who'd just released their single, 'Gabrielle'.

"Dexys were just fucking amazing. The whole look was there, the beanie hats, the leather jackets. They blew me away. So I went back to the office and said, 'I've got to write about this group.'" Convincing his paper to run a feature, Hewitt began to doubt their 'anti-musician' credo considering their overwhelming on-stage power.

Seventeen-year-old future Proclaimers twins Charlie and Craig Reid caught the group at St. Andrews University in early February. Anticipating a ska-derived Midlands collective, they were surprised at what they encountered. Charlie Reid told Radio Two: "Dexys came on, and I've never been as kind of shocked by anything I've seen on stage, just the appearance. And then they started up, and the noise they made was incredible. The way that they confounded expectations really is something that will stay with me forever."*

Introduced by Radio One DJ Simon Bates, Dexys made their breakthrough *Top Of The Pops* debut with 'Dance Stance' in January 1980 following the single's breach of the Top 40. It was a momentous occasion. The Pretenders also appeared, performing their current number one 'Brass In Pocket'. Spooner recalls: "I can always remember being struck by the audience coming in, and thinking, 'There's only 30 people!' If you look at old clips of the show, you see the kids not looking at the stage, but looking all around while this army of red tracksuited geezers are shoving them from stage to stage as the cameras were driving through."

Rowland told Channel Four he concentrated more on his fear of the millions-strong television audience than proceedings in the studio. "I remember the intro of the song, and I was doing my little dance to it, and then I started singing. And I thought, 'This is going okay,' you know, first verse in, I'm miming, but I was still singing the words. And then I thought, 'There's 10 million people looking at me!' as I was singing. And I just started to crack up, and my jaw locked stiff, and as I look back at that performance, I can see myself getting more and more serious. People used to think I was really angry, but honestly I was just terrified!"

"It was a good, confident performance," Spooner insists, "but knowing us all we were pretty nervous. I can remember standing there thinking, 'Fuck, I hope I don't fluff my mimed lines!' It was a big deal," he emphasised, "our first time on the telly."

Paterson also felt the significance of the moment. "I watched *Top Of The Pops* every week and never missed it," he told Radio Two. "And

---

* Rowland's appreciation of the Scottish duo's music has also persisted. He outlined his enjoyment of their work in a 2001 Scottish documentary.

when it did finally come it was a bit overwhelming for someone like me, who was from a little village."

"Doing *Top Of The Pops* the first time was great, when we did 'Dance Stance', that was fantastic," Williams recalled in 2003. "Just a great experience, a programme I'd grown up watching."

"I think that was a big achievement because it came from nowhere," Archer said to True, recalling Dexys first chart success.

Dave Corke was back in the frame when *Sounds'* Phil Sutcliffe interviewed the band in January 1980 for their first feature, going some way to promoting the band's working man's caff-dwelling, tea-drinking habits. "We'd all sit around and spend a lot of time at the Apollonia on Broad Street, which at the time was a real run-down part of town," Spooner recalls. "The canals were derelict and there were loads of empty buildings. Now there are lots of little bistros and canal systems."

Dexys insisted that contractual clauses stipulated a healthy tea quota on tour riders. Short-lived member and chain-drinker Mick Talbot happily embraced the group's tea culture. "It was always little greasy spoon caffs because we were all skint," Spooner recalls. "But you had to be somewhere, and that's how it all came about. We kind of liked it, I always have and I still do. It wasn't a conscious thing. The press ended up making it into a romantic thing. It was just a place to meet up."

On the subject of their activities on tour in early 1980, Rowland told *The Face*: "We stay in guest houses. There's too many temptations around in those big hotels late at night. Bars open to all hours. You'd never get to sleep. We have to go out on stage and know it's us playing, not alcohol and drugs."

"A lot of bands seem to do the gigs for the sake of the ligs," Blythe said in the same interview. "They're not dedicated enough. But I need to play to people. I feel a lot better for it."

"The idea was not to drink before we went on stage, no drink, no drugs before we go on stage," Archer recalled in 2000. "We wanna be different, this is the idea. All these other groups are making the mistake of doing this, so let's not do it." Yet drugs and drink weren't completely off the menu. Playing the Camden Music Machine in January, Rowland admitted that the group consumed uppers and downers, but insisted their drink and drug intake was a far cry from what transpired later that year.

"When we started to get more successful, I tried to rule with an iron fist and that's when I started to ban all the drink and drugs," Rowland told *Record Collector*. "I was obviously just very scared of losing control and what would happen to me if I started taking drugs again."

Archer points to the brass section as the main culprits. "We'd do a show and afterwards they'd be propping up the bar. Kevin used to go mad at them even if they were drinking after a show." While on the 2-Tone tour, Spooner was inducted into the dubious joys of Special Brew on the host's rider. Paterson's whisky consumption was a theme Rowland addressed in his mid-song monologue during 'Respect'.

During a brief tour break, Dexys recorded a four-track Radio One Peel session on February 26 in London. With Growcott's relentlessly impressive drumming, 'The Horse' was a pummelling soul rout. 'Tell Me . . .' oozed a rarely captured menacing momentum while 'Breaking Down The Walls Of Heartache' illustrated their telepathic ability to lock into a groove. Only a slightly leaden and lightweight 'Geno' sounds unrepresentative of the group, its live pulse sapped of strength in the studio.

"I don't think we actually saw John Peel for a start," Spooner recalls. "We went to a standard BBC studio, I think it was at Maida Vale. I can remember going home and listening to it later on the radio. I can't remember John Peel's comments, but I don't think he was particularly keen on the band.

"We did meet on another occasion, I guess it was at a John Peel roadshow. We missed so much in a sense because we were such an insular group. I'd love to look back and think, 'I had this chat with John Peel,' but we thought everybody else was shit, John Peel included."

"I think we're becoming more intense," said Rowland following a confrontational appearance at the Bournemouth Stateside Centre in early March. "Musically we like to swim against the tide. Taking risks is very important to us." Dexys undertook a brief Irish tour, playing dates in the province in Coleraine and Belfast. Arriving in Dublin to find their University College appearance cancelled, *Hot Press* reported the group amused themselves filming in a city studio before enjoying a pub crawl.

With their touring commitments finally fulfilled, a party was planned for March 18 at Birmingham's Zoo Club on Water Street. Rowland later admitted that their first national headlining venture incurred a deficit of £4,000 in miscellaneous pre-tour bills. At a Liverpool show that spring, Dexys waited to play their new single until almost the close of the set. "This is for those people who were here last time we played Liverpool," Rowland announced. "Only 10 people came to see us."

"The band started shouting 'Geno, Geno, Geno' and all those who had waited for it were suddenly delirious," Eddie Cooney recalls. "The whole performance had been really tense, you felt that violence could spark at any moment. The tension was turned into sheer adoration."

Chapter Eight

"I don't know if you know this, but Geno Washington is the greatest soul singer that ever lived."

— Kevin Rowland, 1979

IMPRESSING the virtues of an education in soul music upon their audience became part of the Dexys live experience. Frequent, "typically arrogant" proclamations were made on behalf of American club soul singer Geno Washington, whose raw-edged vocal and stage persona had fired Rowland's imagination.

Born in Indiana, William Francis Washington earned his nickname from New York Giants footballer Geno Marketti. Following three years service in the US Air Force stationed in East Anglia, he opted to remain in the UK and in 1965 became the singer in a band led by guitarist Pete Gage. This soon developed into Washington's own Ram Jam Band with Gage on guitar, Lionel Kingham on tenor sax, Buddy Beadle on baritone, Jeff Wright on Hammond organ, John Roberts on bass and Herb Prestige on drums. The key to their act was a fast-paced, action-packed, medley style delivery, which saw one soul classic merging into another. Audiences barely had time to catch their breath before the band launched into the next song, keeping up the pace for an hour or more. Much of a typical show was captured on their frantic debut album, *Hand Clappin' – Foot Stompin' – Funky Butt – Live!* which became a primer for semi-pro Sixties soul bands up and down the country.

A self-confessed rocker inspired by heroes Little Richard, Fats Domino and Chuck Berry, Washington described their choreographed act as "hot, live hardcore soul". An Anglophile attraction in his adopted homeland, Washington's personality and spirited voice made his belligerent live performances something to cherish. Like most British R&B acts of the early to mid-Sixties, they were regulars at London's Flamingo and Marquee venues, where they garnered a strong contingent of mod support, and at Brixton's Ram Jam Club (from where the band got their moniker). Former Olympic Runner Pete Wingfield, who shared numerous bills with Washington, was well placed to assess their appeal. "He brought an

American-style soul showmanship and stagecraft to Britain, and I don't think people had seen that before. He didn't really have the vocal chops for it, but he's a pretty cool guy. He was geared to giving you a good show, which is what you want."

"I know he blew it, played the cabaret circuit and pissed everyone off but he's criminally underrated, especially the band he had about '65. The fire and emotion . . . he performed with total conviction," Rowland informed *Sounds* in early 1980. "It's that strength and aggression we try to put in."

"It was the way he was a brilliant entertainer and there was a sadness to it as well," Archer told the BBC, "where he was kind of doing all this stuff and he was nowhere really." Wingfield watched the Ram Jam Band in a less celebrated, early Seventies incarnation, featuring a vertically challenged trumpet player and lanky, baritone saxophonist. "The people were obviously chosen for their looks, rather than their chops!" he laughs. Including Blythe in their mid-to-late Seventies ranks, the Ram Jam Band's momentous driving rhythm was a marked influence on Dexys' live sound. "I went to see them [Dexys] live and they seemed to know what they were doing," Wingfield recalls. "I was always keen to check the rhythm section because if they aren't good, the whole thing's no good. But they were strong. The drummer was really on the money."

Still on the backburner, 'Geno' had yet to figure in Dexys' set. Yet Mick Talbot immediately sensed the influence upon the group's material and musical arrangements on his first encounter with Dexys in mid-1979. "I had a chat with them and said, 'You remind me of Geno Washington,'" he recalled on *It Was Like This*. "There were a couple of really good live albums, cult soul albums, that were around and I had one of them." Archer was reputedly enamoured with the group's 1966 *Hand Clappin'* . . . LP. But it was the single 'Michael (The Lover)', peaking at number 39 in early 1967, which enthralled an adolescent Rowland.

With music and fashion always hand in hand, joining the hip, short-haired coterie of Washington's well-groomed, sharp-suited fan base had meant everything to this aspiring 15-year-old. Yet Washington's music was a scarce commodity. "His records weren't in the charts, they weren't on the radio, he wasn't on *Top Of The Pops*, so I saw he was playing at the Railway Hotel and I was desperate to go," Rowland informed Radio Two. He would narrate the story of that pivotal night on stage a quarter of a century later. "Well, it was back in 1968 with my brother John, at the Railway Hotel in Harrow. The room was full of smart young men and I was proud to be one of them. Geno took the stage with his towel swingin' high, and as he did the crowd went wild . . . And one of the songs he sang, it really spoke to us . . ."

"I was totally fed up with everything else at that time [mid-1978], and so I started listening to all of Geno's old records and any other soul singles I could pick up for 10p around the markets," Rowland told Roy Carr. Penning initial lyrics that summer, Rowland drew upon a decade's worth of hindsight on an unforgettable night. Suitably dressed for the occasion as possibly the Railway's youngest patron, he steered clear of any aggro while awaiting Washington's dramatic stage entrance. In a laudatory, semi-poetic evocation, Rowland relayed the adrenalised excitement of his experience. Highlighting a growing ambition and self-belief, the second set of lyrics revealed an element of condescension towards his former hero, and a growing sense of destiny. The imagery was arguably the finest of Rowland's career.

"He did have a real gift with lyrics," Spooner admitted. "I can remember thinking about 'Geno', 'That's really smart, singing a song about another guy but saying, "Look at me looking down on you."'"

Paterson later called it a 'thank you' for a memorable night out. The nostalgic glow dimmed, yet Rowland vowed never to forget Washington's example.

Rowland remembered working separately on 'Geno' during the early summer of 1979 with Archer. "On first hearing the music I felt jealous of Kevin's, by this time, stunning songwriting talent," Rowland confided, "and was relieved when he asked me to write the lyrics." Bearing a passing resemblance to Zoot Money's 'The One And Only', 'Geno''s melodic progression was also reminiscent of The Turtles' 'Happy Together', with Rowland's vocal reflecting Norman 'General' Johnson's tongue-rolling delivery.

Washington's Sixties audiences had frequently been whipped into pre-gig frenzies by DJs. "Who do you want?" they'd ask. "Ge-no! Ge-no! Ge-no! . . ." the crowd cried back. This chant was later incorporated into the record's introduction and fade-out, while Archer admits the parping sax riff was derived from '(I Gotta) Hold On To My Love', the B-side to the Ram Jam Band's 'Michael'.

Alongside a cover of Johnny Johnson & The Bandwagon's 'Breaking Down The Walls Of Heartache', Dexys' second single was recorded in February at John 'Tokoloshe Man' Kongos' Tapestry studios in Mortlake, south-west London. "I'd done a few records there and it seemed the logical place to go," Wingfield recalls. "In retrospect it probably wasn't, because it was kind of cramped. But we got the results."

Having previously remixed 'Dance Stance' and 'I'm Just Looking', Wingfield undertook a re-recording of 'Thankfully . . .' featuring Andy Leek on keyboards at the 'Geno' session. Original organist and writer Pete

Saunders was horrified with the results. "It ['Thankfully . . .'] got recorded with a horrible plastic-y little synthesiser. I remember Pete Wingfield playing it to me and I said, 'What's that? What have you done to my song?!'"

Despite being attracted to the catchy assault of 'Geno', Wingfield had reservations. "I did like the horniness of it. And the horns sure as hell were loud. I mean, the way it ended up, which I think was a bone of contention at the time, you had to put the horns to the level they'd normally be and then basically double it. And that was the sound of the record!"

Wingfield's successful translation of 'Geno''s live, rhythmic pulse incorporated the opening strains from Van Morrison's double live album *It's Too Late To Stop Now*, a work Rowland later cited as an all-time favourite, which provided the introductory expectant crowd applause. Rowland had no qualms over 'Geno''s quality, while Archer was taken by its warmth and optimism. "I think it still holds up today," Wingfield told the BBC. "You can hear the attitude and the power of it, and it still sounds unusual, you know, it's got its own personality, but within the influence of soul music."

EMI had wanted Dexys' cover of Johnny Johnson & The Bandwagon's 'Breaking Down The Walls Of Heartache' released instead.* Blythe and Spooner's regal sax interplay made Dexys version one to savour. With its catchy chant, the record company considered 'Geno' only as a suitable B-side. The compromise idea of a double A-side was mooted. Yet Dexys stood their ground. Released on March 15, the picture sleeve of 'Geno' depicted a stern, no-nonsense outfit awaiting their next assignment. Its unique swagger was delivered with a thrilling ring of confidence. However, *Record Mirror* considered 'Geno' a turgid eulogy with few redeeming qualities and felt Dexys had missed their chance at the kind of chart success The Specials and Madness were enjoying.

Justified in his self-belief, Rowland sensed Dexys were destined to succeed. "First of all, as it was moving up the charts, we were like, 'Well, of course it'll be number one.' And when it was number one, there was no kind of jumping up and down."

This attitude is one Spooner now partially regrets. "I look back and I think, 'You should have been jumping up to the sky about it!'"

"When it got into the Top 10, I think everybody felt, 'Well that's it,'" Archer told Jim Irvin, "but it just kept going higher and higher." The

---

* Pooling their resources in 1967, former solo singers Johnson, Terry Lewis, Arthur Fullilove and Billy Bradley's debut single reached number four in the UK charts in October 1968.

At the dark end of the street. An early shot of the eight-piece Dexys line-up, taken in late 1979 in London, left to right: trombonist 'Big' Jimmy Paterson, alto saxophonist Steve 'Babyface' Spooner, drummer Bobby 'Junior' Ward, tenor saxophonist Jeff 'JB' Blythe, organist Pete Saunders, co-vocalist, songwriter and guitarist Kevin 'Al' Archer, bassist Pete Williams and leader, lyricist and vocalist Kevin Rowland. *(Mike Laye)*

Band on the run. Dexys captured hopping another train station ticket barrier. An essential means of early survival, their fare-dodging tactics became ingrained in group legend. *(Mike Laye)*

The group found in purposeful stride after another bunking escapade to the capital, late 1979. *(Mike Laye)*

A rare glimpse of Dexys as a sextet in late 1979 following the departures of Ward and Saunders. Left to right: Paterson, Spooner, Blythe, Archer, Rowland and Williams. *(Mike Laye)*

The teams that meet in caffs. Founding members Kevin Archer and Kevin Rowland listen intently as Dexys plan their next move in 1980. The checked, lumber-jacketed figure of new drummer Andy Growcott is featured in the background. *(Mike Laye)*

The last gang in town, mid-1980. "It was more than a band. A band would not be a word to describe it adequately," Blythe (centre) later admitted. "A tribe would be a better word, a small tribe." *(Mike Laye)*

A pensive-looking Kevin 'Al' Archer, Rowland's talented lieutenant. *(Mike Laye)*

Classically trained and college-educated, cropped-haired trombonist Jim Paterson rehearsing hard. *(Mike Laye)*

Experienced tenor saxophonist and gifted co-brass arranger Jeff 'JB' Blythe. *(Mike Laye)*

Lean on me: Brass-blower Blythe supports a characteristically impassioned Rowland stage performance during 1980. Sax partner Spooner wails on in the background. *(Mike Laye)*

'If there is *someone…*' Blythe looks on as Rowland makes his point to Archer in mid-song on stage, early 1980. *(Mike Laye)*

Dexys make their first nerve-wracking television appearance in January 1980 with an otherwise fiery *Top Of The Pops* performance of debut single 'Dance Stance'. *(LFI)*

On the waterfront. With kitbags in hand, Dexys ward off the biting chill of Leith docks on tour in Scotland, January 1980. New keyboardist, teenager Andy Leek, is pictured on Rowland's right. *(Mike Laye)*

An early glimpse of a re-constituted and re-fashioned Dexys Mark Two, rehearsing in spartan conditions following the original group's split in November 1980. Left to right: drummer Seb Shelton, pianist Mick Billingham, young guitarist Kevin 'Billy' Adams, bassist Steve Wynne, Rowland, tenor/alto saxophonists Paul Speare and Brian 'Maurice' Brummitt and Paterson. *(Mike Laye)*

Dexys warm up on stage amidst the more salubrious surroundings of London's Old Vic Theatre, ahead of their magical three-night residency in mid-November 1981. The proceeding shows were later acclaimed as arguably the finest of their career. *(David Corio/Retna)*

guitarist fielded calls each Tuesday, enquiring of the single's latest chart position from his dad, who then shared the news with his factory colleagues. Saunders remained aware of its steady weekly ascent while working in a CBS record distribution plant warehouse during his Easter University holiday.

Transatlantic messages left Geno Washington flabbergasted at Dexys' tribute. "They sent me over a copy of the record and I just couldn't believe it!" he told Channel 4. "I'd been in England so long I hadn't gotten back into that American vain thing, 'Oh, about *me*? Man, I'm cookin'!'" As the benefactor of Dexys' tribute, newspapers, promoters and record companies showed an immediate interest. Although grateful, Washington wasn't too enamoured with the Dexys brass, as he told Spencer Leigh. "I'm a Stax freak and you listen to Otis and Arthur Conley for horns. Other than that, no problem."

'Geno' reached number one for a single week on May 3, 1980 and Dexys celebrated their achievement on *Top Of The Pops*. Meanwhile, interviews announcing Andy Leek's sudden departure were soon reported in the music press. Ahead of his forthcoming solo single, 'Move On In Your Maserati', he told the national press: "There was no ill feeling with the rest of the group at all. I just didn't like all the attention." Leek had actually left the group at the end of March when 'Geno' was trailing the lower reaches of the charts.

Rowland later claimed that he had been unable to relish (and ill-equipped to handle) their success. "That had been my dream as a kid, being on *Top Of The Pops*," Rowland confessed to Irvin. "It was great to do that, I just wish I could have actually experienced it and savoured it. I thought if I got on *Top Of The Pops* no one would put me down, but it didn't work. I still felt unworthy of everything."

Archer found the reality of the situation bewildering. "We had lots of people coming up to us and asking what it was like to be on *Top Of The Pops* and being number one. 'Can you explain the feeling?' And it was such a difficult question," he told *Mojo*. "You just felt like making it up and saying, 'Oh, it's brilliant, limousines and all that kind of thing,' but it was nothing like that."

"With this insular thing, it made us very arrogant," admits Spooner, who celebrated his 21st birthday as 'Geno' reached number one. "I was watching it on the telly and celebrating with a girlfriend. We went out to the pub for a quiet drink. 'Geno' came on the jukebox. I thought, 'That's great!' It didn't suddenly change the group. It was just a culmination of the plan."

Saunders scotches the notion of an actual agenda. "It wasn't like the band had built up to it, and it wasn't what the band wanted. Once we'd got a number one, this thing started to happen. It was too much, too soon. We weren't really in a position to become a pop group."

In the dreaded grip of children's TV appearances, Dexys played *Tiswas* and *Cheggers Plays Pop*, which featured a cameo from a trumpet-wielding impostor called Darren. "When I wrote it I never thought it would get to number one," Rowland stated in 1981. "It was just another record to us, I just happened to like Geno Washington – I thought he was great, so I wrote a song about him, and the next thing I know he's on tour . . ." Rowland's reaction to seeing Washington live 12 years on was unsurprising. "It was horrible, it was pathetic. I went to see them and they were awful. That'll teach me."

As rugged underdogs, Dexys had battled from nowhere to the top of the charts. But Rowland felt uneasy in the growing glare of media attention. "All those insecurities that you think are going to be cured by success are actually just highlighted, magnified," he informed Jim Irvin. "People really *are* looking at you now. You just had a load more problems and a load more pressure and I thought it was shit."

"I was busy acting the rebel," he told Jon Wilde. "There was a part of me that wanted to sabotage the whole thing. So that's what I started to do. Just don't expect me to say I'm proud of the fact."

Chapter Nine

D URING their 'Straight To The Heart' tour in the wake of 'Dance Stance', producer Pete Wingfield was put forward as a potential producer for Dexys' debut album. Rowland had been rather enamoured with Wingfield's 1975 Top 20 solo single 'Eighteen With A Bullet', and EMI's A&R chief Roger Aimes sensed their mutual soul reference points would prove creatively productive.

A member of various Van Morrison touring ensembles since the Seventies, Wingfield was second in line for the producer's chair behind Morrison himself, who attended band rehearsals to assess his potential charges at work. Rowland introduced Van to the group. "He came down to see us play at the Cedars Club in Birmingham. It wasn't like a proper gig," Spooner recalls. "We were just up on the stage playing through songs. He didn't say anything to us. He sat there looking miserable with his hat on, having a cup of coffee. He watched us, didn't say a word, got up and he walked out. To this day, I still don't know what he thought. Maybe he decided it just wasn't his thing."

Despite not hiring Morrison, Rowland was thankful that Wingfield oversaw proceedings. "We were lucky with Pete," he told Jim Irvin. "We knew we were good live, but being good in the studio is a very different thing."

"I could see they were all of one mind," Wingfield recalls, "and there was a tremendous kind of drive there. Quite what they were in one mind to do, I don't know, but you knew they were onto something." In May 1980, Dexys decamped to the picturesque Oxfordshire village of Chipping Norton to begin work. Housed in a converted school building, the band was well catered for and entertained.

Rowland felt that forsaking their fabled insularity for an American studio experience would have proved detrimental. "I'm glad we didn't go to America," he told Everett True, "it would have been really wrong for us, we couldn't have done it. It would have been too overwhelming."

"They were a self-contained band, they could stay and it made sense economically," Wingfield pointed out. "I knew it would go well there."

"It was weird staying in this lovely little complex in Chipping Norton, beautiful little cottage," recalls Saunders, who spent hours putting the studio's genuine Hammond organ to good use. "There were barrels of beer, everyone could help themselves." A soul fanatic, Wingfield arrived armed with dozens of American import albums. "I just sat there listening to them and put them all onto tape," Saunders smiles. "Pete was a fantastic musician. He was a very good choice and he had great taste in music."

Ever the experimental, resourceful enthusiast, Wingfield brought an old school ethic to the record's production. Keen to administer what Rowland coined "traditional soul inflections" in Dexys music, the singer was wary of the songs losing their edge. Archer maintained that Wingfield's approach essentially put the group in order.

Eager to foster a recording environment that reflected Dexys at their best, Wingfield became an integral part of the team. He could be found on the studio floor, instilling a requisite vibe or feel: instigating the mid-song breakdown section on the incredibly accomplished 'Seven Days Too Long'; playing piano on 'I Couldn't Help If I Tried'; adding atmospheric falsetto harmonies on 'Keep It' and suggesting fresh backing vocals and piano parts for 'There, There, My Dear'. Saunders remembers Wingfield's flash of genius on what became the album finale. "I was playing the organ. He [Wingfield] said to Barry [Hammond] the engineer, 'I've got an idea.' And he came in, sat there playing the piano, and he stuck the chords right in the middle of it. And they changed the middle of that song completely."

"I don't think you'd have heard all those neat touches live on stage anyway, so what Pete [Saunders] was playing on stage was good for that," Spooner attests. "I think Pete Wingfield thought maybe Pete wasn't quite up to playing on the record. So what you hear on the album is mainly Pete Wingfield's piano playing."

"I don't like to steam in on things unless I feel objectively that I can do a better job for the benefit of the track," Wingfield argues. "And there were a few things that I had in mind that Pete didn't do, so I did do the odd thing."

Saunders admits: "I could have imagined a lot of producers with keyboard abilities saying, 'We're not going to use you, fuck off.' He was quite respectful considering I was 20 years old."

The producer was a little bewildered by Rowland's vocal delivery, despite his stylised approach suiting the overall sound. "The lyrics were very important to him and it was all like this big statement," Wingfield emphasised to Radio Two. "So it had the lyrics, and then to my mind, he sang it so sort of stylised as to make the words virtually unintelligible. I remember saying, 'Listen, if the words are so important, people should hear what they are.'" They agreed to disagree.

Regardless, *Searching For The Young Soul Rebels* captured an essentially positive period. Casting a critical eye over the material, Wingfield was confident that a decent, varied record was possible. He recalls the studio session for album outtake 'The Horse' as an "absolute cracker". It's likely the group also undertook a version of the two-year-old 'Definitely Not Down On The Farm' for good measure.

"When we recorded it, everyone was happy, everyone was stable," Archer told True. "We'd actually achieved it, and it was coming out, and we already had 'Geno', so we knew it was going to be quite successful." A swift 10- to 12-day operation, the group spent four days recording a handful of strong rhythm tracks before capturing the horns later in a day's session.

"Pete realised what sort of band it was," says Saunders in admiration. "He worked with the fact that the horn section are, in fact, out of tune. He worked with the fact that certain things speeded up. A lot of producers would have said, 'Let's do it again, let's get it spot on.'"

Wingfield witnessed the group's dynamic, "rebellious vibe" at work. "There were the 'vision' people within the band, like Kevin Rowland and Kevin Archer, who were very clear on what they were doing, and Archer was the great lieutenant," Wingfield recalls. "And there were the muso types as well who took care of that side of things. They were doing their own thing but with reference to classic soul music which we all shared a love for."

With a comprehensive grasp of a relatively small quota of material, thorough rehearsals and dedication served Dexys well in the studio. Wingfield applauded their industrious approach and dedicated work ethic. "They were a hard-working band. Kevin certainly knew what he was doing. It was more a matter of willing some subscribers to his cause. He was the guy that was driving it in the studio."

The group were also indebted to house engineer Barry Hammond's work. "It was a real education for us, and I don't think we really knew what an engineer was," Spooner insists. "We weren't really that musical, and didn't really know that much about studios. But that wasn't how we sounded live onstage."

Wingfield feels that it was a pretty faithful representation of their stage material. "One of the things that attracted them to me was that they were a bona fide, exciting live band. And it was my job to translate that onto tape. I think the horns were a little louder than they were live, which is fine." His fast-paced modus operandi captured the spark of now-or-never musical tension. Yet it wasn't a case of making a quick record. "That was how I recorded," Wingfield laughs. "I didn't know any other way! I soon got a reputation as a producer who didn't like to hang around. I was starting out as a producer, and your approach develops over time. You get totally into the thing when you're doing it, give it everything you've got and try and make sure the artist is reflected in the best way possible."

An unequivocally powerful statement, . . . *Rebels* boasted an attention to detail and startling sense of identity arguably unlike any other UK pop album of the time. Rowland seized on the novel idea of album sleeve song notes for individual tracks from the unlikely source of a Steely Dan album. "[. . . *Rebels*] was the most fascinating album I'd heard in ages," Jim Irvin declares. "I loved the graphics and the lyrics are different from what you're hearing. It gives the impression that there is confusion in the ranks, and there was work to be done."

Rowland informed *Hot Press* that the key to Dexys' music was emotion and confusion, reflected in the album sleeve's closely cropped photograph of a bewildered Belfast youth, caught in the midst of the sectarian Troubles in Northern Ireland. Conveying a desired "picture of unrest", its Irish origin was a double blessing. Reverting to its original title, this keynote topic was readdressed on 'Burn It Down'.

Later lauded in some quarters as the greatest debut seven-inch since 'Anarchy In The UK', the dynamic unorthodoxy of the brass harmonies in 'Dance Stance' set the standard, a mouth-watering appetizer to the main event. Having declared rock'n'roll a "totally spent creative force", Dexys signified the destruction of the old guard with a final blast of Deep Purple's 'Smoke On The Water' and a cry of "burn it down!" Wingfield recalls that Rowland's conceptual nous accounted for the twirled radio dial overdub at the top of the track. "I think we just got a radio going and put a mike up against it," he recalled.

The Sex Pistols' 'Holidays In The Sun', and former touring accomplices The Specials were then dispatched following a snatch of the chorus to 'Rat Race'. Looking back, Rowland feels that much of his old bravado is indefensible. "I personally now feel that I was nasty," he admitted to True. "I was always doing that sort of thing. There's no need for it really."

Having addressed cultural stigma, personal conflict and redemption were also explored. Rowland admits the first half of 'Tell Me When My Light Turns Green' remained unfinished for some time. The introduction provides a clue to its gestation. Singing of an accumulation of life experiences over his first 23 years, Rowland was almost 27 when the album was released. It evinced an unsoothable anger at the vagaries and frustrations of life. "Yeah, there was an awful lot of that [resentment]. It was focused mostly on the past," Rowland told Irvin. Reining in depression and intimating a belief in God, these testifying sentiments were reflected in both the quasi-gospel rhythmic drive and biblical tract quoted on the record's sleeve.

Dexys time as *habitués* of the Broad Street Apollonia cafe provided the title for the self-congratulatory, cinematic four-minute instrumental, 'The Teams That Meet In Caffs'. Having blossomed during the winter of 1979, '. . . Caffs' evoked "memories of endless rounds of teas, phone calls to promoters, waiting on information and planning our next move," Archer recalled in 2000's . . . *Rebels* reissue liner notes.

"I suppose we had a sort of six-month period around that area, and if we weren't in rehearsal we were in the caff," Spooner adds.

The song provided a fresh dimension to the group's repertoire. While the composition was credited to Archer, Spooner acknowledges that in a group of songwriters, Blythe's and Paterson's efforts have been overlooked. Archer had also written half-formed lyrics, an idea Rowland questioned once he'd heard his partner's vocal. "I might have just been jealous because I always liked to sing everything myself," he admitted to Johnny Rogan. "You never know with me. I hope not. It could have been good." An exquisite epiphany, Blythe's majestic sax solo directed the song towards a climactic finale. The Hammond work sweetened and soothed an emotionally powerful exercise in showcasing the group's dynamics.

Given a clearer, crisper production, 'I'm Just Looking' caught *Musicians Only*'s ear, its elegiac organ lines compensating for what the periodical felt was an overwrought, sobbing vocal. It was a less abrasive performance than Rowland's scowling yelp on the original single, despite the chilling, whispered introduction which conveyed neither warmth nor intimacy.

As a renewable source of joy in spite of its familiarity, the immediacy and glory of 'Geno' remains untarnished. . . . *Rebels*' momentum was sustained in a stunning cover of 'Seven Days Too Long'. While its vibraphone-led introduction and a cappella chorus chant during the song's breakdown deviated from the Harrell/Bailey-penned original, Growcott's propellant percussion lent an addictive feel to arguably the record's strongest performance.

Dexys were clearly transcending their stock of familiar influences. "It wasn't a pastiche Sam & Dave record," says Wingfield. "Kevin was too strong a character to slavishly follow someone else's stylistic thing, or lyrical thing. He was definitely using that as a springboard or a basis of projecting himself." No longer pointing an accusatory finger, Rowland's lyrical obliqueness characterised a struggle in search of empathy, even salvation, on 'I Couldn't Help If I Tried'. Against the emotional ebb and flow of a bittersweet brass tide, Rowland's dextrous, well-executed delivery found a powerful middle ground between understated and overwrought.

"To give Kevin his due, the great thing was we had something distinct and instantly recognisable. No one else sings like that," opines Wingfield, whose thrilling piano lines raise the song to a higher plateau. "He wrote the book on that. It [. . . *Rebels*] shines like a beacon because it's completely different, something that has become clearer with hindsight."

Long in gestation and initially entitled 'Jim's Song', this exquisite trombone-led ballad witnessed the blossoming of the Rowland/Paterson songwriting partnership. Beside the album's brazen salvos, this poignant slow-burner proved one of Dexys' finest moments on record. With a glint of neo-punk venom, the pace quickened considerably. Turbo-charged brass rode the percussive Northern Soul gallop of 'Thankfully, Not Living In Yorkshire It Doesn't Apply'. Rowland's frantic, gasping falsetto illuminated one of the group's strangest cuts. Restating the album's 'searching' theme, the song was topped off with a catchy, defiant chorus. Eddie Cooney witnessed this live favourite's unusual appeal in Liverpool that spring. "The larger part of the audience started to laugh [at Rowland's falsetto] but Kevin just carried on singing. His concentration was immense and his performance fantastic. When he got to the 'ooh, ooh, ah, ah' chorus the whole audience was hooked."

The mood darkened with 'Keep It'. A late addition to their original material, Rowland was instantly enamoured with its economic, effective chord progression. Wingfield's wavering harmonies brought the song towards a tumultuous point of departure. The producer was concerned about retaining the expletive "fuck" in the original lyrics. Having persuaded Rowland to jettison it, it was subsequently used intact, on the following track. Eloquently addressing a sense of ignorance, inertia and of shutting out the world, Blythe's contributions represented the only example of a Dexys song lacking Rowland's unique lyrical stamp. Its tasteful tenor work backed onto the abstract, jazz-inflected narrative, 'Love Part One', Rowland's first serious venture into spoken-word terrain. Under a harsh, atmospheric sax spotlight, Rowland sought to clarify an anti-love perspective in a stark monologue, bereft of intonation.

"Didn't you find it weird when you first heard it?" Archer asked True. "I thought, 'What's this?' because I had a girlfriend at the time and I liked to think I loved her – as it turned out, I didn't. Then when I heard it, I was like, 'Hang on, he's done it again!'" Frequently noted as the record's weakest link, it demonstrated yet another facet of Dexys' musical character.

As imaginative and inflammatory a climax to any album, before or since, 'There, There, My Dear' remains a stellar moment. In an 'open letter to our fellow musicians', Rowland's nigh-on indecipherable lyrics were crammed into vocal phrases of punk-like urgency. Framed in an epistolary fury that would resemble the form of their forthcoming anti-music press diatribes, Rowland's attention to the media fawning of early Eighties acts like Sheffield's Cabaret Voltaire often took precedence over actually hearing the artistes' work.

A track that book-ended an album opening with a laudatory roll call of Irish writers, Beat authors Jack Kerouac and William Burroughs figured in a contemptuous litany directed at a pseudish branch of stereotypical, middle-class musicians under the collective alias of 'Robin'. A last-minute addition, Rowland had asked Saunders for a selection of his Moseley associates' choice reading material. "These people [the 'prototype indie crowd'] were dropping Frank Sinatra's name and I didn't believe they understood him," Rowland opined to Irvin. "I heard a track on John Peel where this bloke sang 'Fraaaank Sin . . . arrr . . . tra' very slowly and I thought that sounded good, so I put that in." Rowland couldn't resist a sly dig at the "anti-fashion" poseurs either, recommending that they adopt the flared look of the previous generation. The fluid bassline to John Fred & The Playboy Band's 1968 hit single 'Judy In Disguise (With Glasses)' was mirrored in 'There, There . . .'s brass herald and urgent rhythm. Backed with dynamic harmonies, Williams' watertight, brooding bassline steered the song to a roaring climax. "The stuff that I play on that [. . . *Rebels*] I wouldn't play like that now," he told *It Was Like This*, "but at the same time it grooves, it added something to it."

In true concept fashion, having returned to the album's opening sense of bravado, the fully attentive listener was urged to embrace a new soul vision. It closed with Rowland's short take on New Orleans R&B hero Lee Dorsey's 1969 cut 'Everything I Do Gonh Be Funky'. Was this a tongue-in-cheek promise of a future direction? If so, any plans for a funkified . . . *Rebels* reappraisal went unrealised. One of the song's penultimate lines, concerning the elusive search for the young soul rebels, was interpreted as heralding a new youthquake. A scornful Rowland scotched the idea in *Hot Press*. "I *hate* movements . . . we've been accused in the British press of trying to start a movement, the soul rebels, and they've compared it to Rude Boys and Glory Boys." While Rowland was vague on the meaning of the album's title, a lyric concerning errant soul rebels from the track 'Last Gang In Town', from The Clash's 1978 *Give 'Em Enough Rope* album, may have provided a frame of reference. The *real* soul rebels were already in place, the ones responsible for making this glorious music.

Searching For The Young Soul Rebels arrived somewhat belatedly that summer, appearing on July 19, and eventually peaking at number six in the UK charts. Danny Baker's constructive *NME* critique championed the work as one of the finest of its era. Colleague Phil McNeill applauded the album as an illuminating, precedent-setting work. In Ireland . . . *Rebels* was also hailed as one of the decade's defining musical moments. *Sounds'* Alan Lewis praised the group for injecting some modern adrenaline into the archetypal Sixties soul formula. "I can't deny that there was something really extraordinary to that record," Rowland told True. "It was much more than music, and it was very real."

"It's a great thing that the music that I was a part of 23 years ago, and a record that I made then, is still very resonant with so many bands that are around now who cite Dexys as a major influence," Williams proudly stated on *It Was Like This.*

While Archer considered it a powerful artistic statement, Saunders believes the album's multidimensional appeal is what made it distinctive. "You've got different ways of looking at the same sort of music through different people. That's why it's a highly rated album. Jimmy came up with beautiful melodies and Jeff was writing lyrics."

"I've learned how people do rate that record. In its day, it sold nothing," Spooner exaggerates. "People didn't know what to make of it, and we didn't see it for what it was at the time."

"It was quite astonishing to think that that was a debut album," Talbot said in 2003. "Even listening to it today, every track seems to make sense. You think, 'Okay, they're new, they're fairly young, there's a lot of potential, it's in development.' It actually reflects how much work they put in before they did it."

Unlike most early Eighties records, hindsight widens much of the album's appeal for Jim Irvin. "It's not what everyone else was doing, it hasn't dated. It doesn't sound like a record of its time. But neither did it sound what they were trying to go for, that sort of Stax-y sound. That's part of its appeal."

"It was fantastic, I still listen to it now," says Paolo Hewitt. "The melodies are amazing, the lyrics are really good. It's such a great statement."

"It's funny," Wingfield ponders, "how an inordinate amount of people hold it in incredibly high esteem. From my point of view at the time, it was just a good job. 'We've had a hit, here's the album to follow it up.' I was completely unaware of any classic status."

"I remember thinking, to be honest, that it was perfection at the time," a fully vindicated Rowland told Radio Two. "And that's all you can ask for."

Chapter Ten

NEWS of Andy Leek's departure had reached Pete Saunders through a university colleague. Confirming his interest, the organist made a speculative phone call to Pete Williams. The bassist admitted he'd personally welcome his return. Saunders was subsequently invited to rejoin the fold that May. The various members seemed relatively unfazed by the new found effect of chart success. "I'm pleased, but it's no big deal. It's like a bottle of whiskey, a fag or anything else," Jim Paterson told *Sounds*.

Saunders immediately sensed this was a different Dexys he was re-entering. "People were able to do things they weren't able to do before. There seemed to be a bit of money around. I think people had been having sexual experiences. The band had become a little bit sexier generally." Saunders observed that the group's dope smoking (tolerated if not approved by Rowland) was more widespread, with a degree of separation between the group and their leader, despite spending greater time in each other's company. "You suddenly realised that a certain unity about things wasn't there now. People were looking after their own a bit more. There was a sense of people thinking they knew what they were doing. And there had been this move of only signing three members of the group to the record company, and it was all supposed to be negotiated." Dave Corke, who had previously only organised gigs, suddenly had some real organisational clout.

Rowland told *Sounds* in May that their short-lived Late Night Feelings vanity label represented an unhealthy "ego trip". "We're not into that, but if we find any bands we like we'll get them deals with EMI like ours." He also praised the company for their working relationship with the group. However, negotiations to improve their six per cent royalty rate following the success of 'Geno' failed to materialise. Dexys resolved to take drastic action to convince their paymasters they meant business.

"If they didn't re-negotiate," Williams confirmed in 2000, "then we were going to take our LP, our work, which of course they laughed at, and didn't believe it. 'Come on, this is EMI!'" the group were scolded. "'You're joking, you don't do that, this is EMI!'"

"But we said, 'We're gonna do it, we'll do it.'"

Dexys realised they weren't getting the deal they deserved. On completing the recording of their album, they resolved to steal the mastertapes and hold EMI to ransom. Rowland insisted in 1993 the manoeuvre was also designed to re-instil collective resolve. "I think I'm one of those people who like a battle to fight, a cause," he admitted to Jim Irvin. "There didn't seem to be one, we'd just made a great album, all we had to do was put it out. Too simple. I got into this thing, 'Big record company's not going to screw us — it's us against EMI.'"

During amiable conversation outside the group's Birmingham rehearsal rooms prior to recording their album, Wingfield sympathised with their plight. Saunders recalls: "Pete said, 'That's the worst deal I've ever heard of.' He said, 'That's an appalling deal. It was seven points.'"

Rowland appeared to savour the impending confrontation. "I didn't give a monkeys about the royalty rate," he later admitted to Radio Two. "I think I really just liked the idea of nicking the tapes to be honest."

Recalling events in 2004, Wingfield laughed. "It's sort of assumed the status of music biz myth. The only difference being that, unlike some of those myths, it's all true!"

The . . . *Rebels* tape-stealing episode occurred at the beginning of June, just days before the start of their second headlining nationwide tour. "It was incredibly well-planned. Everyone was involved," Saunders admits. "We all knew we had to leave them with a certain amount of stuff so that they knew it was good. I wanted nothing to do with it. But they were all geared up for it."

"It had been recorded," Steve Spooner recalled, "and it was down to the mixing, and we'd decided we were gonna do it."

"It was right at the very last moment, we'd finished the project," Pete Wingfield recalls. "Everyone was like, 'Yeah, great.' As I recall we were running off copies from the multi-track to two-track."

With Wingfield out of the control room, the door was locked. The *NME* reported engineer Hammond being "lured" out of the studio. But one group member in the studio had physically restrained the helpless engineer. "And at a given signal, which I think it would have been Steve Spooner coughing, all hell broke loose," Williams laughed. "We all knew exactly what we had to do. There were six or seven two-inch cartons of magnetic tape, so everybody grabbed a tape and ran through this maze of corridors that's in Chipping Norton."

"We just thought, 'What did they do that for?' We thought it was going so well!" Wingfield told the BBC. Group members hastily clambered into their roadie's van, stationed outside. Roaring in anticipation of a swift exit, the back door flung open where the 24-track mastertape was stashed on the back seat.

"We were just about to pull away, and Pete [Wingfield] leaned in and grabbed the tape." Saunders had been warned to use violence if necessary. "I thought, 'I've been working with you, I'm not that person.' I should have at least fought for the tape, but I let him do it. Which I don't think did me any favours." Wingfield had attempted to halt the getaway as they accelerated from the crime scene. With SAS-like efficiency, diversions were already in place to shake off their hot pursuers as the group headed for Birmingham. "Getting chased by a police car up the A40 at 90 miles an hour is not my idea of fun," Paterson told the BBC. Most of the appropriated tapes were secreted at Rowland's mother's house. An *NME* news story related the furore. Corke told the press his charges would file their own account of proceedings. EMI assured the paper that any group statement could prove counter-productive.

Spooner recalled the subsequent, near-fatal decision to ferry the tapes on the tube to EMI's London HQ. "We could well have ruined them because of the magnetism, I dunno what it would have done, but it could have ruined the tapes. Luckily, it didn't. We took them into EMI. They said, 'They're ours, you've gotta give them back.' And we said, 'No, what are you gonna do about it?' "

A label spokesman insisted that press allegations over Dexys' actions could be bad for business. While on tour, the EMI chairman eventually delivered some good news to the group. "In the end they put us up to nine per cent I think," Spooner recalls, "which isn't very good anyway!" A fractious episode that would assume romantic industry legend was wrought with a bitter twist. EMI never forgave the group. Rowland was soon pondering their next adversary.

"We're just totally disillusioned with the press. We've never really been represented properly. If we're not represented properly this time, it'll be the last one," he warned the *NME* in June 1980, his final UK music press interview for almost two years. Coinciding with . . . *Rebels'* release, Dexys' first full-page advertisement had appeared in all four major music weeklies. A missive was fired in *Brum Beat*, outlining Dexys objection to being co-opted into any Birmingham rock movement. Shunning media interviews after little more than six months, sporadic essays were now their sole source of communication with journalists and fans alike. Music journalists, Dexys argued, were "so out of touch, they should be frightened."

Utilising advertising space for these opinion pieces, their opening salvo revealed disillusionment with the "dishonest, hippy press" and their decidedly amateur, cliché-ridden portrayals of the group's musical philosophy. Writers were berated for their lack of originality and "insincerity". It was all but impossible for any self-respecting group to communicate effectively with their audience. "They [journalists] like to put across the idea that they're somewhat above the bands they're talking about," Blythe opined to *Hot Press*. "In fact they don't know what the fuck is going on. They're all afraid to step out on a limb – all reviews are just conglomerations of others – so now we've got a problem getting ourselves across." As Kevin Pearce observed, their latest press missive could create fervour among fans that no other group could incite.

"I was fascinated by the fact that they would put an advertisement in the paper that was a screed of text," said Jim Irvin in admiration, "and the malleability of the meaning of the words and the search for meaning in what they were doing was so unusual." In ex-communicating the Fourth Estate, Dexys were keen to address the confusion over the group. They wouldn't be misunderstood. They were too important for that.

In May, Rowland hinted at their forthcoming agenda in, ironically, none other than the *NME*. "There's not much point me coming out with them [thoughts] in *Sounds* or *NME* because the kids who read them are already converted, or at least quite broad-minded. I'd rather say them in papers like *The Mirror* or *The Sun* 'cos that's what the real people read."

Rowland was as good as his word, as Paolo Hewitt recalls. "I called up EMI and the woman said, 'Look, I'll be straight with you. He [Rowland] is up here talking to *The Sun*.'"

"'He's talking to *The Sun*?!' So I went rushing up to EMI and I saw Kevin there and had a go at him and had a really good chat actually. He said he didn't like the way we'd talked about them, saying it [*Melody Maker*'s April article outlining their train-bunking feat] made us look like criminals."

Making their point with a pre-emptive strike was a guiding philosophy. "Undermine the press, that was the idea," Archer later told Johnny Rogan. "If they wrote something derogatory there was nothing you could do about it." The group were decidedly in favour of this new strategy. Ironically, being adept at English as a pupil, Rowland briefly considered a career in journalism.

"We all just thought, 'Yeah, fucking fantastic,' we were definitely up for that!" Spooner recalls. "We'd told the press we wouldn't be talking to them, and then we were on the front page of every paper the next week. They were saying, "Who do they think they are, how dare they say this?' It was great publicity. Any publicity was good publicity."

Instead of getting on with being a group, Rowland later told Radio Five Live, Dexys succeeded in making admirers "jump through hoops" in a test of their appreciation. Made with the group's support, Rowland admits he came to regret the move of submitting didactic essays. "I don't think what I did was right, putting adverts in the music press, slagging people off. I was too extreme, but I just thought we were being antagonistic and awkward. It seemed like the right thing to do at the time, but it was hard going against the grain.

"Some bands used to say, 'It's alright for you, you can do this, you can do that, we can't because they won't let us.' But nobody let us, we fought for our freedom."

Chapter Eleven

HAVING instigated a battle of wills with both their paymasters and the press, the group then had to contend with the repercussions. "There were all sorts of funny things going on. The mood in the band was a bit strange then," Saunders admits. "The whole of that ['Intense Emotions Revue'] tour was coloured by the fact we should have been releasing an album, with all these weird negotiations. I was on £50 a week on that tour. I might have held onto the tape if I felt that was my percentage."

Traversing England's motorways crammed into a minibus, their 40-date, two-month itinerary began on June 10. An exhaustive agenda included pier pavilions, ballrooms and two-to-three-thousand capacity Locarno dance halls. Rowland argued three years later that the venues were not suitable for Dexys' purposes. "We had been planning to do a tour but I didn't realise it was 40 dates," he told *Jamming!* "I'd said I wanted to play in theatres and unusual venues like St. John's Ambulances or bingo halls, but the agents booked places that weren't right for us."

Saunders argues that Rowland attempted to "screw up being successful by not playing proper venues."

"It's easy to see with hindsight, to look back now and see it was a bit of self-sabotage," Rowland told Irvin, "but I couldn't see it at the time, and probably wouldn't have listened to anyone if they'd mentioned it."

Supporting Dexys' hour-long headlining set were the Rhodes-managed soul outfit The Black Arabs, tone-setting, audience-baiting compere Keith Allen and new four-piece The Upset, fronted by singer Archie Brown. "We got to know The Upset quite well and they were the only group that stayed on that tour with us. We thought they had something special," Spooner recalled.

The *NME* witnessed their Brighton Top Rank show on June 14. While outlining the difficulties Dexys appeared to face in communicating their message through the constraints of a 'soul' show, their tenacity for turning up the temperature and cooling their on-stage ardour was admired. "We were still going down a storm and I think we were as hot as ever," Spooner emphasises, "but this was when things started to get a bit tense." At their Newcastle show a fortnight later, *Sounds* related the sea change since Dexys' descent on the city in March, an occasion resembling a Ram

Jam Band appreciation society. The paper lamented Dexys' paucity of material and criticised their elitist choice of covers. With original songs now proliferating, the dramatic brass tension and their hard-hitting presence were praised.

The third instalment in Dexys' ambitious agenda to see the charts "filled with soul" appeared on July 5. Detecting a Northern Soul influence, *Sounds* later applauded 'There, There, My Dear' as one of the most bizarre, roller coaster lyrical outings ever released. "It's a brilliant three-minute pop record," Chris Roberts affirms. "Great words, full of opinion and contrariness. The references to writers and poets made you, as a young man, want to investigate. This guy was singing about them so passionately it made you want to take a closer look." Backed with 'The Horse', it peaked at number seven in August. Rowland drew little satisfaction from its success. Due to a lack of TV coverage through an industrial strike, a single appearance on Saturday morning kids show *Tiswas* was scant consolation.

The release of 'There, There . . .' made further sense in its lyrical nod to Sinatra. An Oscar-winner as Maggio in the 1953 film *From Here To Eternity*, Ol' Blue Eyes' co-star Montgomery Clift played Prewitt, pictured on the sleeve in trumpet-wielding mode. All avenues of the creative process were explored in promoting the cause. While filming an accompanying video in the city centre, Rowland was subsequently embroiled in an altercation with local group Troops, who rehearsed next door to Dexys in Birmingham's Whiteheath district. Charged with assault, Rowland was fined and given a nine-month suspended prison sentence for two years at a Birmingham court in 1981. New Dexys manager Paul Burton later harboured real concerns over the singer's liberty. Burton had entered the fray during the summer after Dave Corke's sacking against a backdrop of financial problems.

Remaining at the Dexys helm until the bitter end, the late Burton was a dyed-in-the-wool Geordie, then in his early thirties. Single, self-made and successful, he owned a chain of upmarket hairdressing salons in Nottingham, Newcastle upon Tyne and Birmingham. Loyal to his closest friends at his local Tyneside pub, Burton would later become a popular member within the subsequent Dexys fold. His position in the summer of 1980, according to Rowland, was one of equanimity.*

"Now we've two managers – there's 10 people in the organisation,

---

* Burton was later reunited with former charges Blythe and Paterson backstage when they performed as the TKO Horns on *The Tube* with Elvis Costello in 1983. After having been diagnosed with cancer, Burton sadly passed away during 2004.

eight musicians and the two managers, and we're all on an equal split," Rowland informed Dermot Stokes in July. "We all have 10 per cent each, rather than the usual situation where the manager gets 25 per cent of your gross earnings. Hopefully we'll all be part of a creative team. No decisions," Rowland added, "are ever taken without consulting us."

Having worked hard to win their audiences' respect yet now facing instantaneous acclaim, Rowland berated fickle crowds for their drunken jubilation and persistent clamour for 'Geno'. "I was so fed up," he later told Gavin Martin. "I was getting ideas but on the road they just get scrambled, and I thought, 'Fuckin' hell, this just isn't working, y'know?'"

"We were suddenly playing gigs with people that only want to hear 'Geno'," Saunders recounted. "They thought that Kevin was Geno. We were doing gigs where the crowd are shouting for it during the whole set. It was best to play the song right at the beginning, and then play it again at the end. Kevin was careful not to be too churlish about not playing it at all."

While the majority of the group were proud of their achievement, Saunders insists Dexys had been set on achieving critical respect before their sudden chart success. "I think it would have suited everyone if 'Geno' had gone to number 20, 'There, There, My Dear' had gone to number 10 and an album had done reasonably well over the course of six months, with the band being taken on because of its identity, rather than being a one-hit wonder."

Archer later admitted that the adverse side to success helped sour group relations. "I couldn't believe that that was all there was," he told Jim Irvin. "We were really catty with each other and it had an effect on the group. It had gone to our heads a little bit and we started to think differently."

"I felt lousy and I didn't know how to say to anybody that I felt lousy so I just stayed in on me own," Rowland told Irvin. "I reckon that there was that feeling within the group of, 'Oh, is this it? Is this what he promised us? Let's just do what we want.'"

As the pressure began to take its toll, things grew tense. Spooner recalls one heated post-gig argument. "One night on tour, me and Kevin came to blows. We had to be split up by [security man] Tommy 'The Con' Fisher. I was always mild-mannered, even as a kid. But that was one occasion when Kevin and me had a fight, and I don't think he ever forgot that. He tried to get rid of me once."

It had started over the sound at a gig. "Kevin was adamant that he had to hear his own voice coming through the PA, but that was all you could hear," Spooner insisted. "We couldn't hear anything of ourselves, 'cos you can't play in tune otherwise. That's how he started to act." Spooner argued that Rowland began to enjoy the attention he was receiving. "Kevin listened too much to the people who told him he was wonderful and he started believing it all."

"I relished it," Rowland admitted to Irvin. "I took too much of the limelight really, more than was good for me and more than was good for the group as a whole."

A home town Cedars Ballroom show provided welcome respite in mid-July, followed by a triumphant evening at Oxford's Apollo Theatre. "We'd gone on early, 8.30 or something," Rowland recalled to the same journalist, "and no one was pissed, and I thought, 'This is weird,' and we started playing and they were still sitting, but over that hour it built." By the end, Dexys were faced with an admiring audience. "We'd won them. I remember thinking, 'This is good.'" Hereafter, Rowland resolved to play only theatre shows, standing down from "a conveyor belt of groups playing dance halls."

"The gigs on that tour were amazing. That [Oxford show] was something magical," Saunders recollects. "It was a theatrical event, and it went where we wanted it to go. The set was designed as a journey. They [the audience] went down when the set dropped and they listened and we came away thinking, 'We got it right.'"

Yet Archer admits he had reached breaking point. "I just didn't want to do the tour. I went home and I didn't do anything. I felt like I was going mad," he told Irvin. "I didn't want to be on the tour, didn't care how it was going, didn't care how the record was going, I just totally switched off."

"I noticed," Rowland told *Mojo*, "but I don't think I felt much at the time because I was so fucking driven and I was fearful of Kevin and I thought, 'Oh, that's alright, I'll play a bit of guitar.' But now I feel sad about it, it shouldn't have happened, we were a good group." With Rowland looking to further his fascination with Ireland, Dexys embarked on a short sojourn there in late July, beginning in Sligo. He told *Hot Press*: "I've met some really extraordinary people here. I spoke to one guy after the show for nearly three hours. Obviously, with all the Troubles and all, it must have some effect on people – there seems to be a lot of thoughts buzzing around."

The possible dangers of driving around Northern Ireland in a bright orange van with Republic of Ireland number plates, carrying eight short-haired, donkey-jacketed young Englishmen were all too real. Nevertheless, modest crowds provided genuine enthusiasm and commitment, illustrated in a glorious triumph at Dublin's Mansion House. The press championed Dexys' empathy with Ireland, one of unprecedented depth

among English groups. At their final show, the young subject of the
. . . *Rebels* cover appeared backstage in Belfast, waiting to meet the group.
He was given a large cardboard replica of his image to carry home.

It was on this tour that Saunders believes Archer was beginning to see
the dynamics of his partnership with Rowland start to change. "They
were like partners at first. 'We are going to be a two-pronged attack with
guitars.' Kevin [Rowland] turned up for a gig and said, 'I'm not going to
play guitar, I'm just going to stand and sing.' So suddenly Kevin Archer
became the guitarist, and not the singer." Bizarrely, rancour stemmed
from Archer's colourful choice of stage headwear. A messenger relayed
Rowland's orders for Archer to dispense with his red hat.

Williams recalled the farcical *Spinal Tap*-like incident. "They were
screaming at each other just before we went on stage, 'You're not wearing
that!' And there were a few things – the strain was beginning to show," he
told the BBC.

"It was just fear digging tighter and I think that the band found that hard
to deal with," Rowland admitted to Irvin. "It was the tensions of that tour
that really brought it out for me." Unwinding after a show, six or seven
members would congregate in a dressing room to smoke dope. Rowland
abstained. "Maybe the dope would have calmed me down. I don't know.
But I was just terrified out of my life and felt way out of my depth."

Despite their bohemian indulgences, Spooner insists the group's priorities
and professionalism remained intact. "Because a few of us liked to smoke a
bit of wacky baccy, the only unwritten rule we would all adhere to
because of our self-discipline was, when we played, we played *straight*. It
wouldn't be fair not to be in a straight state to play the gig. Afterwards,
you can have a few beers and all the rest of it. The gig was the most
important thing."

With scant resources being squandered on drugs, Archer felt a pang of
guilt. "I tried to stop it and rejoined the tour a different man," he told Jim
Irvin. He believed that outside influences were creating an unhealthy
atmosphere. "People had all kinds of hangers-on, all kinds of people
coming in, changing people's minds. I didn't know who they were."

"I would try and exert power, saying, 'They can't travel with us, the
band are travelling alone,' and it didn't work," Rowland admitted to
Irvin. "People didn't want to sit in the bus, eight of us together, any more.
It was a false situation trying to enforce that."

"We were stuck in a really uncomfortable transit van for eight hours a
day. I used to sleep all the time," Saunders recalls. "Kevin was sitting up the
front deciding which records were cool and which weren't on the radio."
Artificially sustaining the group's insularity was now beyond Rowland.

Upon his return, Archer observed a group in the early stages of dissolution. "And I felt a bit better, but the rest of the band had gone by then, completely gone," he told Irvin.

In August, Rowland outlined the group's post-. . . *Rebels* future. He told *Hot Press'* Dermot Stokes that constant change was their guiding principle. Dexys would not issue . . . *Rebels* Part Two. Why revisit already conquered territory? "We'll want the next project to be totally different. Next year we might want to make a film," he proposed. Rowland later confessed to being confused as to where to go next.

Having returned from Ireland, and finished with The Upset, Dexys finished the tour at the Kilburn National Ballroom on August 7. The previous night, Rowland had penned a second, after-hours press missive at Birmingham's Apollonia café. It stated that an honest approach from their audiences was required. Drunken ecstatic crowds were drowning rather than lifting their spirits. Normally reserved for Irish dances, the press heralded the venue for hosting its first 'rock concert'. With their musical muscle and flair spotlighted on 'Burn It Down', Rowland's distaste for 'Geno' was noted in a mid-set appeasement to the audience who, *Record Mirror*'s Gill Pringle felt, deserved better. A tumultuous 'There, There, My Dear', a recent addition to the set-list, saw Rowland's enigmatic preacher routine culminate in a startling climax.

A short Dutch tour followed, with Dexys playing Groningen on August 17. After a huge festival show and with the rest of the group otherwise engaged, Rowland celebrated his 27th birthday with Saunders at an uncensored screening of *Caligula*.

On a self-appointed quest to locate "*the spirit of Brendan Behan*", Rowland had trawled the streets of Dublin in early August. "I've quite a romantic vision of Dublin, and of its bars! The last time I was here I tried to find some but I couldn't find any good ones," he recounted to *Hot Press*. "I wound up in Grafton Street, and places like that! People kept directing me there when I asked them – they thought I wanted to go in young, hip places. But I didn't."

Rowland would later reflect on this venture in his 1983 composition 'Reminisce (Part One)'. In the song, he pondered whether a trip across the Atlantic would be necessary to realise his quest.

Chapter Twelve

STATIONED at New York's midtown Gramercy Hotel, eight young men emerged from a graffiti-strewn subway, dodging yellow taxis while being awestruck by Manhattan's skyscraper horizon. "New York has changed a lot in 25 years. It was a lot rougher then," Saunders insists. "You really knew you were out of your depth." He later drove down 42nd Street in an American girl's automatic, pursuing a 3 am *Taxi Driver*-style escapade through the city's streets.

"We went for two or three days," Spooner reminisced. "I remember me and Jeff [Blythe] walking the streets, exploring the city one day. I thought, 'What a fantastic place!'" Certain "young, red-blooded" members scored a little cocaine. The typically indifferent hotel staff showed little pity after Archer's room was broken into. Seeking air-conditioned respite from the searing August heat and multichannelled American TV, the band members chanced upon actor, and Dexys fan, Ray Winstone in the hotel bar. On a Stateside trip to promote *Scum*, Winstone complained that the American distributors had subtitled the film.

Williams recalls Dexys' New York dates with genuine affection. While performing one night at Hurrah's, north of Central Park, the presence of a certain James Osterberg at the bar impressed the bassist. Iggy Pop's reaction was never successfully gauged, although Spooner recalls the group earning a strong reception.

"The [gigs] were a fucking disaster," Rowland complained to Jim Irvin. "I felt we weren't really ready, but the Hurrah's club offered to pay for us to go out so we thought we'd go. This used to happen to me a lot, by the time I got on stage I would feel so tense and wound up, people would think I was angry but I was just terrified, and I felt like that in New York . . ."

At one night's show, Saunders' nerves also got the better of him. He completely fluffed the organ solo in 'Breaking Down The Walls Of Heartache'. "I managed to fuck it up, every single line. I don't know how. It was weird. I didn't screw things up like that. It was such a big, prominent thing. It's like you only screw things up like that for a reason." On their return in late August, Saunders was aware of a strange sense of foreboding. "When we came back, there was something in the air, an awareness that things weren't right." He was sacked. "In some ways I had been regarded as someone who had betrayed the trust of the group. I knew in a sense this was always round the corner."

Saunders attributes events to an incident that occurred during a tour break earlier that summer, when he had been dispatched to London with Corke and Jimmy Fisher to visit EMI. Corke emerged from the meeting, concerned that Dexys' debut album might never be released, and lamented the fact that the tapes had not been returned. "And I said, 'So do I, then we'd be out promoting an album.' It was reported back by Jimmy 'the Con' Fisher that I'd suggested Dave get hold of the tapes surreptitiously, and give them back to EMI," Saunders recalls. "One of the reasons I was sacked was because of the things I'd said on this trip." Saunders is also adamant that one particular member of the brass section was instrumental in his dismissal.

Corke broke the bad news and handed Saunders £200 to move back to London. It was a bad day for Pete all round. After watching a screening of *The Great Rock 'n' Roll Swindle*, his girlfriend Madeleine disclosed her infidelity to him.

In early July, just before the release of 'There, There, My Dear' and with The Merton Parkas having disbanded, Rowland approached organist Mick Talbot, who recalled on *It Was Like This*: "And he [Rowland] said, 'I remembered that you knew quite a lot about soul stuff and you were playing that Ray Charles tune, and I think you've got the right roots for this. Do you fancy it?'" Talbot accepted. His membership lasted approximately three months, covering Dexys fateful European excursion. "I only ever did one gig in England and that was a closed door EMI beanfeast at the end of term. It was a brief tenure and I loved that [. . . *Rebels*] album," he recalled in 2003, "and the chance to play that live was really good." Prior to a forthcoming continental jaunt beginning in Scandinavia, Rowland declared the group's intention of continuing to deliver on their winning live formula. "It's no good being yourself at home and compromising somewhere else," he told *Hot Press* in July. "You can't live like that."

"When I look back to the tours we used to do, they were 50-date tours," Williams recalled in 2003. "And then half a week off and then Europe for 50 dates, often back to back. I mean, we were really worked in those days."

"We were pretty tight and insular right until the end," says Spooner, "but when we went to Europe things had got really bad. Kevin had become estranged from the group, rather than it having split down the middle."

Rowland's detachment from the rest of the group was increasingly apparent. In the dressing room, he would sit in one corner, away from the others, not talking or discussing the show. Spooner remembers waiting in a hotel lobby before departing for a show. "We were all there, and I can remember him [Rowland] perched on that chair looking all intense, not looking at us, not talking to us. And that summed it all up on that European tour." Internal tensions were channelled into a furious rendition of 'There, There, My Dear' in a startling Scandinavian TV performance in early October. Dexys then proceeded to enthral their German fanbase at the Cologne Funkhaus on October 11.

"I don't think that that band ever played a bad gig," Talbot maintained in 2003. "There was always that extra something which just used to come across every night." 'Respect' showcased the unified horns' unmistakable power, while the instrumental segues highlighted Growcott's and Williams' intuitive rhythmic prowess.

Doubts began to fester over Growcott's abilities. "The drummer thought he was great by then, we kept saying that he was slowing down and it just got to paranoia," Archer told Irvin. "We'd look at each other during gigs and say, 'Is he slowing down?' We'd got no faith in each other by then."

Rowland had apparently attempted to sack Growcott back in August. "Stoker was physically willing to stand up to Kevin, he wasn't frightened of him," Saunders says.

Against both record company and group opposition, Rowland insisted on releasing a re-recorded version of 'Keep It' as Dexys fourth single. "They didn't want to play it and the fact that we'd re-recorded it made it even worse," Archer told *Record Collector*. Subtitled 'Part Two (Inferiority Part One)', Rowland's lyrical reappraisal transformed the Blythe/Archer original into a terrifying work. Entering a German studio, the 3:44 sequel represented a proud, ambitious stab at creating Dexys masterpiece.

"That was about the break-up of the group. The group was obviously breaking up on a European tour and we just felt it couldn't go on," Rowland confided to Johnny Rogan.

"We played those gigs as a professional unit, but it was at the back of my mind, and probably everybody else's mind, that it couldn't go on like this," Spooner concurs. Archer maintains that Williams and Growcott were unhappy playing with him alongside Rowland in the control room. "Someone would say, 'The bass drum's out,' and they weren't having it from that person," the guitarist told Jim Irvin. Despite the difficult atmosphere, performance standards were clearly not an issue. A desperate dual vocal dialogue produced a dramatic coda, with Archer acting as Rowland's saviour. Augmented by Wingfield's sobbing falsetto, Rowland's vocal prominence rendered the music almost secondary. His anguish reflected escalating tensions, communication breakdown and his own insecurities. "It was definitely recorded at the right time because I hadn't spoken to anyone in the group for three or four dates and when it gets like that, it gets sort of tense." Reference was made to the 1969 film *Midnight Cowboy*, starring Dustin Hoffman and Jon Voight. Promotional adverts quoted film dialogue, reflecting the song's air of paranoia.

Capturing this dark and foreboding moment, the record sleeve's dramatic artwork (a profile from an original mid-19th century Il'ia Repin painting based on Ivan The Terrible) reflected the tension. Rowland considered this wracked epic his finest hour, telling *Mojo*, "This is how I feel, inferior. This is who I really am underneath it all. That was like, I want to say it now. I was having a kind of breakdown."

This exercise was one of purely personal vindication, Spooner feels. "Towards the end, Kevin was getting very self-obsessed. And he really showed on that. Why do you think he re-released 'Keep It'? He hadn't written the original [lyric], Jeff had."

"We thought we didn't need a producer," Rowland sheepishly admitted, convinced that 'Keep It' would be a hit. Yet Wingfield's empathetic touch at the controls was sorely missed.

Archer blamed delusions of grandeur for the single's underwhelming self-production. "I think it was the success that did it," he told Irvin. "Because it was a number one, everyone felt, 'I know what I'm doing.'"

"And at the same time," Rowland argued, "the rest of the band were coming in separate to me, saying: 'We don't want this released – we're the new Dexys, we're going to get a new singer and throw Rowland out.'"

Archer insists dressing room discussions had centred on a group plan to oust both himself and Rowland and resume work under the Dexys banner as the European tour rolled on. "We had thought about carrying on as Dexys Midnight Runners," Spooner admits, "and we had sat around and said, 'Can we split the group up? Can we carry on?' And of course that came up in the conversation: 'Are we still gonna be Dexys or not?'"

"I would have thought that the others were aware that they're not signed and Kevin was becoming more and more isolated," Saunders points out. "It concentrated people's minds on a band life without Kevin." Rowland outlined in Dexys' subsequent March 1981 press essay that this conspiratorial plan had been foiled, insisting the dissenters had been dismissed. Blythe, Growcott, Spooner, Talbot and Williams resolved to jump before they were pushed. The dissenting quintet wanted their creative freedom back.

"By the end of the group, it was just falling apart," Spooner opines. "It was becoming about posturing and posing, as opposed to real belief in what you were doing. As musicians and a band, we were starting to feel really restricted. It was going too much down one channel, which Kevin wanted to go down." Rowland later intimated that the group no longer felt inclined to listen. He felt he had unwittingly relinquished, or attempted to exert, too much control. "No doubt in Kevin's mind was the notion that, 'Well, I did start the group, it was my idea.' I imagine he started wanting to get some control back," Spooner stresses.

Blythe later told the BBC that Rowland had failed to surrender sufficient control in order for the band to develop. "It was like he had a pathological need to go back to square one."

"It wasn't about progressing or developing," Saunders reflects. "It was about setting the foundation for Dexys Mark Two, which was whatever was in Kevin's head."

"Obviously the rest of the group felt that I was becoming very insular and paranoid," Rowland admitted to *Record Collector*. "Pete Williams said that. It couldn't go on really."

"His behaviour got so bad and he definitely wanted to split that incarnation of the Dexys up," Williams told the BBC. "Really, I think it was quite a calculated move."

Crossing the Swiss border, events finally reached a head. "I remember doing that last show in Switzerland, and I heard them all say, 'This is the one. This is the last one!'" Archer informed Jim Irvin. "They didn't want any part of it any more and I think they thought they'd learnt enough to get by in the music business." Approached by Williams in his Zurich hotel room to join their new venture, Archer sensed it was a futile prospect.

"They wrote us [himself and Rowland] both a letter on Dexys notepaper saying, 'We have taken over the name Dexys Midnight Runners'. They all signed it," Archer recalled. "I thought it was a joke really." His old friend told him that they would continue regardless.

Informed of their intentions by Archer over tea, Rowland's initial hurt was tempered with relief. "I suppose that was my fear, that everybody was going to go," he told *Mojo*. Rowland disclosed news of the group's demise to Paterson. "All of a sudden, the band were no more," Paterson informed Radio Two. "I actually started crying onstage, and to be honest, that was one of the best gigs we ever did." He had admitted to *Keep On Running*: "I felt like it was the end just as we were getting started, but I took things far too personal and felt like packing in music altogether."

"Jim was going to come with us," Spooner recalled. "The two Kevins were gonna do something together, so I guess Kevin somehow persuaded him to stay." Archer later admitted his surprise at Paterson's initial involvement in the defection. In Archer's conspicuous absence, Dexys summoned one final, dramatic act with a compelling rendition of 'I Couldn't Help If I Tried' alongside 'Tell Me When My Light Turns Green' on BBC2's *Something Else* on November 10.

Rowland expressed his remorse over Dexys' dissolution to Jim Irvin. "I feel sad at the way I treated other band members and that I blew such a good opportunity for everybody. But having said that, could it have been any different? I don't know."

"It's a tragedy that that band was so short-lived when it actually got somewhere," Saunders reflects. "Everyone had worked so hard in building the project. In a sense, I wonder if when we got what we wanted, perhaps it was right to split up once we had achieved that thing."

"There were a lot of strong feelings, a lot of strong feelings," Rowland told the BBC in 2000. "Oh, there was a lot of hurt there, a lot of hurt." And that sense of hurt persisted. Despite having made their peace, when Rowland and Williams were interviewed together in 2003, the bitterness that surrounded the split was still palpable. It had not been pleasant.

"Pretty ugly, really," Williams told *Word*. "Just . . . just . . . a breakdown in communication as they say. It was not a good atmosphere." The bassist clearly hadn't mourned the subsequent void. "It was a fuckin' relief really . . ."

Released posthumously in mid-November, the sleeve for 'Keep It (Part Two)' illustrated the new athletic, boxing-booted Dexys aesthetic. The shift in Rowland's visual emphasis was a sure sign of things moving forward. Dexys' latest dispatch stalled outside the top 75. *Smash Hits* suggested the group's fracture was perhaps a blessing, given its overwrought vocals and lyrical self-obsession. "It was one of the hardest singles ever released to listen to," Jim Irvin recalled. "I don't know what they were thinking of, but I loved them for it."

"I thought it would be a smash," Rowland later insisted.

The flipside, a forceful interpretation of Cliff Bennett's 'One Way Love', was equally unbearable for some. "That was terrible," Spooner opined. "Kevin Archer was trying to imitate Kevin's voice."

A failure of what Rowland called "truth of emotion" was crushing. "This was the first time in Dexys when I found myself to be widely and unknowingly out of sync with commercialism," he admitted in 1996's *It Was Like This* liner notes. "The mighty Kevin Archer supported me through to the end, though I know he found it hard." "No more teardrops", Archer sang on 'One Way Love'. It became a sad epitaph.

On November 15, an EMI press statement announced that Dexys had been unable to agree over future plans. The reasons for the split were not discussed. The following January, Rowland outlined how unrepresentative the group's philosophy had become for his colleagues. "Basically there were four people left and the rest felt creatively stifled 'cos they weren't getting their ideas across, although I don't know exactly what 'cos they never told me. I can understand how they feel – I'd hate to be in a group and be dominated by someone else's ideas."

"When it split," Spooner recalls, "the two camps went away saying, 'We're Dexys, and you're not.' We started to think about what we'd be playing and if we'd do the old songs, because they had Kevin's name on them. A few weeks down the line, we came to the decision that we wanted to start afresh, we didn't want to be Dexys." Intent on regaining their own musical identity and demonstrating their potential, Spooner, Williams and Blythe approached a disinterested EMI, announcing their plans to resume action. In a conspiratorial act laced with poetic justice, Corke's managerial services were re-employed. An initially nameless group inducted Upset guitarist Rob Jones and singer Archie Brown. After sifting through a handful of candidates, a newly christened eight-piece, The Bureau, eventually settled on trombonist Paul Taylor in early 1981.

Regret over the original Dexys' split seems thin on the ground. Sitting in a café with Rowland, months before their disintegration, Spooner was asked what he considered to be the group's natural lifespan. "I said, 'I think we've got a while left in us yet.' But we were never gonna be a U2 or a Pink Floyd. It always felt like that right from the start."

Archer sensed an almost unavoidable fate awaiting Dexys. "I think it was destined to be that way," he told Irvin. "And I don't think we could have done it without Kevin at all. If we hadn't have had Kevin we would have been just another group, wouldn't have had any success, might still be playing now. I think he really set us apart from any other groups . . ."

"It was a short era but it was a great era. Two years, the best years of my life," Paterson informed Radio Two.

"We burnt too bright, almost," Rowland told Everett True. "The feeling was so intense. We couldn't go on. I couldn't go on, not like that."

Chapter Thirteen

DEXYS' turbulent final missive had offered aural evidence of Archer's role as Rowland's rock of support during the group's split. In a songwriting partnership founded upon a healthily competitive edge, not unlike many other duos, Rowland later intimated a sense of creative rivalry. Notably all single releases, the sum of the Rowland/Archer-credited output, stretched to just three songs.

"We were very fierce in the songwriting department," Archer told Jim Irvin. "We had some great ideas."

Steve Spooner always sensed that Rowland had the upper hand in this relationship. "I think that Kev Archer was his lieutenant, and highly influenced by Kev Rowland. Not to say that he wasn't a talented lad, but Rowland was definitely the main man."

"Kevin was a massive part of Dexys," Rowland acknowledged to Phil Sutcliffe in 1993, citing Archer's role in writing 'Geno' and 'There, There, My Dear'. A tentatively performed, re-recorded rendition of Dexys number one hit marked Rowland and Archer's final appearance together on the 1980 Christmas *Top Of The Pops* special. Meanwhile, Rowland had temporarily reverted to his earlier calling as a hairdresser at Burton's Birmingham salon in late 1980, with the shop's profits later used to fund group operations. Instead of taking stock, he had already set his sights on Dexys Mark Two.

Rowland later regretted his impetus for reconstructing the group. "It was only the motivation of wanting to do them [The Bureau] down that made me carry on. Which isn't a very good basis for anything. I thought, 'It's my fucking group, you're not gonna do that,'" he told Keith Cameron. "'I'm gonna form another Dexys Midnight Runners, and beat those bastards.' But it was the wrong thing to do, for me to carry on at that point." Following The Killjoys' dissolution and in the wake of the recent defection, Rowland conceded: "I hadn't stopped to say, 'Well what's happening, what is it I do that's twice caused this reaction?'"

Archer assisted Rowland in recruiting suitable new personnel. His eventual replacement, in January 1981, was long-time fan and guitarist Kevin 'Billy' Adams. "I met Billy and helped him with a lot of things. I just wanted to leave properly," Archer told the *NME* in 2000.

"I moved to Birmingham and joined a group and they knew Kevin and it went from there. It just seems like it's always changing and it's always good," Adams later told fanzine writer Tony Beesley. Adams had originally informed Rowland of his interest in Dexys during their earliest Birmingham shows and he accepted the offer to join without hesitation. Rowland assured Adams that changing his name would ease confusion.

"I instantly liked Kevin when I met him – he seemed to have a self-assurance and determination I'd never seen before," Adams told Ted Kessler. "I knew he'd be successful – never doubted it at all."

Archer, too, had been completely taken by Rowland's confident persona. "I was an expert at hiding it. It was a life's work. Where I grew up, I didn't think I was allowed to have any vulnerability. It wasn't on the menu. I didn't think I could show any weakness," Rowland confided to Johnny Rogan. As the youngest, most impressionable member, Adams was a relatively inexperienced guitarist who, not unlike his predecessor, hit the strings hard. The 20-year-old turned his life upside down for the cause. Subsequently cast as Rowland's most ardent disciple, Adams gradually took a more active and prominent part in decision-making. A Slade fan before immersing himself in soul music, he was also a Status Quo and later Cure aficionado.

Previously part of mod-derived, chart act Secret Affair and also Archie Brown & The Young Bucks, drummer Seb Shelton's acquaintance with Dexys had stemmed from his association with support act The Upset, from the previous summer. Having played in a variety of local bands after leaving school, Shelton never earned beyond £60 a week from Secret Affair's limited chart success of three Top 30 records in 1979 and 1980.

Approached by Rowland in August to replace Growcott, Shelton agreed to join Dexys the following month. Yet a fortnight before his tenure was due to begin, Dexys had splintered. Shelton kept a flat in Muswell Hill at the time. "I joined Dexys when Kevin was having his final rows with EMI," he told Q in 1993. "He'd refused to accept wages from them because he wanted a lump sum advance for the second album."

After asking EMI for financial assistance in resurrecting the group, but with little or no help forthcoming, Rowland, Paterson and Shelton were determined EMI would not dictate their precarious future. Had they not persevered, the group could easily have been torn asunder before the year was out. With a renewed sense of purpose, the trio began auditioning new recruits in late November.

Steve Wynne, a laid-back, wry-humoured, inventive bassist, joined not long after Shelton's induction. New Hammond organist was Mick

Billingham, a self-taught classical pianist, inspired by Genesis' Tony Banks and ELP's Keith Emerson ("he made me realise it was possible to make the organ sing"). Incongruously, Billingham was also a reggae and ska fanatic. His membership of copious small-time Birmingham rock bands had been juggled around a job in the building trade.

Having met Rowland during The Killjoys era, Billingham later played with Ghislaine Weston and Mark Phillips in Out Of Nowhere. The keyboardist had also been approached to join during Dexys' formation. "I'd heard so many negative things about Kevin that I turned him down." Following the split, Billingham was contacted again. With . . . *Rebels* representing a pinnacle of sorts in contemporary pop music and enraptured with 'There, There, My Dear', he now decided it was the right move. "Kevin was very forthright, but all the main ingredients for success were there," Billingham said. "He was obviously a man who knew what he wanted and how to get it. I was very impressed by his approach. It gave the group meaning and it all seemed so special."

After auditioning on 'I'm Just Looking', 'Tell Me . . .' and 'Keep It (Part Two)', Billingham was asked to join. While his commitment was unquestionable, he sensed Rowland's reservations over his musical past. Yet Billingham's consummate musicianship was one of the most under-stated and crucial factors in the Dexys formula. "He was an excellent Hammond player. I've never heard anyone to match him. He had a really good feel for it," said fellow recruit, alto saxophonist Brian Brummitt. Hailing from the North East and about to fly to the States to join his girl-friend, the 25-year-old Brummitt had been telephoned by Shelton, who had watched various local bands on the live circuit before Christmas. An admirer of sophisticated jazz-influenced work by the likes of Stan Getz, Stanley Turrentine and Steely Dan and a huge fan of Van Morrison, he was asked to audition, and after a successful second rehearsal in January, he was in.

Smethwick-based Paul Speare was a London College of Music-educated flautist/tenor sax player. Enthralled by multi-instrumentalist/sax session man Jimmy Hastings and jazz experimentalist John Surman, as well as Herbie Hancock, Caravan, Soft Machine and Junior Walker, Speare had been involved in a trio of small Birmingham jazz-funk bands before Outlaw Studios engineer Phil Savage had passed his contact details on to Rowland. Handed a copy of . . . *Rebels* by Archer and Rowland at the Apollonia café prior to a two-song audition, Speare was offered the job on the spot. He accepted but it was a tough decision for him to make as he was then holding down a respectable teaching job.

With the group unaware of his intention to leave Dexys until the last minute, Archer's loyalty was sorely missed as he left the fold. "I just wanted to do my own thing really, I think that's what it boiled down to," Archer explained to Keith Cameron. "I wanted control over what I was doing, like Kevin wanted control." Drawing on a sense of achievement through their creative alliance, it was a pivotal parting of the ways for Archer.

The previous summer, the two men had discussed utilising stringed instruments. Adams recalled a later conversation with Rowland on this topic. "He mentioned that he and Kevin Archer had talked about trying out strings instead of brass and experimenting a bit with different instrumental line-ups, before the first band had split up," he told Ted Kessler.

Rowland insisted that another reason behind the original group's split was his ambitious proposition for the sax players to master violin. "It takes years to learn to play one instrument, and he expected us to learn another within a few days? We weren't having any of that shit," Spooner asserted. "I can remember at the end of the group, all the violin ideas had come out. Kevin Rowland had already said to us as a brass section, 'I want to do something with violins.' So that proved that he hadn't nicked the idea off of Kevin Archer." Andy Leek later maintained that "ideas man" Archer's departure left a creative vacuum. If Archer was now out of the immediate picture, he was by no means out of the frame. While The Bureau rapidly assembled new demo material during January and incited a major record company scramble between Chrysalis, Island, Warners, and Phonogram for their signature, an intensive rehearsal period for Dexys' initially entitled 'Open Heart Revue' ensued.

Housed together in a hotel, Dexys spent six weeks rehearsing at Paul Burton's privately owned Royalty art-deco cinema in Gosforth, near Newcastle. Forced to clear the stage before the daily 5 pm film screenings, Speare recalled the moving experience of hearing a new composition 'Until I Believe In My Soul' echo around the empty auditorium of this atmospheric venue. Musical discipline was rigorous: switching off was not an easy option. But during the group's occupancy, their full live potential began to surface as performance and presentation were constantly being fine-tuned. "We really needed to have the space to breathe properly. I can remember being quite excited because the group started to sound quite powerful and the stage movements were looking visually stunning," Billingham enthused. "I can also remember it being incredibly hard work."

"It *was* hard work," Brummitt recalls. "But we were hammering things out and generally feeling we were getting somewhere."

Conditioned responses to the physical demands of rehearsals became second nature as a disciplined regime developed. The gigs would prove to be arduous affairs. Initially at Rowland's behest but increasingly encouraged by the keener members, their time in Newcastle marked the start of a fabled fitness regime, including lunchtime swimming and evening runs, crucial in diffusing tension, honing physiques and raising stamina. "We all rehearsed hard," Adams told Radio Two, "but there were a few of us who worked out too and we'd go out running every other night."

"I don't think Kevin enjoyed doing it but it was a crucial period for the group," Billingham concedes. An image of sweat-encrusted musicians returning to their rehearsal room, attempting to capture this energy and devotion, was not quite the reality.

"I tried it once or twice," Brummitt recalls, "but the novelty soon wore off. Seb used to go on his own, Billy Adams used to go on his own. I remember trying it early one morning, and I thought, 'I feel worse, not better!' I was a smoker at the time so it wasn't too easy." Rowland's self-discipline set the standard, giving up smoking through sheer force of willpower. Members subscribed in their own way. Wynne and Billingham were keen swimmers.

"It seemed logical to do it as a group. No one was pressured into anything that was slightly like a demand from Kevin. I *would* have minded that. It also helped with our 'pure' image," Billingham added, tongue-in-cheek. While in Newcastle, Burton laid down some ground rules as Rowland issued his set of commandments to the group. Gathering his colleagues around him in rehearsals, Rowland made it clear this was *his* group. A *group*, he hastened to stress, and not a *band*. Any illusions of democracy within the fold were effectively crushed.

Rowland's disgust for conventional rock etiquette was emphatic: they would perform shows as opposed to gigs, and record LPs, not albums. "It was clear from the outset that Kevin was the driving force and that he had his own agenda," Speare confirms, "not all of which was clear to me at the time. It became apparent fairly early on that he perceived the group as being outside the mainstream pop/rock arena." Pre-show alcohol consumption and dope smoking was strictly prohibited. Any guilty party who flouted the strict criteria was out.

"I got the impression that drug-taking was quite popular with the first line-up," Billingham recounted, "so maybe it was a good thing."

Attempting to convey the image of a clean-living lifestyle, Rowland effectively corralled a committed group towards self-restraint. But the strongest motive behind this mindset was Rowland's fear of his own "addictive tendencies". "That's why I banned the group from doing those things," he told Jon Wilde in 1999. Four years later, he told *Mojo*. "I

remember as we were getting the press release together for the Projected Passion Revue, I said to the manager, 'Say soft drinks will be on sale at all the venues.' He said I was sounding puritanical. 'Yeah, great, I am a bit.'"
"We were certainly trying to achieve something pure, but it wasn't a regime," Rowland insisted.

It wasn't all self-discipline and puritanical zeal. Post-gig dressing rooms would often be full of crates of beer, and post-rehearsal players frequently propped up bars. Dope smoking also prevailed. "Self-improvement and self-preservation, that's what's important," Rowland assured fans.

Adams told Keith Cameron that a modicum of spiritual fulfilment was the reward for their devotion. "It was self-development through physical training. After a show, we'd say to each other, 'Did you get there? Did you reach that high?'" When Dexys hit their musical stride, a spirit of comradeship prevailed.

"We knew that when we played well, that was a sort of high in itself," Brummitt insists. "Sometimes you'd do something, and you'd think, 'That really hit the spot.'"

Past members acknowledge Dexys music was built on foundations elevated to a "semi-religious ideal". Billingham felt inspired to quote from The New Testament's Book of Revelations in the group's 1981 tour programme, which cited the gospel inspiration of Aretha Franklin's 'I Say A Little Prayer' and The Edwin Hawkins Singers' 'Oh Happy Day'.

Kung-fu devotee Shelton also acknowledged this "religious fervour" when Dexys were in full flow. "The band didn't like it," he told Q, "but they did understand and they were inspired."

The group's dedication was praiseworthy, despite bemusement at some of the requirements. "I did largely subscribe to it and actually felt that I'd changed as a person in some respects," Speare argues. "But I became aware, quite early on, that I possibly wasn't one of Kevin's favourites." Shelton, in 1993, defined the old Dexys ethic as being "big on commitment, small on favours."

Indeed, Rowland had the uncanny ability to persuade his loyal charges to enter into the unlikeliest strategies and, moreover, make them work. Wearing shorts and T-shirts, they were later filmed jogging on a freezing winter's day in an Oldbury park. With the group struggling to stay on their feet in the snow, the TV crew failed to contain their amusement. Rowland continued to promote this work ethic as late as October 1982, turning up for an interview clutching his running shoes and training kit. "To me, it was a joke," Brummitt admitted. "And I wasn't the only one. If you wanted to stay in the band, you had to go along with it."

Despite everything, Shelton recognised Dexys unique potency. "No matter how much any of us moaned, we knew it was the best band we could ever have played in."

In perpetuating this image, Dexys clearly offered an alternative to the cliché-ridden rock lifestyle. Enacting a physical, imposing image in made-to-measure designer threads, contemptuous observers of their latest sartorial statement clearly didn't understand. "I think it was just right for the music," Rowland told the *NME*. "It had a physical look about it as well with the boxing boots and those sort of trousers. There was also a religious feel to some of the music, so the hoods looked a bit sort of monastic. And the ponytails had that sort of discipline that came over with it . . ." The inspiration for boxing boots and ponytails arose from when Rowland had visited Liverpool and seen local "scallies" in anoraks. Dexys resembled an ascetic gang of athletic musical gladiators waiting to enter the ring. Group members who walked the streets in full stage regalia were greeted with mirthful contempt and no little curiosity, none more so than in pubs and clubs.

"I went to a nightclub in London called Heaven one night with Kev," Brummitt recalls. "Me and him were dressed in the full get-up, and we attracted a crowd of people. And it was dangerous. I thought, 'We're gonna get murdered here. There's a lot more people here who don't like us than do like us.' We managed to get out, and dived into a taxi before they caught up with us."

Having tightened their repertoire into a workable set-list, the subsequent stage show's attention to detail centred on choreographed moves. Brummitt and Speare and Wynne and Adams practised balancing on precarious speaker cabinets at the front of the stage during the full force of performance. Adams' string-breaking stunts were also a feature of the anti-rock convention of the shows. During one rehearsal, he ran forward onto the cabinet, overbalanced and somersaulted off into the auditorium with his guitar in tow. Miraculously, he was unhurt. The other Dexys collapsed in fits of laughter. While an abortive attempt was made to introduce an electronic drum kit, Billingham, keen to lighten the tense mood, delighted in performing cheesy Hammond instrumentals out of Rowland's earshot. "I think everyone was a bit wary of Kevin," Billingham admits. "He was very quiet and brooding in those days, understandably so, I think."

"I was always concerned about some of the tensions," said Speare, "particularly between Jim and Kevin. But, taking everything into account, it's amazing we stayed together as long as we did. Kevin was sometimes sullen, sometimes humorous, sometimes difficult to please, and often prickly. He was unpredictable. We would never know what mood he would be in on any particular day, but this would be made apparent from the moment he arrived."

Paolo Hewitt held the same view. "He was a prickly guy. Other times he was really warm to you. There was a definite charisma, there was something special there. There's a few people who had it, and he certainly had it."

Meanwhile, Dexys' woeful finances blighted early proceedings. "We were broke, completely broke," Rowland admitted. "We had no money or anything, nowhere to rehearse, really, and I kind of liked that."

"It was hard," says Shelton, "but I've always thrived on hardship."

Illustrating their unflinching devotion, in an interview with *Q*, the drummer recalled "living on about £20 a fortnight while we rehearsed in a derelict factory with no heating." Dexys had found a rehearsal space – a warehouse off Bristol Street in one of the city's less-than-salubrious districts – they dubbed 'The Fridge'. With a single electric bulb for light and heat, its lack of creature comforts typified Dexys' bleak outlook. Enduring the perishing cold, Dexys grafted on a cigarette-butt strewn, sparsely carpeted floor. Their music rebounded off bare-bricked, paint-flaked walls, disappearing out through paneless windows. Office hours were the order of the day. Speare remembers the strange intensity that characterised those rehearsal sessions. "Everyone would stand looking at each other," he told the BBC, "waiting for Kevin to say something. And then we'd say, 'What do you think, Kevin?' And he'd go, 'Well, it was good, but not *great*.'"

Brummitt and Speare were encouraged to rehearse without the aid of microphones. "'That's how you learn,' Kevin would say," Shelton recounted in 1993, "but they'd become better players who could hit notes they didn't even know existed before." Gradually, Dexys Mark Two became a close-knit, workmanlike unit. Billingham claims a sense of rapport was built as the group grew more comfortable in each other's company. They convened for Wimpy Bar breakfasts prior to rehearsals at new premises in Birmingham's Dale End. Fresh material was soon forthcoming, but it was a painstaking process. Rowland invariably had a basic tune, or sometimes a lyric ready. If not, he'd sing through a number of wordless styles, with Paterson introducing a basic brass arrangement. With rhythm and brass sections working separately, the whole group would undertake a full rendition, developing the change from verse to chorus until something suitable was found. "Play like you mean it," the group were often told. Working on two new songs simultaneously, the creative ethos centred on quality control.

"Everything to do with the group followed this important tenet," Billingham recalls. "It helped to wheedle out the obvious and the clichés."

Apart from the aforementioned gospel influences, the new group's sources of musical inspirations included Marvin Gaye, Nina Simone, Bill Withers, Don Covay, Curtis Mayfield, the Philly soul of MFSB, jazz giant Miles Davis and saxophonist Grover Washington.

Also in January, at Outlaw studios, Dexys recorded demos of a new Paterson/Rowland original, 'Plan B', as well as 'Show Me' and a cover of The Bar Kays' 'Soul Finger'. Their intrinsically tight sound was seemingly devoid of its characteristic passion. Dexys then performed as guest band on BBC2's *Boom Boom, Out Go The Lights*, a show featuring emerging alternative Comic Strip acts.* The group gathered at Mick Billingham's flat to undertake a miming session to tracks from the . . . *Rebels* LP. Each member took it in turns as the rest looked on. Brummitt and Paterson in particular looked somewhat embarrassed pounding the floorboards as their efforts set the stereo jumping.

Having recorded backing tracks at Morgan studios for the BBC show, the producer offered the brass section future session work. Brummitt and Speare were eager, but Paterson interjected: Dexys operated a strict rule that no session work would be permitted. It was an early inkling of what was to come.

---

* MC Alexei Sayle, a huge Dexys fan, released his own, Alexei's Midnight Runners homage entitled 'Pop Up Toasters' the following autumn.

Chapter Fourteen

IN late January, Dexys recorded their new single 'Plan B' and 'Soul Finger' with Babe Ruth guitarist Alan Shacklock, in Abbey Road's Studio One. Work took just a few days, and with little money in their pockets, it was clearly a labour of love.

"We all felt it was a great record," Mick Billingham recounts, "but we were a bit concerned as to how it was going to sound. We knew it was crucial." Studio proceedings, he recalls, were overshadowed by "clashes" between Rowland and Shacklock. The final product, he surmised, suffered as a result. "It was a big blow, considering there was nothing else like it at the time."

The distinctive brass section were still fusing their tight sound. "People soon began to mention the unity of the horn sound, and record producers started to ask if they could use us," Brummitt recalled. "But it was refused."

Signalling a desire to play theatre venues, Dexys' Projected Passion Revue was tentatively booked for a February unveiling. "I imagined the shows and the intensity of the shows, and how we'd have the audience on their seats and then we'd whack 'em, and take it down again and hold 'em," Rowland admitted to the BBC. "I kind of visualised all that stuff."

"Kevin was a person who definitely had vision," Speare understated. "And everyone else in the group was expected to pursue that vision." With healthy disregard for standard rock practices, dance troupe Torque and comedians Nigel Planer and Peter Richardson (a.k.a. The Outer Limits) were hired, part of a 'spiritually in-tune' theatrical revue. Flouting the group's philosophy, the duo frequently visited Dexys' dressing room to take advantage of their post-show rider.

For Rowland at least, the labour-intensive work rate and enervating, musical *modus operandi* eventually wore them down. "We definitely suffered eventually, it was fucking hard work," he admitted to the *NME* in 1993. "We were very, very committed to doing something good – and that was both good and bad."

In March, seven months after their last music press missive, Dexys felt compelled to defend their honour. "The *NME* seem intent on making Kevin this year's whipping boy," their essay scolded. "You won't do it chaps; he's stronger than you." Despite doubting Rowland's theory of press misrepresentation, the group backed his stance. These wonderfully intriguing, attention-grabbing exercises came with a price.

"Basically what he did was alienate the press against us," said Brummitt. "No one's under any obligation to speak to anyone. But [Rowland] put his own essays in, like he was lecturing them. It didn't achieve anything."

"Kevin backed out of the attention and the spotlight did come off them," Jim Irvin points out, "so that people did just go, 'What are they playing at?' and just left them alone."

"I don't really feel like celebrating my behaviour in those days. I can't say it was great doing that in the music press," Rowland told Johnny Rogan. "That's how it was then and the only thing that really stands up for me now is the music really. That's what I'm interested in." Speare feels Rowland's motives, often inciting ridicule, were difficult to fathom: the press' response was not at all surprising. Gavin Martin and Paolo Hewitt were notable sympathisers.

"I think what really pissed the press off was their whole culture and value system was being attacked," Hewitt argues. "'We don't want alcohol at our gigs, we don't want pissed up people, we want it to be serious.' They [the press] hadn't seen anything like it. Rock culture is a drug culture in some respects. But Dexys were so anti all that."

Music press news stories on April 11 announced Dexys' departure from EMI, with Burton insisting they'd parted company over the contentious release of 'Plan B'. The record company argued it was sanctioned with both the group and management's compliance. While no A&R representative had visited the group in rehearsals, an EMI office party was thrown to celebrate the record's release on March 9. Appearing to wrestle great positivity and resolute self-belief from its grooves, 'Plan B' boasted a lyrical debt to Bill Withers' 'Lean On Me'. Yet the song revisited the themes of 'Keep It (Part Two)'. Rowland underlined his paranoia over the original group's split in a spoken-word admission on unbearable breakdown in communication. However, with the bluster of a new band behind him, Dexys' fifth single was a barnstorming effort. Rowland's cry of 'Jimmy!' heralded a gallant Paterson solo, a great Dexys moment. Yet the reviews were far from glowing: Paterson's trombone work inspired mirth, while *Smash Hits* questioned both a straining horn section and Rowland's vocal display. Thankfully, Gavin Martin applauded Dexys' depth of conviction and noted an inspirational debt to Smokey Robinson & The Miracles' 'Come Round Here (I'm The One That You Need)'.

Rowland now views the song with a more critical eye. "How fuckin' pompous! I'm saying to someone, 'Hold out your hand, trust in me' like a fucking God or something," he informed *Word* in 2003. Peaking at number 58 and lost among the latest offerings from Elvis Costello, The Jam and The Specials, 'Plan B' was a true jewel in the singles crown, deserving a far better fate than its lost classic status.

Bereft of significant promotional weight, EMI informed the group that the company hadn't pressed enough copies, sensing it simply wouldn't sell. "It was the final straw," Billingham maintains. "EMI wouldn't budge an inch on anything, and neither would we. It was frustrating but we were going to carry on whatever." Having clarified their intention to leave the label, their record company issued a legal challenge stating they were under contract. In fact, they were free agents: EMI had overlooked their option on the group. Burton spent two weeks studying their contract before finding the loophole.

"If it wasn't for him," Rowland insisted to the *NME* the following year, "we'd have never got out of it."

After a High Court judges' panel reading declared in Dexys' favour, the way seemed clear to sign with Phonogram. Then EMI placed an injunction on the group from releasing further material. Effectively in limbo, Rowland surmised that EMI were keen to punish him for his stubborn antics. "I'm not saying what I did was always right. I did loads of stupid things . . . I just look back now and wonder how I would have reacted to some prick coming into my office shouting and kicking things over," he admitted to Gavin Martin in 1982, "at the time it was fucking pandemonium."

Dexys convened at Burton's Birmingham shop to hear the verdict on 'Plan B' on the BBC Radio One's *Round Table* record review programme. The show also featured The Bureau's debut waxing, released on Warners following their signature for a generous £95,000 advance. With a ska-inflected bassline and alleged Rowland-baiting lyrics, 'Only For Sheep' and 'Plan B' were both subsequently starved of airplay and promotion. The panel, including Kirsty McColl and Malcolm McLaren, were less than complimentary about Dexys' efforts. The ex-Pistols Svengali derided Rowland and co's latest vinyl offering. "They previewed 'Plan B' and McLaren said he was still waiting to hear 'Plan A'," Billingham recalls. "So obviously it was an incident waiting to happen."

Rowland regaled the *NME* with news of Burton embarrassing McLaren in front of EMI's top brass on a visit to their offices, with Dexys "using him [McLaren] to get our feelings across to EMI." It had worked, Rowland admitted, but had soured Dexys' reputation. As the group stood surrounded by stage equipment outside their Newcastle rehearsal space ready to depart for final tour preparations in Birmingham, Burton broke further bad news: the majority of their national 'Projected Passion Revue' tour had been cancelled. Although promoters and slow ticket sales were mentioned, Burton appeared reluctant to discuss the reasons. From an April itinerary of a dozen theatre shows, only their Chelmsford Odeon, Dominion Theatre and Birmingham Odeon dates survived. With the disappointment over 'Plan B''s failure to chart still fresh, the timing hurt. Hopes of inking a new recording deal were hampered by slow progress. While negotiations with Phonogram were under way, CBS A&R man, Muff Winwood (brother of Steve), was also rumoured to be interested.

"We hope to get a single out fairly quickly, and then we'll see about rescheduling the dates," Burton optimistically informed the press.

Dexys had recorded 'Show Me' and 'Soon' in March independently, with legendary Bolan/Bowie producer Tony Visconti at London's Good Earth studios. Visconti invited Brummitt, Paterson and Speare to stay behind in the studio, playing them unreleased Bowie tapes and showing them some of his production tricks. Keen to employ an in-house horn section, the tempted trio were forced to decline Visconti's offer. The experience proved a highlight. "Kevin was pretty much in awe of Visconti, as we all were," Brummitt conceded.

"'Show Me' is quite a big production, considering its simplicity as a song, and was just what we needed as our first single with Phonogram," said Speare.

Funded largely by proceeds from Burton's businesses and still without a contract, Dexys needed all the help they could get. Still on a regular, if modest, £60 per week, they were embroiled in a no-win financial scenario as promoters sought to recoup debts accrued through cancelled appearances. The Bureau appeared to be winning any speculative battle hands down. Sustaining their early momentum with dates in Holland and Belgium, they recorded their eponymous debut LP with Pete Wingfield, effectively capturing the group in its creative infancy, and embarked on a 25-date UK university tour in mid-April. Meanwhile, Dexys swiftly attracted something of a cult following, receding into the commercial margins as their solidarity was put to the test. The Projected Passion Revue was finally aired in a tense performance at Chelmsford on April 13 in front of a half-empty theatre. Having stood in the wings coursing with adrenaline, Rowland ordered his troops to run on stage.

Tensed and frowning towards the rear of the hall, no direct communication was permitted with the crowd, who surged forwards to the stage. Feeling the pinch of first-night nerves, the group breathed a sigh of relief when their awkward debut was over. Phonogram housed the group at a bed and breakfast, The Stagecoach, in Kilburn, north London, prior to their thrilling, full house Dominion Theatre performance. In a vibrant atmosphere, the capital's audience were suitably captivated. Opening with the instrumental 'Spiritual Passion', their set included 'Tell Me When My Light Turns Green', 'Dance Stance', 'Breaking Down The Walls Of Heartache', 'I Couldn't Help If I Tried', 'Plan B', crowd favourites 'Geno' and 'Respect' and Rowland's explosive, theatrical performance during 'Until I Believe In My Soul', greeted with hushed silence and contemptuous mirth. A fiery new number 'Let's Make This Precious' and 'There, There, My Dear' closed proceedings.

A precursor to greater things, *Melody Maker*'s Adam Sweeting felt the show had been a success. *Sounds* witnessed a group triumphant in a battle to regain their old majesty. *Record Mirror*, meanwhile, focused their antipathy towards a tuneless, prescriptive set. "Most of the new members have never played in groups before, and it shows."

"Untampered pure inspiration. We are spiritually more in tune, we are strong, we're a group," Rowland responded.

Record Mirror was also critical of the group's apparently anti-publicity approach. Chancing upon Rowland at a New Order gig days before Dexys' subsequent home town performance, reporter Kevin Wilson was brusquely informed he'd have to pay to attend the Birmingham Odeon show. Dexys received a rousing reception. Playing a Multiple Sclerosis benefit gig at The Venue in London, below bill-topper Adam Ant, a celebrity-studded audience were decidedly nonplussed. While Dexys marvelled at his impressive stage set, Adam was quite taken with Dexys' brass section. Their appearance proved a shrewd move. Radio Luxembourg later played 'Show Me' on thrice-hourly rotation, a contributory factor in its impressive summer chart placing.

"It was so good for us to play live after looking forward to it for so long," Rowland proudly told the Dexys faithful following their stage baptism. "We've put far too much effort, time and thought into it to let it go to waste." His confidence in the group's future remained undimmed, despite the lack of a new record deal or significant live exposure. While his former colleagues The Bureau released their second single, the excellent 'Let Him Have It' in May, Rowland's determination to produce a superior successor to Dexys' landmark debut LP was clear.

"It's only over the last few months through meeting the new members of the group and gradually assembling new ideas that I can see past *Young Soul Rebels*. The new LP will be better, it has to be. We'll rewrite it, re-record it, won't release it until it is better." Dexys illustrated their on-stage prowess at a BBC Radio *In Concert* show at London's Paris Theatre on May 20, unveiling a formative, brass-driven 'Liars A To E' under the working title of 'Your Own.'

For Paolo Hewitt, it was a defining moment. "I saw Dexys doing the BBC Radio One show down Regent Street when I first heard 'Until I Believe In My Soul'. He got to that bit where he said, 'I'm gonna punish my body,' and he just dropped to the stage. It was riveting. I'd never seen anything like it." Yet bemused cynics felt Rowland's passionate, zealous delivery often reduced the show to a melodramatic meltdown, lacking the traditional warmth of soul.

Rowland countered his critics' opinion in 1982. "People say to us, they tell me that I overdo things, that I go over the top and overplay things onstage. I don't fuckin' care because that's how it is, that's how I want it to be."

Dexys finally inked a new deal with Phonogram, resuming their relationship with A&R man Roger Aimes. The subsequent advance didn't last long. Burton had worked hard in attempting to ease a frequently hand-to-mouth existence: group members had often slept on sofas or floors of their friends' flats. It proved oddly momentous too. One Phonogram executive noted that it was the first time they'd signed a group whose single was already climbing the charts. "I felt that whoever the manager was while all this was going on was obviously pretty good," said Jim Irvin. "To manage to get them another deal and then get that label behind them."

"He [Burton] was bashing his head against a brick wall a lot of the time because of these record company types," says Brummitt. "We had to make the progress and they would reap the rewards from it." Brummitt and Speare's frequent roadie/transport duties were temporarily suspended as a short European tour was undertaken in late June and early July. Dexys played open-air dates in the Netherlands, with Dutch national radio taping two shows from a mobile recording unit. At a rain-sodden, mountainside rock festival in front of a drunken audience, two veteran hippies manned the mixing desk, capturing the group at full throttle. Having sampled some of Amsterdam's sights, on an Oslo-bound plane Dexys indulged in a tea-swilling, flat-cap wearing Yorkshiremen-aping routine, much to the Dutch passengers' bafflement. Despite other groups' attempts at sabotage, threats of physical violence and a bankrupt promoter, Dexys were determined to get onstage at the Hamar Festival in Norway, where they earned a warm reception. A folk and rock showcase outside Stavanger followed.

A nightclub show at Stockholm's modest and humid Underground venue saw Rowland take the unusual step of playing guitar onstage. Dexys undertook further dates in Bussum and Brouwershaven at the end of June, with the horn section offered further session work in Germany. Treated well by tour promoters, the group had found genuine enthusiasm among their European audiences on this working holiday. Carrying on the momentum, they headed into the BBC's Maida Vale studios to record instrumental 'Spiritual Passion' (later retitled 'Dubious'), a lyrically revised, dramatically charged 'Liars A To E', 'Let's Make This Precious' and 'Until I Believe In My Soul' for Richard Skinner's Radio One show on July 9. These much-vaunted cuts were the closest studio approximation to Dexys' 1981 stage show content from perhaps their greatest live incarnation. However, the public had to wait until 1995 before the *Radio One Sessions* were released.

After its lengthy gestation, 'Show Me' had finally appeared the previous week. A somewhat out-of-character, nostalgic cut driven by a classically belligerent horn riff, the song's strong narrative found Rowland harking back to his youth. He mused on the fate of his "wild" schoolboy peers, with whom nobody merited a chance of survival beyond their domain, the school playground. Rowland never harboured much affection for the tune. *Record Mirror* lampooned Rowland for his implausibly angst-ridden vocal.

While scoffing at Dexys' pretensions, *Smash Hits* took note of the single's sentimental sleeve picturing the band as young boys, while championing the energising brass work. It was backed with the compact, hymnal organ-accompanied 'Soon', Rowland's confessional ode to purity and the negation of violence. Nicknamed 'The Hitmaker', Visconti had proved his worth. 'Show Me' reached number 16, Dexys' only chart success until the following summer. They appeared on *Top Of The Pops* alongside The Human League, who performed 'Love Action'.

Everything suddenly seemed to be back on course. A new confidence prevailed following a successful tour, new record deal and Top 20 single. Dexys' innovative frontline horn sound was becoming increasingly familiar as a brassy pop formula began to infiltrate the UK charts. "Every time I turn on the radio these days I hear a brass section," said Rowland. In the wake of the success of 'Show Me', Dexys' musical agenda was becoming rather safe. It was time to take a risk.

Chapter Fifteen

THE name of Kevin Archer's new group, The Blue Ox Babes, was derived from the traditional American folklore of forester Paul Bunyan and Babe, his blue ox. Formed early in 1981 with girlfriend Yasmin Saleh, and drummer Ian Pettitt, Archer was also keen to re-employ short-lived Dexys organist, Andy Leek.

Their aural prototype included American Cajun music, spirituals, folk strains and soul music. Underlining their rustic intentions, largely acoustic instrumentation was supplemented by jew's harp, melodicas and mouth organs. With image a key consideration, a wild, down-home Romany look was developed.

Archer had also envisaged a string-augmented, Celtic sound. He later approached 24-year-old Helen Bevington, a Bristol-born, classically trained Birmingham School of Music violinist (taught by Pete Saunders' aunt), to play on demo versions of his group's work. Her gypsy-fired fiddle enlivened the barrelhouse Irish folk shanty of 'What Does Anybody Ever Think About?', and the mellifluous, waltz-time 'Four Golden Tongues Talk'. Archer hoped Leek and Bevington would provide a strong musical grounding to develop this new material. "I thought they were terrific," Helen said in the BBC Dexys documentary. "He [Archer] was such a good singer, and it was very relaxed. It was great to play the fiddle with such great music."

Another of Archer's new compositions, 'We Are Back Together', was cited by Rowland as a current inspiration in a *Record Mirror* exclusive in August. He also referenced Tennessee Williams' *A Streetcar Named Desire* and Martin Scorsese's *Mean Streets*. Yet it was 1980's *Raging Bull* that had left an indelible mark on Rowland. The opening, slow-motion black-and-white sequence – of a hooded, boxing-booted Robert De Niro engaging in character Jake La Motta's shadow play – proved a pivotal influence. "It was me against the world," Rowland told the BBC. "I went to see *Raging Bull* and that was just me. It was life or death, actually. That's what it felt like, life or death." In preparation for these live shows Rowland admitted that adopting a Method actor mentality had been crucial. "It was just trying to be professional in a very unprofessional age. It meant a lot to me to get it right."

With a similar press ban, *á la* De Niro, Paolo Hewitt noted this increasingly pervasive influence. "It was always, 'What is he gonna do next?' When I'd read that he [Rowland] had been to see *Raging Bull*, I understood totally. Dexys wouldn't make a record unless they thought it was great. And they wouldn't play a gig unless they thought they were gonna be great." Having blasted Edwin Hawkins and Aretha Franklin's 'I Say A Little Prayer' (Rowland's choice cut of the moment) over the PA system, the crowd were readied for the Runners' dramatic entrance. With Archer looking on, the highlights in a Nottingham Playhouse performance captured for ITV's *Videosounds* on August 16 included a declamatory 'There, There, My Dear', the brooding black blues of 'I'm Just Looking', and a torrential 'Plan B'.

Yet the general group consensus was one of disappointment, with Adams rueing the fact that the following night's superior Edinburgh show hadn't been filmed instead. A *Sounds* account of the following night's Coasters date, Rowland's 28th birthday, found Dexys being hauled over the critical coals, accused of compromising compassion for showmanship and substance for sweat north of the border. While The Bureau embarked on a subsequently curtailed autumn Stateside tour with The Pretenders, enduring distribution problems and financial hardship, Dexys played a record company showcase in Bournemouth prior to the exhilarating experience of performing in front of a phenomenal 100,000–plus crowd in September at the Festo d'Avante in Portugal. The group headlined a bill featuring a Russian ensemble, German oom-pah band and Cuban Latin jazzers Irakere. The group were welcomed by tumultuous applause, walking out onto a gigantic stage book-ended by oversized PA stacks. Rowland was captured leaping in mid-air on a *Melody Maker* front cover in late August.

Brummitt claims Rowland had already shared news of his forthcoming musical agenda with a mutual friend during a Spanish summer holiday. The saxophonist revealed that Clive Dawson had been told by Rowland in July that he was planning to dispense with the brass section and induct strings instead. "I reckon that, to this day, Kevin doesn't know that I knew what had been said." When Brummitt informed Speare, neither man refused to believe their places might be under threat. Rancour gradually surfaced after Rowland's subsequent announcement that the brass trio should learn stringed instruments during the autumn. To their chagrin, it became the focal point of rehearsals.

Shelton recalled to Q the moment Rowland laid down the new challenge. "Kevin handed out cellos and fiddles to the brass section and told them, 'These are your new instruments, you're playing them on the next tour.' They weren't keen. They did it, though." As novices, Paterson and Brummitt were encouraged to master cellos, while Rowland was aware of Speare's self-taught proficiency on viola. The prospect of re-learning his rudimentary skills was nothing less than a challenge.

The implausibility of the task left Paterson dumbfounded. "I'm a musician," he told the BBC, "and I know you can't learn the cello and get on stage and play it properly within two months. Nobody can do that."

"He thought it was like learning a guitar. It wasn't like that at all," Brummitt remembers.

"You have to learn bowing and different techniques. I said, 'It'll take years to learn to do this.' Kevin said, 'I put my faith in you. I know you're gonna be able to do it.'"

While the idea was total anathema to Brummitt, Speare felt the requirements eventually changed for the better. "I suppose I started realising that the brass section were going to start taking a back seat," Paterson concluded. "You know, they were going to be playing second fiddle to the fiddles."

Rowland later insisted they had failed to grasp the "sacred" essence of his quest. Feelings of insecurity, exploitation and a sense of hardship prevailed. Yet a spirit of camaraderie and self-deprecating humour often alleviated tension.

"The burning question of the day was, 'Where's Basher with the money?'" Brummitt recalled with a laugh. "He had a big handful of money, handing out 60 quid to each of us. He said, 'I've gotta laugh. I'd cry if I didn't laugh.' I don't know how we got by. But we didn't do anything criminal and we didn't sign on."

In September, Dexys recorded their new single 'Liars A To E' with Daryl Hall and John Oates helmsman Neil Kernon in a studio in London's West End. The producer appeared to encounter difficulties in delivering a sound conducive to Rowland's ears. Speaking in collective terms, Rowland later explained his propensity for influencing proceedings in the studio. "We would get paranoid about it to the extent that if you listen to our old records, you'll find very little echo or reverb, 'cos we wouldn't let the producers do anything," he told Stuart Baillie in 1993. "It would have been alright half the time. I think we were obsessional, really." The stirring, horn-driven swing of the instrumental B-side 'And Yes, We Must Remain The Wildhearted Outsiders' (co-written by Shelton, Paterson and Billingham) was also taped, alongside the more commercially attractive 'Let's Make This Precious'. One comic, stress-relieving exercise involved Billingham and Speare spending a night in the studio with Kernon to illicitly record the song 'Puke', replete with string-slating lyrics and Billingham's vocal impersonation of Rowland.

"We heard it the next morning and we were killing ourselves laughing," Brummitt smiles. "Kevin came in, and said, 'What's up?' If he'd heard that he'd have sacked the lot of us!"

Aware that their parts were to be replaced by string session players, the recording experience had become dispiriting for the brass section. "I think the strings debacle gave everyone in the group a feeling of insecurity," Speare recalled. "It was the brass section this time, who could it be next?" That question would soon be answered.

'Liars . . .' had been recorded just before Steve Wynne was replaced on bass by Mick Gallick. Although a committed musician, Wynne's time-keeping for rehearsals was cited as a factor in his departure. Another unnamed member alleged that Wynne was also dismissed for contravening the strict group philosophy.

Brummitt and Shelton were staying at Burton's flat in Four Oaks in Sutton Coldfield. One Saturday morning, Rowland arrived to solicit their opinion on Wynne's position in the band. Living in adjacent flats in Moseley, Billingham had a strong rapport with Wynne, and was particularly upset when Rowland later broke the news of the bassist's sacking to his shocked colleagues at Birmingham's Pickwick tearooms.

The group walked to their rehearsal space to find Shelton putting new recruit Mick Gallick through his paces. Hailing from Coventry, Frank Zappa fanatic Gallick (later given the pseudonym Georgio Kilkenny) was a solid bass player, and became an asset, quickly learning Dexys' set. Released at the end of October as the first Dexys single devoid of brass, the Paterson/Rowland-penned 'Liars A To E' was a milestone. Prefacing the strings' entrance, an a cappella group chant was sung in rhythm to Shelton's steady beat. White & Torch singer Steve Torch, whose song 'Live In Fear' Rowland was a fan of, initially received a songwriting credit.

With lines from the chorus of The Killjoys' 'Smoke Your Own' filtered into the song, Rowland also referenced Van Morrison's 'Saint Dominic's Preview' in expressing his antipathy towards the media, goading them into readiness for his latest outburst. It was a judicious affront. "Sometimes, I would sit down to write a song and journalists faces would appear in my head," he admitted to Jon Wilde. "I made out that I hated the press. But I was obsessed with what they said about me." Favourable reviews were still forthcoming, with the *NME*'s Chris Bohn championing Rowland's vocal efforts. *Smash Hits* noted it's cerebral appeal, the transitional sound of a band in the process of mastering a new string-led sound.

Despite Phonogram's concerns that the single would not succeed, Rowland had absolute faith in 'Liars A To E' but the leaden, cello-heavy offering only reached number 72, a disastrous follow-up to 'Show Me'.

"Kevin seemed hell-bent on making suicidal decisions on behalf of us all," Speare said, referring to the song's release in preference to 'Let's Make This Precious'.

"We were getting there and getting there," Rowland later told Gavin Martin. But its failure did little to alleviate tension, instil confidence or boost morale. More than anything, the group craved tangible signs of success and a modicum of financial stability.

With Dexys seeking a viable commercial formula in moulding soul and strings, Archer paid his erstwhile songwriting partner a visit that autumn and shared some of his Celtic string-augmented Babes material. With Archer's blessing, Rowland retained the tape. "I heard Kevin's demo," Rowland informed Johnny Rogan, "and I remember listening to it and being very impressed, thinking, 'Wow, how has he done that?'" He admitted in a BBC interview that its sound and style had "subconsciously" influenced him. "I wasn't getting what I wanted," Rowland confessed to Phil Sutcliffe. "He [Archer] found it and I stole it."

With their old friendship in mind, Archer insisted in 1997 he'd had no reason to suspect any underlying motives on Rowland's part, but he later felt aggrieved. "Well he just nicked the idea, yeah," Archer made plain in the BBC documentary. "I think he thought, 'This is my direction!'"

Chapter Sixteen

LOOKING to the outside world, at least, like the last gang in town, Rowland relished Dexys' wild-hearted outsider status in a largely synthetic pop world. "I wanted to be alone and try to let Dexys find their strength in isolation," he told Paul Evers. "That's a much more creative breeding ground, I think. We also were underdogs, and out of that position we got our strength." Examining what a 'day in the life' of a Midnight Runner entailed, a colour-page spread in *Melody Maker* on November 21 found the group snapped running, rehearsing, and biding their time, while holed up in a Birmingham caff over an urn of strong tea. Each member brought something special to the party. With his charisma, fervent vision and drive, his colleagues suggested Rowland's sense of humour was concealed under an unpredictable demeanour. While his dedication and determination remained indisputable, he expected the same in return.

As the 'hardest working man in show business', Shelton proved a rock steady, no-nonsense percussionist who undertook his authoritative 'Sergeant Major' role with relish. His business and organisational strengths were clear. An intuitive player with a fantastic ear and an underrated songwriter, Billingham often found his ideas quashed. A warm, genuine and quick-witted character, he was renowned for his humorous storytelling. Brummitt was enthusiastic, experienced and accomplished; his ability to replicate a tune was impressive. Providing Celtic spirit and irrepressible loyalty, Paterson consistently rose to the occasion as a songwriter. Being groomed for a future role as chief co-songwriter and right-hand man, guitarist Adams had grown into a trustworthy lieutenant. Speare, meanwhile, was a naturally cautious, talented multi-instrumentalist who Burton felt offered a stabilising influence. "I functioned well within the group when I felt my contributions were valued, but as time went on, there was the distinct feeling this was no longer the case. Paranoia set in."

What group members have described as Rowland's 'inner circle' of Adams, Paterson and, to an extent, Shelton gradually developed. Billingham, Brummitt, Gallick and Speare had built a friendly sociable rapport in their compulsion to escape the group's rigorous intensity, frequenting the city's Holy City Zoo club. "It was this thing about certain people being more included than others. We were just the blokes who played the music. We were outside looking in. Kevin and the rest became the group. They were in charge," Brummitt reiterates.

Yet Rowland was adamant that this was the definitive Dexys cast, telling Phil Sutcliffe, "That was the one, make no mistake. It was the most powerful Dexys, the purest, the most meaningful."

Having announced the London Old Vic Theatre shows late in October, an exhaustive, enthralling set of early staples and fresh compositions was in place. A cover of Van Morrison's 'Jackie Wilson Said (I'm In Heaven When You Smile)' and new originals 'Yes Let's', 'Old' and 'I'll Show You' were respectively euphoric, virile, meditative and oddly sentimental. The three-day residency over November 13 to 15 showcased the group's live gospel feel, and the theatre's traditional ambience provided an appropriately dramatic setting for the finale of this incarnation's short stage life. "By now, it was devotion time," Paolo Hewitt enthused, an eager witness. "It was all alienated, isolated working-class Catholic boys, and they were tapping into that. People loved them. That was the great thing about Dexys. You either loved them or hated them. They split people down the middle."

Backstage, journalists attempted to interview Rowland. They found a man who simply refused to yield. Jim Irvin noted the charged atmosphere. "There was a tremendous sort of buzz about the place. Because there had been some chaos around the tour, you were lucky to be there, lucky to have got a ticket and know the show would happen." On an elegant, sparse white stage, a plain black curtain formed an unlit backdrop, veiling the amps and sound gear. A podium was situated on the floor for Shelton's drum riser and Billingham's keyboards and organ, while the rest of the group were bathed in stark theatrical lighting. Bill Withers' 'Lean On Me' was played on heavy rotation before Capital Radio DJ Gary Crowley rallied the crowd, introducing the main event. The red stage curtain withdrew. A startled audience were confronted with the incredible sight of the brass section, clutching barely mastered cellos and viola, fronting the stage for the unfamiliar, wistful melancholia of 'Old'. Rowland began to sing, seated way back on the drum riser as Dexys prepared to turn up the heat onstage.

"While the guys were sawing away at the front on these cellos and me on the viola," Speare told the BBC, "there was a session player in shirt and braces sat behind the curtain backstage, miked up with a 60,000 quid cello pumping through the PA system."

"Nobody ever spotted that one, for some reason," Brummitt laughs. "We got a sound out of it but we were never gonna be good cello players onstage."

Paterson coped manfully with the task. "I just played the root notes of the chord but I really laid into it. It made a good sound," he told *Q*. "Not unlike a cat being strangled, I'm told."

"I thought it [the brass/string interface] was really good," Hewitt enthuses. "It took it away from just being a soul thing and brought a new element and you just thought, 'This is interesting,' opening up with a ballad."

"They finished the song," Irvin recalls, "literally threw the strings into the wings, and the brass got picked up. The podium seemed to magically slide across the stage. I understood the theatricality of the venue and the event, and the stagecraft at that show was amazing." The band tore into the regular, brassy set-opener 'Spiritual Passion', featuring Speare's jazz-funk, middle-eight sax solo. "I was always a little surprised that Kevin allowed it to be used, but it was perhaps a sweetener for Jim who wrote it," he admits.

"One of the remarkable things was that the sound was so hard. And we achieved that by pushing players way beyond what they thought they could achieve," Shelton told the BBC. Segueing into an authoritative reading of 'Tell Me When My Light Turns Green', Dexys hit their stride.

"It's like when we go onstage, the first couple of songs are always faked a bit. I think you have to do that to get yourself really going," Rowland enthused to the *NME*. "Then after a while it becomes absolutely natural. As soon as I play 'Tell Me When My Light Turns Green', I look up and I don't have to think about anything else. I just know that it's there. And it takes off from there and there's no faking it." A personal entreaty on Catholicism, later described by Rowland as his "version of spirituality", 'Let's Make This Precious' followed hard on its heels. Having grown in stature, the song's new precedence was realised in this august setting.

A peerless version of 'Jackie Wilson Said', Van Morrison's nod to the soul man, premiered next. Over crystal brass, the effect of the music's fury was such that, as Irvin reasoned, "It was clear the deal was: 'buy into this and we'll all be transcended somewhere else.'" The crowd suitably trans-fixed, Dexys dropped the pace. His band's heads bowed, Rowland pro-ceeded to deliver the confessional 'Soon'; Billingham's solemn keyboard chords reverberating against a reverential silence. Its elusive beauty segued into 'Plan B's blazing, horn-filled backdrop. 'Burn It Down' was delivered with a latent knockout punch and rekindled intensity. Cascading horns poured forth as Shelton's thunderous drumming accompanied the chant of 'Yes Let's'. This work-in-progress exhibited a rampaging libido on Rowland's part, projecting his passion in an evocation of carnal pleasure. Having already urged the audience to envisage Rowland in the guise of Bill Withers on 'Plan B', "as ridiculous as it seems," he offered during

'Respect', "imagine I'm Al Green," inspiring devout fan Adam Ant's lyric for 'Goody Two Shoes'. The brass salvos of this soul chestnut retained its place throughout Dexys' career. When they blew at lung busting full-tilt, nothing could compare.

" 'Respect' was a killer, a lot of perspiration," recalled Brummitt.

"It was always full-on," Speare concurred.

"People say, 'Oh, they're just ripping off Otis Redding,' " Rowland later remonstrated, "And get it totally fuckin' wrong."

Ridiculed for his pained articulations on spiritual and physical purgatory, the true believers clung to Rowland's every word. With Paterson's 'Last Post'-esque solo sounding a salutary note before the battle between body and soul, hecklers invaded the solemn silence on 'Until I Believe In My Soul'. "On those quiet bits, you could hear a pin drop. We had the audience in the palm of our hand," Rowland would later enthuse to Radio Two. "I used to bounce down on my knees, you know that 'yes, yes, yes.' I'd seen James Brown do it." Testifying as he dropped to the stage, Rowland's act was theatrically captivating. 'Show Me' found Speare and Brummitt revelling in the occasion. Their insurgency was fully unleashed on 'There, There, My Dear', culminating in Rowland's vociferous sermon from the on-stage pulpit. Brothers and sisters, welcome the new soul vision. This was the real thing. A breathless band left the stage to emphatic applause.

Returning for a five-song encore, Dexys reprised their new string-led vision. Chanting the intro to 'Liars A To E', Dexys sawed away through their new offering. *Record Mirror* was impressed, while a scathing *NME* found the lyrical focus offensive. "It looked incredible. It all worked, and again it was a very punchy sound," Jim Irvin argues. "And they were really good players. We came out of that gig saying the new album is going to be so good. All the new songs were amazing. And that was why it was such a shame that *Too-Rye-Ay* took so long to come out." Indeed, an LP captured then would have proved an inspired prospect.

With the horns back on stage, the instrumental snap of 'Soul Finger' followed. Easing back on its originally overwrought delivery, 'Keep It (Part Two)' provided a trembling edge to the set. The new requiem, 'I'll Show You', proved a more sobering sequel to its elder sibling 'Show Me'. While still perfecting his roll-call of outcasts, Rowland delivered a touching paean to innumerable lost souls as raging saxes drove the song to its climax. And as the yearning horn refrains of 'Seven Days Too Long' drifted away, the musical and emotional torrents the band had invoked left an indelible impression. "Those three nights at the Old Vic were all I wanted to say in '81," Rowland later admitted.

"The first night was pretty good, the second one was better and the last one was brilliant," Brummitt acknowledged. "It seemed like a turning point. The public were beginning to catch on."

"It was like their time had come," Hewitt enthuses. "They'd got the audience, and we were like disciples. We were gonna let them do what they wanted. It was a time of the group coming into their own."

Gavin Martin witnessed an unprecedented performance running the whole gamut of emotions. Mike Nicholls garlanded a display of regal musical power.

Floored by the show's concept, Jim Irvin was resolute in his admiration. "To this day, I've never seen a band do anything quite like that." Voices of dissent included *Melody Maker*'s Adam Sweeting, who felt the group's over-rehearsed performance drained the show of its spirit. The *NME* wrote off the whole concept, castigating Dexys' lack of subtlety, soul and humour. In 2003, *Mojo* lauded this incarnation as one of the all-time great lost bands. It was appropriate, if belated, recompense.

By way of preserving its integrity after this exhilarating display, Rowland called time on the Projected Passion Revue. "Yeah, it read well," he later reflected. "But I'm not going to romanticise that period."

"I was someone else then," he informed *Record Collector* in 2000. "I was very unhappy, very driven and had no life at all. The music was good but that's about it, really." By 2003, he'd relaxed his opinion on this awesome live legacy, telling *Mojo*: "We seemed to have an edge, what we achieved was kind of spiritual, for want of a better word. It was pure. We worked hard and there were tensions, but some of those shows . . ." In the fall-out from these hallowed dates, the group's commercial considerations remained a pressing problem. Merchandise sales had been particularly good during their London residency, and the group were paid for the first time in weeks. But while Dexys were rehearsing at the rear of an ice cream parlour at this time, Christmas 1981 was the most miserable a penniless Speare ever experienced. Unable to pay bills, heat his flat, buy food or petrol, he was forced to cash up his teacher's pension as a final resort. A formal dissolution had begun to look a distinct possibility.

Easing pressure to pay wages, Rowland suggested signing on the dole. Uneasy about effectively severing all concrete ties to the group, they persevered in a crucial display of commitment. "We could easily just have disbanded right there," Speare insists. Burton was resigned to calling it a day.

"I always thought it was a necessity to keep changing," Rowland told Phil Sutcliffe. "After we'd done the Projected Passion Revue at the Old Vic it seemed a good idea to wrap it up."

"If they were his thoughts at the time he never told any of us,"

Brummitt argues. "He was probably thinking of coming back in another incarnation. Which is what he did in the end really.

"Kevin said, 'Well, I don't think we should. Let's give it one more try,'" Brummitt recounts. "So we did."

Suitably impressed by Archer's string experiment, Rowland resolved to bring three new violin players into the fold, in place of the viola and cellos. He acted upon Archer's encouragement to make contact with Bevington to recruit suitable players. With the proviso that she didn't want to join The Blue Ox Babes, Archer even suggested Bevington. Rowland went one better. Contrary to previous accounts, it was Speare who was sent to find Bevington at the Birmingham Conservatoire. "When I walked in she was practising a piece by Stravinsky. I explained that she'd been recommended by Archer and that we'd be interested in her coming to a rehearsal with two other violinists of her choice."

"Helen and Steve [Shaw] and Roger [Huckle] came back. Steve and Helen stayed, and they suddenly became part of the group," Brummitt recalls. "That was when the die was cast."

Initially learning by ear, Bevington had begun playing violin aged nine, featuring in local Bristol orchestras and travelling to America and Europe in her early teens. Following stints in a jazz-rock and hippie rock bands, she engaged in months of rehearsal before enrolling at Birmingham School of Music. Initially struck by their serious demeanours, she recalled her first Dexys rehearsal with a shudder in a fan club dispatch. "The impact of the music and the high level of commitment was what hit me first, and second was the cold! I can remember keeping my coat and scarf on all through the rehearsal and also wishing it was possible to play with gloves on."

Twenty-year-old Shaw had played fiddle in Liverpool since the age of nine and had focused on a classical career in operatic and orchestral music. He found the idea of playing Puccini in a sun-kissed Sicilian summer (as opposed to punchy soul in a wintry, semi-derelict warehouse) rather appealing.

"But me and Helen thought about it and it seemed like a really exciting opportunity," Shaw insists. He decided to take his exams early the following February. "I didn't want anything to stand in the way, or any college commitment hanging over me. And I didn't want to run the risk of having spent three years at college and end up leaving with nothing."

While Speare's flute-playing skills were utilised, Adams swapped string-busting for banjo-plucking, Billingham traded his organ for piano, while Brummitt and Paterson felt their places were becoming increasingly marginalised. "There's a lot to be said for dictatorship within a band when it works well," commented journalist Peter Paphides.

"With people changing their names and wearing clothes they might not ordinarily have worn, you just get this shared purpose," Rowland explained. "And that's the whole point of being in a band. The moment that shared purpose disappears, you may as well not be a band." Yet Rowland's vision for the group left Bevington somewhat bewildered.

"I remember Kevin coming into the rehearsal room one day and saying, 'Okay, the three of you are now called the Emerald Express,'" she told the BBC. "I thought, 'Great name, fantastic.' And then he said, 'You are now Helen O'Hara, you are Steve Brennan and you are Roger McDuff.' And all I can remember thinking is, 'Thank God I didn't get the McDuff name!'" With far greater interest in a classical music career, Huckle's tenure was short-lived. While the strings were subsequently applauded for their Gaelic authenticity, the truth was a little more prosaic: none of the trio were Irish. Nonetheless, their impact was striking.

"Helen O'Hara and her Emerald Express made the group sparkle, she brought the show to life. Up to six months previously, I would never have had a girl in the group, it was nothing to do with being sexist, Dexys had been a male thing," Rowland would later admit. "Much had changed."

With the group honing their new sound at the turn of 1982, their previous devotional, cultish appeal now held little attraction for Rowland, as he told Jon Wilde, "I really wanted to have mainstream success."

Chapter Seventeen

I think it has to change every year, I want it to be ever changing and ever challenging. Not just the music, but the group, the whole fuckin' thing, always challenging and a little bit threatening at times as well, to kick things up once in a while, and just be . . . good, always good.

— Kevin Rowland, 1982

IN December 1981, when production duo Clive Langer and Alan Winstanley were brought into the fold to oversee Dexys' first new material, their brief on this 'one-off' mission was clear-cut: resurrect the group's ailing chart fortunes. "That's why Roger [Aimes] would have got us in there," producer Langer affirms. "We were doing well at the time with Madness and The Teardrop Explodes and so we were sent off to see them, got the train to Birmingham and saw them rehearse."

Langer and Winstanley became arguably the leading British new wave production team of the early Eighties. Having helmed Madness' early work and both Teardrop Explodes LPs (*Kilimanjaro* and *Wilder*), they worked on Elvis Costello's *Punch The Clock* (featuring Blythe, Paterson and Speare as the TKO Horns) in 1983 and Lloyd Cole & The Commotions' *Rattlesnakes*. Under the duo's auspices, Dexys would eventually enjoy their most consistent run of commercial success.

Conceived in Oldbury, co-written with Paterson and Rowland and recorded at London's AIR Studios on Oxford Circus, 'The Celtic Soul Brothers' found organist Billingham making his songwriting mark. Tamla and often obscure Sixties soul was a consistent inspiration for much of the group's material and Billingham admitted the influence of The Whispers' 'Needle In A Haystack', with its funky percussive feel, insistent rhythm, piano and serene strings. "It was played as a demo and it was really good," Langer recounts, enamoured with the strong, unusual melody of 'The Celtic Soul Brothers'.

"This was a far more uplifting style," said Speare. "There was a renewed feeling of optimism around at that time. Helen and Steve had provided a breath of fresh air, both musically and as people."

"Helen always had this sort of spontaneous edge about her," Brennan

117

elucidates. "She seemed to like to have a go and take a chance. She was a bit more experienced than me and was considered to be a versatile player." Rowland's vocal performance and the song's melodic playfulness were singled out for praise in reviews upon its release in March. *Record Mirror* felt the curtain-raising, stand-aside sentiment comparable to a rallying cry. The single was backed with the ivory tinkling, pseudo-philosophy of spoken-word sequel 'Love (Part Two)'. Recorded the day after the group's gruelling demo session for what became 'Come On Eileen', 'Love' was a 1:43 diatribe against the meaningless banalities of marital contentment and yuletide festivities. A rejuvenated belief and confidence in the group's latest work was clear and Rowland told the Dexys' fanbase in early 1982 that the group were evolving in a fresh, Celtic direction.

"There is a real sense of nailing things together in those records," Jim Irvin insists. "The Irish fiddles/soul thing shouldn't work, and it doesn't really beyond a couple of songs. But it's a sense of, 'Right, we're gonna make this work and sod the consequences.'"

Dexys struggled to garner significant radio airplay. "How could anyone buy it if they didn't know it was out?" was Adams reasoning.

"People heard 'Celtic Soul Brothers' and they didn't make any sense of it," Paolo Hewitt recalls. Peaking at number 45, its failure to breach the charts left the group crestfallen.

Langer felt the group's disappointment stemmed from their own inflated expectations. "They always created their own pressure. Kevin wanted success but he never thought about money. And he'd talk about it in a different way to the record company; he'd just want stuff to be really good, and to be proud of it. Obviously having a hit is important to everyone, but as long as he felt it was good, that was probably enough."

While there was poverty, Brennan claims, an unspoken, unstinting allegiance to Rowland's vision was apparent. "Kevin wanted people in the group who were committed. No flakiness, certainly no half-heartedness. It reinforced the belief that we were doing something special. It was quite emotional, because of the intensity of the level of work and commitment that people were putting in."

O'Hara recalled the 'last chance saloon' atmosphere. "I remember someone in the group saying that if there wasn't another hit single then the group was probably going to have to close," she told Radio Two in 2004. Salvation was closer at hand than anyone suspected. During the mastering of their latest single, Rowland had played the production duo a demo version of a new song in the cutting room.

"Even then, ['Come On Eileen'] sounded like a strong single,"

118

Winstanley insists. "We did the guide vocal, and that stayed on right until the end before he went out to do the real vocal."

"We played Roger Aimes the song," Langer recalls, "and Alan was saying this is definitely going to be a massive hit, but Roger and I were quite concerned because 'Celtic Soul Brothers' hadn't been a hit, even though it was a hit later."

Dutifully named in honour of James Brown and Van Morrison, Rowland tacked a self-referential note to the end of the song's working title, the eulogistic 'James, Stan And Me'. The original Dexys line-up used an early photoshoot among Birmingham's concrete monoliths as an opportunity to demonstrate their love for Brown, warding off the cold by chanting the blatant lyrical entreaties of 'Sex Machine'. Following this pre-gig vocal ritual, Rowland had admitted: "We try to go onstage feeling like most bands do when they come back for an encore and that warm-up session certainly works."

Rowland's presence and Dexys' musical dynamism had already earned favourable comparisons to the pinnacle of James Brown and his Famous Flames' live revue's powers in the early Sixties. Around the time the group demoed 'James, Stan And Me', Brown played Birmingham in early 1982. Rowland enthused over seeing the Godfather of Soul on his knees singing 'Prisoner Of Love', telling the *NME*, "I thought that was really great because it was getting through to people."

An early clue to Rowland's admiration for Van Morrison, meanwhile, had appeared in an early 1980 interview with *Record Mirror*. Championing the Irishman who'd inspired supposed new-wave pretenders Graham Parker, Joe Jackson and Elvis Costello, Rowland dismissed them as "petty imitations of the real thing." Rowland counted *Astral Weeks*' exploratory nine-minute track 'Madame George' as an epiphany. He has also cited 'Into The Mystic' (from the 1970 follow-up *Moondance*) as an all-time favourite.

Crucially, Morrison's vocal improvisations and ululations left a deep impression on Rowland, whispering his heart's intent into the microphone or bellowing from the bottom of his soul. The Man's *It's Too Late To Stop Now* double live LP from 1974 ("the deepest, most powerful record I've ever heard") had the biggest impact on Rowland. It featured the acclaimed Caledonian Soul Orchestra, augmented by a string quartet. The employment of the Emerald Express violin trio indicated something of this record's influence.

On tracks such as 'Until I Believe In My Soul', Rowland's stage delivery and exuberant testifying had already drawn comparisons with Brown, the illustrious Soul Brother Number One. But it was Paterson that

Rowland identified as his own soul brother. " 'The Celtic Soul Brothers' was me and Jim, Jim being Scottish and me being Irish," he explained to Radio Two in 2004. "The strong devotion was the band, or was supposed to be anyway. That was my ideal."

Rowland and Paterson would often work through the night, testing ideas, thrashing out new songs and developing arrangements. The Dexys songwriting discipline was a 'continuous process', each song taking six weeks to two months to complete. "I have one of these little recorders and I go around with it, taping ideas into it all the time and writing ideas in a little notebook," Rowland told Gavin Martin. "But I certainly don't think they're instant and they have to be out right away."

Rowland always needed a partner with whom to collaborate and translate his ideas. Various Dexys' members have underlined Paterson's vital role. "His classical training was a great help to him. He really rose to the occasion," said Billingham.

"Jimmy was a massive part of the songwriting team, and he was just as passionate as Kevin was about the group and about the music," Brennan attests, "but so was everybody else." Overwhelmed by the rest of the group's musicianship, Brennan was particularly impressed by the organist. "Micky was very academic, he was very thorough and he could include every kind of nuance. The arrangements had every kind of detail and dynamic in them, and it was Micky and Jim who would write these parts out."

Speare observed the many "peaks and troughs" in Rowland and Paterson's working relationship. "Kevin handled Jim with kid gloves," Speare maintains, "and rightly so, because Jim had been the only original member to resist the temptation to leave."

"It was a pull-push relationship," Brummitt agrees. "Jim was very loyal to Kevin. But on one hand we had Kevin berating us, and on the other hand we'd have Jim berating us on behalf of Kevin. And then the next thing you know, Jim would be in the pub with us. There were a lot of undercurrents."

Having not played on 'Celtic Soul Brothers', Brummitt was all too aware of his diminishing role in an increasingly marginalised brass section and resolved to leave of his own volition. "The worst of it was being left in the dark. Things were being decided without consultation, not being told. And it wasn't just the direction of the group. That's the way it was, from start to finish." A week before leaving the group, Brummitt was enjoying the sun at Paterson's house. Turning to the trombonist, he argued that their days were well and truly numbered. Steady offers of session work, from Langer and Winstanley among others, continued to present themselves. Brummitt suggested they strike out on their own. Just weeks before Dexys were due to record their second album, Brummitt walked out of rehearsals for the final time.

Returning to Paterson's house, he broke the news. The trombonist's emotions overwhelming him, he headed for the studio. Rowland arrived and asked where Brummitt was. 'He's left, he's packed it in,' the Scotsman told his songwriting partner. Paterson then informed Rowland he was leaving too. "I went into rehearsals and I don't know what happened. I just started crying and said, 'I'm leaving,' and just walked out," he told the BBC. "We were still in the middle of writing 'Come On Eileen', and although I'd co-written all the songs on the LP, it just wasn't enough to keep me there."

Rowland told Radio Two that Brummitt, who had appeared "troubled" during rehearsals for 'Come On Eileen', had been invited to leave. Paterson's departure, he insists, was an act of support for his colleague. Brummitt and Burton returned home to the North East, the weekend of the former's departure.

"I went back to Newcastle on the bus, took me about 11 hours," Brummitt recalls. "I got back to my flat and I thought, 'That's it. I'm virtually destitute. I've got virtually nothing to show for it, but I've made the right decision.'" They visited O'Hara en route, with Burton paying her session fees. She would later consider a place with the Bilbao Symphony Orchestra in Spain. Opting to stay with the group, she eventually started a relationship with Rowland.

Three weeks after his departure, Brummitt was at a friend's music shop in Newcastle when he received an unexpected phone call. "Don't ask me how he got the number. Kevin rang up the shop, and said, 'Is that it then?' We had a bit of banter, exchanged a few insults, and then he said, 'Would you consider coming back to do the album?'" Brummitt offered to return on one condition: that the brass trio would record together. Rowland agreed. Seeking to capture something of the fervour and drama of their live shows, Rowland's determination to top . . . *Rebels* remained a strong motivational force. Following three days of meticulous preparation, the songs were in rude health.

"They wanted to play together like they did in rehearsals and we let them," Clive Langer insists.

"We went, 'Great, see you next week,'" Winstanley recalls. "But they said, 'No, no, no – we want to play you the whole album!'"

Dexys performed their new material in a Birmingham rehearsal room. "We were kind of like pinned to the wall while they rehearsed it," laughs Langer. "They did all the movements that they would later do on stage.

They were still wearing the kind of boxing gear, but were in a transition visually. Their performance was incredible." While it was a largely productive period, tensions simmered below the surface. The *Too-Rye-Ay* sessions have been painted as a somewhat desultory experience for certain members. The shift towards strings at the horns' expense had already created an uneasy atmosphere. Paterson and Brummitt had returned to record, while Speare felt isolated and uncertain of his future.

Brennan, unaware of the horn players' earlier string 'tuition', admits: "It was clear that there was going to be a new sound, and not everyone seemed overly ecstatic about it. I think people sensed that there was a major metamorphosis coming on. Being realistic about it, Jim must have thought, 'Who are these kids coming in with violins? Is this gonna rock the boat and affect our future?' "

With neither of the production team party to Dexys politics, Langer argued that the strings were not taking priority. "The brass section was there beforehand, so they were like an older dog when a new puppy comes along and everyone loves the puppy. Maybe the string players were more naïve to the situation and they needed more attention, but I didn't feel there was any resentment at the time."

Brennan remembers the situation a little differently. "There was a lot of tension at the time. People were sitting around and wondering what was going to happen and which way the record was going. Kevin was definitely doing his best to keep the camaraderie together. He was pleading with a couple of the members of the brass section that things were going to be okay, they'd still be playing."

The pervasive sense of paranoia within the group stunned Brennan. "I'd never experienced it before Dexys. It was incredible." Initially envisaged as separate entities, Rowland was wary of merging horns and strings on certain songs.

"Kevin was really into his soul and his Motown and Stax and stuff," said Langer. "Everyone had always mixed strings and brass, but it hadn't quite occurred to him. I wasn't that aware of this being a string song and that being a brass song. He might have seen the songs in a totally different way. Even if they were written for strings but we thought it needed a bit of brass, then we could suggest it."

"When we started working on this I was really worried thinking, 'Half the LP's going to be new Dexys, half the old – maybe we should have one side for the old and the other for the new,' but I decided that'd be terrible," Rowland revealed to the *NME* that summer. "I just tried to put them together and it surprised me how well it worked – it really did." Rowland later said that Phonogram's impatience for a hit single left him little choice but to consent to commercially driven considerations.

"Kevin was slightly reticent because his mind was set," Langer confirms. "But once we tried it, he liked it. If he agreed that something needed changing, and he liked it, there were no problems. We didn't stifle him in the studio."

Provisionally entitled *Hey, Where Are You Going With That Suitcase?* Dexys' second album was completed at a brisk pace at Genetic studios in Streatley, Berkshire. Working 10 or 12-hour days, the whole project took five weeks during late March and April 1982. Fearing the loss of his vocal power, a solitary day's work was lost when Rowland was taken to Reading Hospital for a throat examination. "Kevin's got a lot of character in his voice, and the melodies are really good," Winstanley feels. "The singing isn't great on *Too-Rye-Ay*. But it's the sound and it works." Quoting the marriage of acoustic instrumentation and well-honed horn lines as it's strongest asset, Rowland continues to single out 'Let's Make This Precious' as a standout track. One of *Too-Rye-Ay*'s abiding strengths is the stirring warmth provided by 'The Sisters Of Scarlet' (a.k.a. Katie Kissoon, Carol Kenyon, and Sam Brown), the first female voices to appear on a Dexys record.

Following abortive attempts to summon a requisite feel on 'Liars A To E', Rowland successfully encouraged the trio to adopt a sassy, Deep South vocal vibe. After sending a two-track demo comprising 'The Celtic Soul Brothers' and a cover of 'Jackie Wilson Said' to Van Morrison, Morrison's contribution was requested on their version of his song. Instead, Morrison intoned a few choice comments for fans in a brief, Michael Caine-style monologue intended as an album coda, which didn't make the final cut. Dexys faced a challenge in recording 'Soon' and a segue into 'Plan B' and 'I'll Show You' in one take. Paterson's brilliant, expressive trombone solo on 'Plan B' was shelved in favour of a dated, tuneless harmonica, while it's equivalent on 'Until I Believe In My Soul' was jettisoned for Speare's tin whistle. Perfecting the latter song's brass harmonies and requisite atmospherics proved problematic. The group's regimented discipline was a far cry from the more *laissez-faire* attitude and random studio processes Langer and Winstanley were accustomed to. "They walked in like an army, recorded like an army," the producer opines, "and went home like an army."

"I think that with trained musicians, it didn't matter how good the violin player was or how good the sax player was. Coming out of punk, it was all about this energy," Peter Paphides reasons, "and it was every-thing." Yet the group's general would soon assume individual artistic billing.

"Within a few years, Kevin Rowland was much more known than anyone else, and unfairly so," Rowland admitted to Johnny Rogan. The product of Kevin Rowland *and* Dexys Midnight Runners, *Too-Rye-Ay* was a consummately eclectic record of ballistic entreaties, contemplative ballads and epic redemption numbers. The group were often found waging a vibrant musical battle to establish some middle ground between past and present.

The album was the product of a period of transition, Speare considered. "It was the new sound and we'd arrived." With hindsight, Rowland felt that Dexys had failed to deliver on what he'd envisaged as being their masterpiece. He would often describe *Too-Rye-Ay* as a soulless, flawed artefact.

"He must have respected what was going on enough to go along with it," Langer reasoned. "If he wasn't happy with it, then why get us to do the next single?"

Aside from the strength of the material itself, Langer and Winstanley's work on *Too-Rye-Ay*, while subject to subsequent criticism, gave Dexys a key to chart success. "When people enthuse about *Too-Rye-Ay*, I am wincing inside," Rowland later admitted to Jon Wilde, "because I never felt worthy of the big success." Yet as quickly as the new record had been assembled, Dexys began to fragment. "I didn't know how to hold it together," Rowland told Ted Kessler. "I was afraid and a bully." His own assessment, that he had been a "monster to work with," seemed an over-simplification of pressures circulating around the group.

"Kevin could be quite intimidating, but nothing ever blew up," Langer insisted. Amidst the determination and industriousness, there were moments of levity. The producer recalled a fitting postscript to the saga. "I bumped into Kevin five, 10 years later and he said, 'The record could have been better, it could have been better.' I said, 'Yeah, it could have been better, but it was pretty good.' Everything could be better in hindsight. Whether it *would* be better, I don't know."

With *Too-Rye-Ay* completed by May, Speare had decided enough was enough. With Rowland about to fly to Spain on holiday, he was left responsible for booking a rehearsal room ahead of his return. It was the final straw. Wanting to call a group meeting in the hope of establishing some moral support and quell Speare's instinct to quit, Shelton felt it was a pointless exercise. He wished Speare good luck for the future. Rowland never contacted him to find out his reasons for leaving. Speare recalled feeling torn over his departure just as commercial, and crucially, financial rewards began to arrive later that summer. "On one hand, I kept thinking that, after all the difficulties of the last year-and-a-half, I'd left just as they'd

Dexys photographed for a 'day in the life' feature in autumn 1981, a period of fractious transition that saw the disgruntled brass section being utilised by Rowland as a short-lived novice string trio. With Speare playing viola, Brummitt (seated left) and Paterson (seated right) attempted to master cellos. Following Steve Wynne's sacking, newly installed bassist Mick Gallick (swiftly awarded the alias of Giorgio Kilkenny) is pictured standing, far right. *(Adrian Boot/Retna)*

Dexys busking their soul message on the mean streets of Birmingham, 1981. *(LFI)*

The Bureau, early 1981, left to right: guitarist Rob Jones, Growcott, singer Archie Brown, Williams, Spooner, Hammond/keyboardist Mick Talbot, Blythe, trombonist Paul Taylor. *(Mike Laye)*

The late Paul 'Basher' Burton, Corke's replacement as Dexys manager in the summer of 1980, pictured at the Avante Festival in Portugal, September 1981. Burton sadly passed away in 2004 after a battle with cancer. *(Brian Brummitt Collection)*

Neil Kernon, producer of the group's Phonogram single 'Liars A To E', aboard the Dexys tour bus en route to the Avante Festival, Portugal. *(Brian Brummitt Collection)*

Original Dexys manager Dave Corke, later re-instated by the former Midnight Runners quintet of Blythe, Growcott, Spooner, Talbot and Williams to oversee The Bureau's affairs in 1981. *(Mike Laye)*

A pre-occupied Billy Adams (left) and Rowland, experimenting with new off-duty headwear, enjoy trademark refreshments aboard a flight from Amsterdam to Oslo during their European tour, June 1981. "This was our phase of pretending to be Yorkshiremen," Brummitt recalls, to the utter bafflement of their fellow Dutch passengers. *(Brian Brummitt Collection)*

A ponderous Jim Paterson at manager Paul Burton's flat in Four Oaks, Sutton Coldfield, 1981. *(Brian Brummitt Collection)*

Rowland replete with guitar on stage at Stockholm's hot, dingy Underground Club, June 1981, an unfamiliar sight for Dexys fans during their Projected Passion Revue live shows that year. *(Brian Brummitt Collection)*

Micky Billingham in relaxed mood on tour in Stockholm, June 1981. *(Brian Brummitt Collection)*

Swapping skins for strings, drummer Shelton is caught in a unique guitar-wielding moment at Burton's abode, early 1981. *(Brian Brummitt Collection)*

Sermon from the stage: Rowland preaching the soul gospel to the Dexys faithful at London's The Venue, May 1981. *(David Corio/Retna)*

The gang's all here. Dexys line up for the camera in early 1981. This second incarnation of the group were hailed in some quarters as one of the UK's greatest 'lost' bands. *(LFI)*

The gypsified, celtic soul brethren, flushed with post-'Eileen' chart success, autumn 1982.
Back row left to right: bassist (and future Status Quo stalwart) John Edwards, violinist Steve 'Brennan' Shaw, Billy Adams. Seated left to right: Shelton, Rowland's then-current girlfriend and violinist/string arranger Helen 'O'Hara' Bevington, Billingham, Rowland. *(LFI)*

A dungaree-clad Rowland strikes a familiar roof-raising pose during a performance of their chart-topping, career-salvaging 'Come On Eileen' on *Top Of The Pops,* July1982. *(LFI)*

Brooks Brothers in arms: A dignified portrait from the *Don't Stand Me Down* photo sessions, the group's long-in-gestation third album. Maligned as much for the look as the music, the work has long since been re-evaluated as a timeless lost classic. Seated next to O'Hara, saxophonist Nick Gatfield had fled the fold by the time the LP was eventually released in September 1985.

Rowland's nerve-shredding return to the live stage, following a near 14-year absence at the Reading Festival in August 1999, provoked controversy. Clad in white mini-dress, stockings and knickers and joined by two dancers for the performance of solo single 'Concrete And Clay', Rowland later attracted derision and contempt for his new sartorial guise. *(Stuart Mostyn/Redferns)*

Returning as the dapper statesmen of British pop in 2003, Rowland (centre) is flanked by the latest Dexys cast, who performed an acclaimed UK tour that autumn, their first for 18 years. Including former members Talbot (centre back) and Williams (far right), also pictured at that year's *Q* Music Awards were drummer Crispin Taylor (far left), stood beside keyboardist Volker Janssen, next to trombonist Paul Taylor. Bassist Julian Crampton is second right. *(LFI)*

The stranger at the door? Rowland in his unique brand of gentrified attire. *(Tony Buckingham/Redferns)*

cracked it," he said. "But on the other hand, I knew I couldn't have stayed any longer as I was at the end of my tether." Suffering from something close to nervous exhaustion, Speare admits, "The group was obviously the source of my problems, but I dreaded having to spend any time away from it because this meant I'd be stuck in my flat with no money.

"There was a lot of resentment within me, but I think I did a good job of hiding it. I was encouraged by the fact that Mick Gallick, a good mate at the time, later decided to leave – things obviously hadn't improved within the group." While Shelton insisted Gallick left later that summer in the belief he had no future with the group, Speare felt the bassist had simply had enough.

Following The Bureau's dissolution and with The Blue Ox Babes in search of a new bassist, Pete Williams was brought in at short notice to play a Stiff Records showcase at Birmingham Arts Centre during the summer of 1982. The record label was impressed with the group. However, Andy Leek subsequently left the fold. Having come this far, Archer felt the show had to go on. "I said we could still make a record," he told Everett True, "but the problem was I didn't want to deal with all the music and all the image as well."

According to Rowland, Archer approached Paul Burton for assistance in securing his group a record deal. Stiff Records boss Dave Robinson appeared to harbour reservations about The Babes' material. "He said, 'It sounds like Dexys, but don't worry about it,'" Archer recalled, attempting to explain he'd been a founder member. "I said, 'What do you mean, don't worry about it?' He said, 'Well, they've made it now with a big single,'" he told Johnny Rogan in 2000. Leek's departure was also cited as a factor in Archer's decision to inform Stiff there would be no single-only deal. Rowland had braced himself for some sort of Dexy/Blue Ox face-off. Why hadn't Archer released a single? Rowland mused. "It was a big relief not to sign," Archer insisted to True, "and then I heard 'Come On Eileen'."

With a generic brass riff and lack of a recognisable chorus marking it as a work-in-progress number, Dexys had premiered 'Yes Let's' back in November. "It was demoed, but it sounded very clumsy in parts. But it didn't go to waste," Billingham insists. 'Yes Let's' offered melodic signposts and intriguing lyrical glimpses of what was to come. On Dexys' summer 1981 Scandinavian tour, an interview on spirituality with an attractive journalist in Stockholm had provided Rowland with inspiration.

"This girl came to interview me," he told Radio Two. "And she was talking about the spirituality of Dexys. But the fact of it was she was absolutely beautiful and I just really fancied her. But I wasn't able to say that 'cos we were having this conversation about spirituality. What I really wanted to do was get next to her." Inevitably, sex entered the equation. 'Yes Let's' most provocative statement of intent found Rowland casting spiritual matters aside, keen to enact his lustful desire.

At the time, Rowland alluded to another, possibly dubious story of a blossoming childhood friendship with a young girl. Set against a natural teenage sexual impulse was the sense of Catholic guilt that informed this tongue-twisting entreaty. With its opening lyrical gambit (concerning Fifties singer Johnny Ray's tear-inducing effect on the female populace) in place, 'Come On Eileen' had developed into its following incarnation, 'James, Stan And Me', early in 1982. By the time Rowland recorded his final vocal during the spring LP sessions, Langer recalled the "weird" sensation of hearing what became the famous chorus lines to 'Come On Eileen' instead. "The lyric had completely changed. It was one of their new songs, so that's why the lyrics hadn't been finished. Which threw us, because we were so used to hearing it as it was."

A laborious proposition in rehearsals, Adams' proficiency had been put to the test. "Billy was great, he had a good attitude, but he just wasn't a great guitarist," Winstanley said. "On 'Come On Eileen', we must have got through a dozen strings for the banjo part from the beginning of the song to the end. But it sounds good."

"You could hear that the banjo gave it loads of life," Langer insists. Boasting a melodic debt to The Isley Brothers and a distinctive Tamla piano sound, Jimmy James & The Vagabonds' 'A Man Like Me' has been repeatedly singled out as the song's strongest influence. But Dexys *did* co-opt the rhythmic and percussive basis of Unit Four Plus Two's 1965 hit single 'Concrete And Clay'.

Rowland admitted the inspirational source for the overly familiar, tension-building mid-song segment to Radio Two. "[In] one of his [Archer's] songs he had a breakdown and a speed-up section. It was a completely different rhythm and melody to 'Come On Eileen' but I used the idea. And it was wrong, I shouldn't have done it."

Intriguingly, this breakdown section proved problematic, and might easily have been discarded. "We did go through a period of questioning whether that breakdown and build-up should be there, when it changes tempo," Langer asserts. "It's really stupid now because it's one of the strongest points of the song." The producer believes Rowland's musicality has been overlooked and underplayed. "I think he gave too much credit to Kevin Archer. But we experienced him, and he seemed very musical."

In an increasingly parlous financial position with Phonogram, a future for the group without immediate commercial success had become untenable.

"If it takes you a long time to get success, you might be £500,000 in debt to the record company," said Shelton in a 1997 magazine interview. "You can quite easily find yourself having Top 10 records and earning £80 a week, because there might be five or six of you, plus expenses. The running cost for the band could be £100,000 per year, so before you even sell anything, you could be massively in debt." Without radio airplay and lacking much needed exposure, if 'Come On Eileen' followed the form of their previous two singles, Phonogram would have had little hesitation in dropping Dexys at this point. The group travelled to Newcastle to prepare for their first live shows since November. It would prove another triumph over the odds as Dexys began a phoenix-like ascent.

Chapter Eighteen

HAVING told the music weeklies of their imminent departure in order to attract session work, Brummitt, Paterson and Speare's first assignment comprised one last live performance with their old band. Through local contacts, Brummitt and Burton organised a successful warm-up show at a Gateshead working men's club. "I knew the people who were on the committee at the club. I said to the Coatesworth chairman, 'Would you be interested in having Dexys Midnight Runners on here?' and he almost fainted! I said, 'We'll do a night here before we do a Radio One Roadshow.'"

"It was a good idea," said Speare, "to play a low-key venue before presenting a whole new sound, with new members, live on national radio!" The following day, armed with new and reinterpreted material, the dungaree-clad Midnight Runners and the Emerald Express made their inaugural live bow on a Newcastle Exhibition Park stage on June 6.

Rowland recalled the perverse adrenaline charge to Paolo Hewitt as the curtain went up on Dexys Mark Three. "I walked on and you could see the jaws drop. I felt, 'Here you are, you fuckers, what do you think of this? You thought we'd have ponytails and the anoraks.' I love that side of it, I must admit." Rowland and Adams had returned to rehearsals one day following a King's Road, Chelsea shopping trip with a large allocation of baggy denim dungarees. Rowland would frequently carry around black bin liners full of clothes, ready to augment their new image. Before long, leather jerkins, tatty cardigans, tawdry pullovers, plimsolls and neckerchiefs became *de rigueur*. In a loose theme of non-conformity, long unkempt hair became the order of the day. Quizzed on the philosophy behind Dexys' new apparel, Rowland told *Jamming!*: "We had the hair from one thing, and the Southern American dungarees, and other things thrown in. It was a contrived image intended to convey a wild feeling, not necessarily a gypsy look."

"Unemployment was rising, Thatcher was in, people were really dressing down and ripping their denims. And Kevin's there with the inside-out dungarees. And he was always trying to tap into this," Paolo Hewitt suggests.

"Kevin got into a boho, gypsy look. There's something very romantic about that fiddler-gypsy image," Chris Roberts insists. "He was building up a mythology and romance around the band. It was very appealing and very inspirational." Most of the group, however, including an initially aghast Adams, weren't too happy with it. Critics of this latest sartorial guise applied the old 'if it ain't broken, why fix it?' maxim.

"Against what was going on, it was a cool, sexy look in the summer of '82," Rowland asserted in 2003. "Being different from everybody else was a factor." With scant opportunity to soundcheck, Dexys were forced to restart their set after a blasé crew of technicians failed to switch on the recording equipment. Yet internal problems and external pressures worked in their favour. With the brass players audibly loaded with extra determin-ation, Dexys gave a thrilling account of themselves.

Only three 'exclusive' live numbers were played on the night, including a cover of MFSB's 'The Sound Of Philadelphia' and the three-month-old single 'The Celtic Soul Brothers'. Significantly, the live debut of 'Come On Eileen' was accorded a rousing reception. "It was brilliant," Brummitt enthused. "It was the best we'd ever done. Much more relaxed, and we were doing backing vocals as well. Everything was sounding good. It was going well, the audience loved it. It was a real good night." A stirring, Hammond-infused 'TSOP' segued into 'Burn It Down', string riffs replacing the rousing brass blasts. The horns on 'Let's Make This Precious' sounded magnificent and a resounding 'Jackie Wilson Said' remained one of the band's great live moments. Paterson signed off with one final trom-bone salute on 'Plan B' before 'Geno' brought a roar of crowd approval. A jaunty 'Celtic Soul Brothers' was followed by 'There, There, My Dear'. Dexys left the stage to resounding acclaim after their parting encore shot 'I'll Show You' followed the percussive flares and squalling saxes of 'Show Me'. *Melody Maker* offered a verbose, prose-heavy celebration, and Rowland had brought the group into a new era.

Following their departure after the Newcastle shows, Rowland sug-gested that it was likely the brass players would work with the group again. "They've never even tried to get session work, which is what they are going to do now," he told the *NME*. "Their loyalty has amazed me, because they stayed around without any real success to speak of."

Backed with the horn-stoked instrumental 'Dubious', 'Come On Eileen' was released on June 12. Rowland's optimism had been dissipated by low expectations and a resignation toward the group's fate, later emphasising how "lack of money" and "lack of will" had brought Dexys close to dissolution. Brennan recalls the group eventually being barred from every sandwich bar in town after fleeing without paying. "Eleven of us would go in and then, one by one, gradually make our exits. We'd say,

'Oh no, they're gonna pay, they're gonna pay,' and it would come down to Kevin and he'd say, 'I'll pay the bill when I come back from the toilet,' and he'd be straight out the window. Everybody was really skint. They used to have a whip round so that they could pay us. It was heartbreaking. The strain on us when the bills came in; being threatened with having electricity cut off, eviction. It was harsh."

With Adams living in Birmingham's Bearwood district, O'Hara and Brennan sharing a flat and Rowland in a house on the city's busy Hagley Road, they would all take a return bus ride into rehearsals each day. As '. . . Eileen' struggled at number 63 in the charts almost a month after the group's triumphant Newcastle appearance, their disintegration began to look inevitable. Dexys entered a BBC studio on July 4 to record a new track 'All In All (This One Last Wild Waltz)', alongside 'Old' and 'Jackie Wilson Said' for 'Kid' Jensen's show. With Gallick about to depart, session player Mark Walters briefly took over Paterson's illustrious trombone berth, while Nick Gatfield contended with both alto and tenor sax duties. '. . . Eileen' roamed the lower reaches of the Top 40 before Dexys made a pivotal appearance on *Top Of The Pops* in mid-July. One Tuesday lunch-time, Rowland heard some good news over the radio. Paolo Hewitt recalls: "I was at his house and he was doing the washing up and the charts had just come out. And he went: 'Oh, I've got a Top 10 record.'"

"At first, 'Come On Eileen' was only played on the radio a couple of times a week," Rowland recounted to Johnny Rogan in 2000. "It struggled up the charts. It was a slow ascent, then bang!"

Sitting in his Birmingham flat, Archer was bewildered upon hearing the fruits of Rowland's labour. "It was my music. There was no mistaking it," Archer told the *Daily Mail* in 1997. "We all looked at each other and went silent. To be fair, he wrote the words to the music. But it was the tune that was so distinctive and made it a success – that tune was mine. I'd left the band and they were carrying on without me with my idea, my music and enjoying success."

"People heard it and it just snowballed," he told Ted Kessler. "We finally got the hit we'd been waiting for, although even I didn't expect it to be that successful." 'Come On Eileen' began a four-week residency at the top of the UK singles charts on August 7, with *Too-Rye-Ay* spending three weeks in pole position until early September.

"At first it was incredible," Adams recalled of their initial excitement. "I remember exactly where I was when I found out 'Come On Eileen' was number one and how I felt like I was walking on clouds for a couple of weeks." Rowland recounted the period of elation stretching from a few minutes to a few weeks.

Dexys commemorated their achievement at London's Embassy Hotel with Burton's purchase of six bottles of champagne. "That was to say, 'You're cracked it lads, you're number one.' That's the only thing that I remember," Brennan insists. "I don't recall feeling it was a massive thing that we'd achieved, certainly not financially anyway. There was no period of enjoyment or congratulatory celebration. It was almost as if, success-wise, it hadn't happened. But we had proved we were worth every penny and Dexys were back on top."

"No matter how many times I've heard 'Come On Eileen', it's still absolutely thrilling," Peter Paphides enthuses. "It's like four songs in one, like a mini-opera. It just all works. It's a fantastic mix of subject matter, and the excitement is mirrored in the music." For the newly departed, this success proved hard to stomach.

"During the weeks that followed, it went straight to the top of the charts. That left a pretty nasty taste in all our mouths," Brummitt admitted.

"Being recognised in the street and hearing your name shouted – all of these strange experiences went with the huge success and I'm sure if I'd been a bit more together, a bit more self-assured then I could've taken it in my stride and enjoyed it more," Adams told Kessler.

Rowland recalls visiting a restaurant also frequented by Boy George when Culture Club were at a similar zenith. "I couldn't walk down the fucking road but here was George, with his great big hat standing outside signing autographs, in his element, really enjoying it," he recalled to True. "He was the exact opposite to me. I was just sidling out, trying to get out. I felt like I was under siege. Some people, it infuses them, makes them grow. It has the opposite effect on me."

With the onset of success and instant recognition, things would in-evitably change. "And they changed pretty quickly. It was quite bizarre," Brennan admits, "because you thought it would have made things more relaxed."

"Kevin had this policy that we'd always wear the uniform, whatever we're doing. And we used to go to rehearsals fully clad in dungarees. And he used to get on the bus wearing his tam-o-shanter, and everybody would always comment that Kevin looked like 'the bloke from that pop group'. And in a thick Wolverhampton, Black Country accent he'd say, 'Oh, I wish I had his money – everyone says I look like him!' I think people thought, 'It looks like him, but he wouldn't be on the bus.'"

By mid-September, 'Eileen' had gone platinum, becoming the biggest selling single of 1982. The song would subsequently garner Brit and Ivor Novello awards. "It was another 'Geno', only bigger," Rowland later lamented. "It just seemed very light, in a very lightweight way."

In discussion with *SFX*'s Max Bell in 1982, Rowland made a colourful comparison between Dexys' previously introspective outlook and the garrulous group now suddenly in the public eye. "It's like last year if we went out in the sun we might have put our shirts on. This time we might go nude sunbathing. We're going to be diving in head first." With heavy-duty exposure naturally following their chart success, the enigmatic, anti-press diatribes had run their course. Rowland had given Dexys' first interview in almost two years to Gavin Martin in June.

Paolo Hewitt recalls Phonogram press officer Colin Bell's phone call. "He said, 'I've gotta take you out for lunch. I've got some bad news. Kevin's doing an interview, but he's doing it with the *NME*.' Which was fair enough because the *NME* was far more popular. He said, 'It's nothing against you.'" Hewitt heard a playback of Dexys' forthcoming album instead.

Too-Rye-Ay was released in August. Opening with the effervescent, stand-aside statement of 'The Celtic Soul Brothers' (complete with MC-like introduction from Rowland) its string flourishes were an upbeat precursor to the following track's introspective content. "At the time when I wrote 'Let's Make This Precious', it was the most important to me. It was so important," Rowland told Hewitt, who recognised the music's religious tenets. "In Catholicism, it being a really forward-looking religion, you were taught that from day one you were born with sin. So you're always struggling. And the thing about those songs is they're all about struggle, alienation and redemption and talking about God and confusion. You're instinctively tapping into that." The album's more extreme submersion in an Irish folk-oriented sound appeared with the dramatic 'All In All (This One Last Wild Waltz)', the persistent swooping strings and Sisters Of Scarlet vocals giving the song an unusual feel, with a Gaelic lyrical coda. "It's not that I love folk," Rowland admitted at the time. "I could not name a folk artist I like, but I think it would be a good idea for the pop scene to play acoustic music. Celtic music."

"It was good to have a waltz on the album," insisted Langer. Rowland felt it a more suitable follow-up to '. . . Eileen' than Dexys' emphatic reading of 'Jackie Wilson Said'.

Yet Rowland was only too happy to accept Van Morrison's praise for their effort. "He quite rightly thinks it's better than his own version," he told Max Bell. "It just felt great when I heard it. It really stood out. I must admit, I thought his version was a little bit underplayed." Morrison had apparently offered to pen fresh material for a follow-up. While arguing that the song perfectly fitted the album's framework, Rowland would later distance himself from it.

Aside from recycling 'There, There, My Dear's reference to dumb patriotism, the introspective lyrical thread of 'Old' lamented the plight of the elderly, a silent majority somewhat overlooked by modern society. "Kevin's lyrics make me cry," Paterson confided to fanzine editor Neil Warburton. "I love that song." Paterson recalled the genesis of its stately, wistful melody. "We were rehearsing one day, we had most of it written, but we didn't have a melody for some of it. When it came to having a break, Kevin said, 'Can you stay here and see if you can write a melody?' I don't know where it came from but by the time the group came back I'd written the melody." Rowland later admitted he was never enamoured with the final, five-minute rendition. A brief instrumental reprise from '. . . Precious' took the first side to a close.

'Soon' was left mysteriously uncredited on side two's track listing, sadly lacking Billingham's enchanting hymnal organ introduction. Featuring a powerful Rowland vocal, this vulnerable soliloquy was a meditation on achieving a 'precious' state without invoking violence or pain. Rowland implored believers to "hold on" during a newly string-embellished 'Plan B' before segueing into the compassionate soul march of 'I'll Show You'. A fine example of Rowland's pop sensibilities and a hidden gem in the Dexys' canon, the song demonstrated his great conceptual skills. Originally intended as a flip-sided sequel to 'Show Me', it was an illustration of the vagaries of time. "I went back to see how the people I'd went to school with had grown up," Rowland revealed. "I've still got a soft spot for the guys in the song because they've still got it in them," he told Gavin Martin. The fates of Rowland's less illustrious peers were transposed over an insistent, vintage brass riff that grew into a stirring refrain.

"Me and Pete [Barrett, Dexys designer] and Kevin were walking down the street," said Paolo Hewitt, recalling a trip to Paris in 1982, "and there was a guy begging. Kevin just put his hand in his pocket and went, 'There you go,' and he gave him loads of money. He always stood up for the down and outs."

"When he runs through that list of the marginalised and the deviants, that was great," states Peter Paphides. "To imagine someone as a child and then to come back and tell them that they're just as human as you are, it showed that no one was above fallibility." Evincing a subliminal sadness that often imbued their work, Rowland bravely wore his heart on his sleeve. Phonogram had apparently objected to the inclusion of a re-recorded 'Liars A To E', arguing that its presence made the album too unwieldy. It stayed, and, thankfully, it fitted. Superior to its seven-inch predecessor, this tense, swooning classic proved a pivotal moment. Shelton's empathetic drumming was worthy of merit in a sultry melange of Hammond, piano and insistent strings. It gave way to the seven-minute epic 'Until I Believe In My Soul'. In dramatic fashion, Rowland vowed to resolve a metaphysical conflict between flesh and spirit by punishing the body. O'Hara's serene violin accompanied Rowland's moments of spiritual contemplation. The key to his spiritual quest rested on the "realisation of the soul."

While childhood expectations were also a frame of reference, Rowland attempted to initiate an emotional awakening, reacquainting himself with his adolescent feelings. The lyrical snapshot of a train ride between Birmingham and London flashed past. *Sounds* underlined the similarity with Van Morrison's journey from Dublin to Sandy Row on 'Madame George', while its compositional qualities drew comparison to Morrison's 'Autumn Song' and 'Snow In San Anselmo'. Having attempted to sate his soul's appetite, Rowland then sang of his carnal desires on the album's irresistible, libido-centric closing track.

As one of the greatest-selling UK singles, no one could have envisaged the impact a career salvaging 'Come On Eileen' would have on the group's subsequent fortunes and musical aspirations. "If that record hadn't been a hit, you wouldn't have had *Don't Stand Me Down*," Hewitt argues. "But that level of success ruined it. I know that Kevin got recognised a lot. With that level of fame, you can't operate in the way that you usually do. You can't go and sit in a café. It really bothered him that that audience was there just for that record."

Even Archer conceded the undeniable strength of the song. "All that 'Come On Eileen' stuff looked really powerful to me, I knew they were really successful once they'd done that," he admitted to Everett True. "After that the time for Blue Ox was a very bad time. It was a rough ride for them. I told them we'd be successful, or at least get a record deal." Archer had even attempted to woo Dexys' old nemesis, EMI. They weren't interested in an "English folk" group. Rowland acknowledged in 2000 that commercial success for The Blue Ox Babes would have been a wholly justified reward. Yet the Babes eventually split up. Pete Williams went on to front These Tender Virtues in 1984 that included Babes' drummer Ian Pettitt in the ranks. They later released *The Continuing Saga* EP.

"He [Rowland] conceded that Kevin Archer was the architect of the *Too-Rye-Ay* sound, but I think he does himself down because it doesn't really matter in a way who thought of it," Paphides argues. "It's how you use it. When you hear those Blue Ox Babes records, it's clear that what's lacking is Kevin Rowland."

"I heard The Blue Ox Babes stuff and, yeah, the idea was there,"

Hewitt reasons, "but it didn't come anywhere near what Kevin was doing."

Rowland later admitted that Paterson and Adams had not received enough credit for their input. "At the end of the day, it's between those two," the trombonist told the BBC. "I'm disappointed that it happened like that, because I felt that I was part of something new. Kevin didn't steal any songs from Kevin Archer, 'cos I co-wrote all those songs, and I certainly didn't steal anything."

The *NME*'s Phil McNeill acknowledged *Too-Rye-Ay*'s emotional framework in cross-referencing old and new material, lauded Rowland's performances and also the group's unique intensity. *Jamming!*'s Tony Fletcher believed the album's epic closing sequence was unsurpassable, while Richard Lowe noted it's vividness amid the ephemeral nature of 1982's pop scene. "To me it seemed like an eternity," Paphides recalls. "But now you think nothing of a band disappearing for two years and coming back with their next album. It kind of seemed like they had started again." *Melody Maker* later accorded *Too-Rye-Ay* its album of the year accolade, while *Record Mirror* applauded the fresh instrumentation. *Smash Hits* homed in on Langer and Winstanley's focused, energetic production. Yet the battle for individual space, as opposed to Wingfield's compartmentalised sound on . . . *Rebels*, was criticised. On re-release in 1996, *Q* felt *Too-Rye-Ay*'s scintillating blend of folk and soul far more appreciable than on initial release.

Too-Rye-Ay closed with Rowland's abridged revision of an Irish traditional song, previously mooted as a potential album title. "I've always liked songs like 'Believe Me If All Those Endearing Young Charms'; my mum used to sing it when I was a kid and she'd had a drink or something," he confided to the *NME*. "Dexys isn't just a collection of any old songs – for me it's a lifetime's experience," Rowland asserted that October. "I'm very hard on myself, and I'll work and work until I get it right. My standards are maybe three or four times higher than people I talk to and I've done the sweating, I'm doing the singing. I want everyone to know about me and my songs and it will happen."

With his Gaelic romanticism in full flow, Rowland bestowed the epithet of 'Ballymena Belle' upon O'Hara. She would now play Scarlet Rivera to his Bob Dylan on their own gypsy Rolling Thunder Revue – The Bridge.

Chapter Nineteen

WITH little time at his disposal, Rowland's selection criteria based on attitude and character proved simply unfeasible in recruiting new members ahead of an imminent UK tour. John Edwards was installed on bass and with alto Nick Gatfield already on board, tenor saxophonist Andy Hamilton, trombonist Spike Edney and additional violinist Simon Walker were enlisted in an 11-strong line-up.

"Simon didn't really have any ambitions about being in the group, but he liked the songs and he liked being part of it," said Brennan. "And at the same time, all sorts of big name session players started appearing. We had this guy playing trombone who was actually the piano player in Queen. They seemed to be very humoured by Kevin's sort of applied approach. They were all older than us and they played really well. But the whole dynamic changed completely. For me, it all became very different. And there was a sax player [Hamilton] who had played with David Bowie and Paul McCartney. And we also had Nick Gatfield. So it had become like a different group."

"The touring wasn't much fun with those people," Adams later admitted to *Record Collector*. "The shows weren't fulfilling. Previous tours had been like a spiritual fulfilment. 'The Bridge' was as much work, but with no satisfaction."

Calling the new revue "our best, most colourful and complete live performance" at the time, Rowland later insisted that the shows had failed to reach previous exalted standards.

"I used to turn round sometimes and I'd see some of the session players, and I think they thought it was a bit of a sort of hillbilly pantomime," Adams corroborated to Radio Two. "We wanted them to give 110 per cent, like we did ourselves. And that is what gave Kevin the reputation for being difficult."

The tour opened with a well-received Glasgow show on September 26 at the Pavilion Theatre, coinciding with the single release of 'Jackie Wilson Said'. In a private *Too-Rye-Ay* recording session for the single, Van Morrison had appeared at AIR Studios. Langer recalls this ultimately fruitless episode. "We went to London because Van was going to come and sing on it. Kevin left me in the lurch 'cos he said, 'We're getting Van

Morrison in,' and we went, 'Great, great.' He was obviously one of Kevin's heroes at that time. "Van came in the studio, and I said to Kevin, 'Well, what's he going to sing?' And Kevin said, 'Well, I don't know. Get him to sing the song!' "

Winstanley observed Morrison's legendary truculence. "He just stood by the microphone, and we ran straight through three times, and he never sang a note. And in the end, Kevin went into the studio to try and nurture him along. And we could hear them having a little conversation." Morrison asked the producer what was required. "He said, 'You've got all the backing vocals on there, what do you want me for?' " Langer politely reminded him that it was his song and he was a great singer. Following numerous run-throughs, and without Van singing a note, the session was over. Morrison walked out.

The record sleeve pictured Rowland in a symbolic pose, bearing a heavy weight on his shoulders. "It was the Catholic thing again," Paolo Hewitt maintains. "That's what Dexys were doing, talking about punishing the body. Some of the imagery that went with it, the bag over the shoulder was like Jesus with the cross. It definitely worked on that level."

'Jackie Wilson Said' reached number five, and a notorious appearance on *Top Of The Pops* occurred on September 30, when the group mimed in front of a huge background blow-up of darts supremo Jocky Wilson. "We thought it was hilarious," Rowland told *Jack*. "The producer said, 'But everyone will think we've made a mistake!'

"We said, 'Only those who don't get the joke.' "

Another practical joke came at a band member's expense in Belfast. "I remember we were staying in the Europa Hotel, historically known as one of the most bombed hotels in Europe," Brennan recalls. "Kevin and Paul Burton had this cassette recorder, and they got this Irish promoter to record a message saying he was part of this military faction who were after me because my name was Brennan. I didn't know they'd done it, but they put this really long tape on a recorder in a biscuit tin under the bed.

"I was always really tired and it was about six o'clock in the evening and I wanted to have a sleep before the show. And as I was nodding off, I heard all this shouting: 'Is that you Brennan? Are you there? We're gonna come and get you!' And I was absolutely terrified. I didn't know what was going on!"

At Cardiff's St. David's Hall on October 6, *Melody Maker* applauded Rowland's growing status as a showman. He compared the live experience to an act of exorcism. "I really do bare myself for everybody to see, and maybe that's embarrassing, but it's real. It's me – not some character

I'm hiding behind. It's a huge responsibility to entertain thousands of people, but then again, I think I'm the man for the job."

Before the first of the acclaimed Shaftesbury Theatre performances three days later, Rowland insisted he'd climbed into the auditorium's darkened private boxes to observe his audience. Stage fright was also a factor before the shows. "I get it every single night," he admitted the following year.

O'Hara told Q in 1993 that The Bridge shows had proved a personal musical epiphany. "It was the soul that got me. Or maybe passion is a better word. Those songs really pulled the heartstrings and made me play with a lot more expression than I ever thought I could. It drew something out of me."

Brennan recalls the inspiring, but exhausting demands of those shows. "We worked really hard on the stage presentation. And when we played, people were physically scared in the audience, being confronted by these angry men. Kevin would be looking around during the songs and expecting you to climb on the monitors and egging you on. Kevin had the detail in mind; what would make it effective, unique." Powerful renditions of 'Let's Make This Precious', 'Respect' and a triumphant, reworked 'Until I Believe In My Soul' found a 'burning' Rowland in monologue mode, contemplating his group's procession across the conceptual bridge.

"It's thrilling when they storm up to the footlights at the beginning of 'Let's Make This Precious'," Peter Paphides enthused, "and when they step forward to do the whole preamble about the bridge: 'its high, but I've gotta get over the bridge' on 'Until I Believe In My Soul'. What a great understanding of performance.

"Kevin grew out of listening to really great performers. The James Brown thing is obviously important. Why would you think you could do what he was capable of? But in his way, Kevin did." A new composition, the fiddle-driven, acoustic hoedown 'Kevin Rowland's Band', was also previewed but when the Shaftesbury Theatre show was re-released on video in 1991, reviewer Stephen Dalton considered the vagaries of time had drained the theatrical show's power.

"*The Bridge* (video) is fucking awful," Rowland winced in 2003. "I didn't want it out, it's garbage, but we got talked into it."

The Bridge reached Europe in late October. Following shows in Haarlem, Hamburg and Berlin, Dexys played Switzerland, the Netherlands and Belgium. November's subsequent Gallic jaunt proved a highlight, culminating in a three-night residency at Paris' Eldorado Théâtre. "The French tour was very exciting. I particularly liked France and the audiences we had were something else," O'Hara recalled.

"Dexys loved performing and hanging out in France," Rowland confirmed in 2002. But by the time Dexys hit the French capital, Rowland had sensed another creative shift was looming.

Dexys' champion Paolo Hewitt had by now jumped ship from *Melody Maker* to the *NME*. "I told the *NME* I'd been to Paris to see Dexys. They said, 'Oh, go on, write 400 words on it,' 'cos they were so big at the time. And I wrote a bit about going to the gig, and afterwards it said Rowland had intimated that the winds of change were coming. And he was really pissed off. And rightly so because he wasn't giving an interview."

The so-called 'hip-hop' wars being fought at the *NME* in the early Eighties had essentially created a divide between the old guard of rock and punk writers, including Nick Kent and Charles Shaar Murray, and the new wave of Ian Penman and Paul Morley promoting, amongst others, New Romanticism and electro pop. Morley was a fan of ABC. The group's *The Lexicon Of Love* had been released on Mercury the same week as *Too-Rye-Ay*. Billingham recalled that the mention of Martin Fry's group could stir antipathy in their leader. "I'm just fed up with people coming up to me and telling me the likes of ABC are a good group," Rowland told Gavin Martin in 1982. "They might be a good comedy group or something, maybe they should develop that angle of it, I dunno."

"It's all been done to death, hasn't it? Duran Duran and bands like that have got to be finished now," Rowland railed at Mark Ellen. "Bands pulling cheap tricks and getting fancy productions 'cos they know they'll get their records played on Radio One." It appeared that few early Eighties pop groups were spared Rowland's wrath, particularly the likes of Spandau Ballet, Soft Cell and The Jam.

Yet Hewitt recalls visiting Rowland's house in the summer of 1982 and seeing a room filled with records, including the latest Madness LP. "You've gotta keep up, see what people are doing," Rowland told him. "Even though he might have been sitting there saying, 'They're shit, they're shit,' he was busy studying music, getting a feel for the times. That was his craft."

Langer and Winstanley's services were retained for the acoustic 'Let's Get This Straight (From The Start)', marking one of O'Hara's earliest songwriting contributions. Recorded in Wimbledon, the resident tape op told the production duo about the studio's autocue system. "When the tape stopped, the talk-back came on automatically. And I remember me and Clive saying, 'No, we don't want to use any of that,'" Winstanley recalls. "For some reason, he put it on. When the tape stopped, we started discussing how bad the bass player was, not knowing that they could hear us! I don't know who he was, but Kevin sacked him! I felt so bad thinking,

'This poor guy has got fired because Kevin had heard me and Clive saying he wasn't really cutting the mustard.' So I've never used autocue ever again! But he did like sacking musicians."

George Chandler and The Brothers Just, Jimmy Thomas and Simon Solace, provided backing vocals on 'Let's Get This Straight . . .' Rowland appeared far happier with the single edit of 'Old' that became the B-side, yet when the single was released in November *Record Mirror* sensed the beginning of the end of Dexys' chart relationship, while *Smash Hits* underlined the single's plodding nature and indecipherable lyrics. "The most Van Morrison-y one was 'Let's Get This Straight . . .' He [Rowland] probably knew it, but he didn't want to tell anyone," Hewitt concludes. "But it made perfect sense as a template, and also in terms of the way he developed his career in an individual way."

"We're not good friends," Rowland told journalist Max Bell when discussing Morrison. "We only met a few months ago. I admire what he's doing. I'd like to make it clear though, that Van Morrison is somebody I respect, because over the last 20 years he's gone totally his own way, regardless of any commercial consideration. But there's no way I'd like to end up like Van Morrison . . ." Rowland's two-year UK music media sabbatical ended, ironically, in the *NME*'s company on the day he chanced upon the media-wary Ulsterman in a Notting Hill café.

Slotting television appearances between tours, an incendiary performance on one of the first episodes of Channel 4's *The Tube* in December demonstrated that Dexys' musical fire was still burning. Their thrilling reinterpretation of 'There, There, My Dear' saw the tempestuous energy of the original ferment into a full-blooded, high-spirited onslaught. Giving his band the green light to take flight, Rowland indulged in a spate of one-armed press-ups.

"For me, that is the absolute definitive version," Paphides insists. "I had the footage on tape, and just watched it over and over again. I didn't even recognise it, because they didn't announce it at the beginning. Rowland just goes off on a tangent at one point. And then he's on his knees, with the microphone dangling down in front of his face. It was pure theatre. I loved them, and it was absolutely what I needed to hear."

Playing '. . . Eileen' on a festive *Top Of The Pops* and venturing into tongue-in-cheek seasonal Slade territory with 'Merry Xmas Everybody' on *Pop Goes Christmas*, feeling estranged, Rowland's place in the pop circus was in marked contrast to his contemporaries. "I saw Duran Duran walking through [*Top Of The Pops*] and they seemed to be enjoying themselves and I remember thinking, 'I understand what this pop business is all about now,'" he told Jim Irvin. "You get some success and you pretend you're enjoying it, that's the deal, you nod and say, 'It's great and you get loads of money. That's what it is. They must be pretending.' Now I look back and think, actually, they probably were enjoying themselves. It was me who wasn't enjoying myself."

"It was like misplaced success. He was successful, but it was as if he wasn't comfortable with it at that time," Brennan observes. Being approached on the street swiftly became a bugbear.

Rowland later insisted that he felt exposed, trapped in what he coined a "goldfish bowl" existence. "I was forever getting people coming up to me, and I did get fed up with it, saying, 'You did a song that really meant a lot to me,' and it would be 'Come On Eileen'," he complained to Everett True. "It was like the only song we'd ever done."

"And the single became so important that it cast its shadow over everything we did," Adams admitted to Ted Kessler.

"The problem was when Kevin got to 'Come On Eileen' and *Too-Rye-Ay* they attracted a whole load of people who didn't really understand the group," Hewitt insists. "With success, which proved to be such a terrible thing for Kevin, I think it actually allowed him to express another side."

O'Hara, on the other hand, savoured the attention that accompanied pop acclaim. "I mean, it was fantastic," she told the BBC. "Walking from the dressing room to the bus and people pulling your hair, and it was a classic pop star thing, which for me was great."

Dexys were rolling on a wave of three successive Top 30 hits in six months. Yet as The Bridge bandwagon pulled to a temporary halt, Rowland sat alone that New Year's Eve in Birmingham and mused on his predicament. "I had nobody to go out with," he told Jon Wilde. "When I wasn't working I was lost . . ."

"It gradually started to dawn on me, even though we were going down well, that it really didn't mean much at all," Rowland later told Keith Cameron. "I just saw all this chaos going on around me and my reaction was, 'Fuck it!' My reaction was *Don't Stand Me Down* really. I was like, 'Okay, people, the party's over.'"

Late in 1982, Paul Burton summoned Billingham, Brummitt, Paterson and Speare to a meeting at Birmingham's Australian Bar to discuss royalties. The brass trio had recently completed a lengthy album project with John Watts and were touring with the Q-Tips before morphing into the TKO Horns trio, with Brummitt's place taken by Jeff Blythe in 1983. Billingham had only recently departed the fold, joining West Midlands 'supergroup' General Public, featuring Growcott on drums, The Beat's Dave Wakeling and Ranking Roger, and Specials bassist Horace Panter.

141

While signing to Phonogram in 1981 had provided them with some security, Burton informed the four musicians that the record company were prepared to walk away without offering any remuneration for their efforts. He outlined the offer. The deal was simple: they could accept an immediate lump sum, signing away any rights to future royalties, or take Phonogram Records to court. Left with little choice, they accepted a one-off payment but, in Speare's view, the four were "definitely bought off cheaply. The deal was struck before the full scale of its success was realised." The sum, around £10,000 apiece, was still a godsend. Speare was able to put a modest deposit on a small house and buy a second-hand estate car.

"Basher made sure we got paid, when we were absolutely skint, desperate," Brummitt admits. "If it hadn't have been for Paul Burton, we'd never have seen a penny of that. I always remember him for that."

Yet while the former members were adjusting to life away from the group, Brennan recalls a familiar pattern emerging among the surviving line-up. "The group kind of broke into two factions. Kevin and Paul Burton suggested it might be beneficial if there was a nucleus which would comprise the key members." Rowland, O'Hara, Adams and Shelton were considered the mainstay of the group. "Kevin, Billy and Helen became really close," says Brennan. "They were together all the time. Helen became part of the songwriting team. Clearly, she knew a lot about writing string parts. And some people's noses were perhaps put out of joint a little. I was always a little bit miffed that I was on the outside."

In January 1983, Dexys prepared to embark on their first US tour, with a major city itinerary opening in New York at the Savoy Theatre. While O'Hara enjoyed the "atmosphere and energy" of the Big Apple, Rowland felt the whole experience had come to resemble little more than a "gravy train". "I felt I was just going through the motions," he told William Shaw. "I couldn't make it real. Stupid, isn't it? I just wish I'd had a bit more fun. I was leading this fuckin' mad existence. I was leading a very lonely life. I remember being in New York in the Eighties and I didn't go out to clubs or anything."

For other members, it was also a strained experience. "I'd never been to America," Brennan said. "It was a new patch for us and we had to play to get recognised. And that was when I started to get fed up. I thought, 'I should be enjoying this, but I'm not.' I know I got on Kevin's nerves. He was preoccupied and I wanted to know what he was doing. I was insecure about it, I suppose. I wanted to keep on doing it. I was only 22, I didn't want to stop yet! It wasn't a happy time for me, which is quite ironic when you think of the fortunate position I was in."

Dates followed in Philadelphia, Detroit, Chicago, Los Angeles and San

Francisco, interspersed with TV work. Returning to England, a Radio One *In Concert* Royal Court Theatre show in Liverpool on March 16 marked the end of their lengthy UK trawl as attention turned towards the lack of new material. Significantly, the 'winds of change' that Rowland had spoken of in Paris four months earlier were stirring. While in the States, his long-held love of Ivy League couture was reignited. "Kevin was busy going around promoting the group and the album and the shows, and doing interviews with Helen," says Brennan. "And he started buying these fantastic Ivy League clothes. He always had a good eye for detail about everything, but particularly clothes. This stuff was all really expensive.

"Instinctively, there was a sense that he was bored with what we were doing, I felt. He'd done the 'Eileen' thing and we'd had the number one, and he wanted to move forward and do something else. And I was think-ing, 'Well, what's gonna happen next?'"

In March, a re-released 'The Celtic Soul Brothers' was coupled with a new, spoken-word Rowland narrative over unobtrusive bass and piano. 'Reminisce (Part One)' featured The Brothers Just's Jimmy Thomas in the conversational mix alongside Adams. Rowland had initially envisaged the track as a follow-up to 'Let's Get This Straight (From The Start)'. "Dexys had often used question and answer vocals on previous records and the musicality of taking it to this stage appealed a lot. It opened things up for us," Rowland acknowledged in 1997, "what could be done with a song." Keen to experiment and expand the group's musical horizons, Rowland had been suitably inspired by the Van Morrison track 'Rave On John Donne' taken from Morrison's 1983 album, *Inarticulate Speech Of The Heart*. Morrison even received a covert name-check in the song, with Rowland approaching a ginger-haired man with an imposing demeanour in a Dublin bar. "That track gave me a real lift," Rowland admitted to *Record Collector*.

In April, Dexys supported David Bowie in Paris, and a potentially lucra-tive touring role on the former Thin White Duke's 'Serious Moonlight' tour was in the pipeline. "We started off the set with 'Come On Eileen' and I remember at the end of the song Kevin was saying stuff like, 'That's it then, you can all fuck off now.' There was a bit of verbal going on about Bowie and we ended up being physically evicted off the stage. Bowie stood there in his lime green suit and he didn't look very pleased. A couple of the group felt it wasn't a good move."

The albatross of 'Come On Eileen' had repeated it's homeland success elsewhere in the world, but over nine months after its initial UK release, an incredible achievement occurred when, on April 23, 1983, 'Come On

Eileen' topped the US *Billboard* charts, ending Michael Jackson's seven-week run with 'Billie Jean'.* Even *Too-Rye-Ay* found itself inside the Top 20 *Billboard* album charts. Yet it all proved a salutary experience for Rowland. "Do you know, I didn't feel any sense of achievement," he told Radio Two. "I think I did really want a career in America and I was desperately disappointed because I knew that by that time we weren't taken seriously. We were seen as a novelty act. They thought we were Dickensian or something."

A second US tour in May was hastily arranged to capitalise on the success of 'Come On Eileen'. "This time, in the aftermath of '. . . Eileen', it seemed many people had begun to write us off already as a one-hit wonder," Adams lamented to Ted Kessler. Their achievement had ultimately proved counter-productive. When the group played New York, Yoko Ono asked to share the stage with Rowland during 'Respect'. Thankfully, he refused. By the end of the trek, Dexys had toured The Bridge for eight months across the UK, Europe and America.

"There was an atmosphere around us when we were successful and going around the world, and I just went along with it," Rowland told Everett True. "I didn't have the courage to ask anyone about the money. I was on my own. Again, I'd gone insular. I didn't talk to anybody and I just felt I've got to keep this going on my own. 'There's all these people working. Isn't it great that we're successful? I shouldn't complain.' But inside I was dying. All I had left was my music."

"Kevin changed drastically," Brennan concurs. "He seemed unapproachable. You'd try to speak to him and he didn't seem to have any time for me. Whether it was my reaction to that Bowie thing but I started to hate being in the group. I just felt more stress than joy from it. I used to talk to Billy and say, 'What's gonna happen to me?' and he'd say, 'Don't worry, we're going to be playing 'Come On Eileen' forever."

"It could have been great but it turned out not very good at all," Rowland concluded to *The Hit*. "*Too-Rye-Ay* wasn't leading anywhere. I could just make money – so what? I have to have a certain amount of self-respect otherwise I can't exist and carry on." With the touring over by the summer of 1983, the idea of ending Dexys had occurred to its leader. Unbeknown to Adams, Rowland resolved to visit old pal Kevin Archer with a proposition of a dual frontman role, not dissimilar to the original Dexys agenda. The timing of his approach was apt. Paterson's departure the previous summer had proven a blow to the group dynamic. "I was

---

* Jackson returned to pole position the following week with his next single 'Beat It'.

very concerned. He'd written all the songs. It was very difficult," Rowland told Johnny Rogan.

"I just wanted to see if [Archer] wanted to do something with meaning," Rowland told *Record Collector* in 2002.

"Kevin Archer was on the scene already, because he lived near Kevin [Rowland] on the Hagley Road and I used to bump into him," said Brennan, who was relieved of his Dexys duties by Burton that summer. "Kevin Rowland used to take clothes around to Kev that he'd brought back from America. He always kept in touch. I always thought Kevin Rowland wanted Kevin Archer involved on the next album. I was always amazed that it didn't happen."

Archer was apprehensive about sharing the stage with his old partner, at that point, still one of British pop's most recognisable faces. "Dexys were too strong by then," he told *Record Collector*. "If we'd have come out, they would have gone, 'It's Kevin Rowland and who's *that*?'"

Chapter Twenty

THE *Too-Rye-Ay* touring cycle during the summer of 1983 had left Rowland feeling unfulfilled, disillusioned and exhausted. Following Dexys' phenomenal success, he felt the group had become a shallow shadow of their former selves. The relentless promotional duties had left Rowland feeling little more than a record company 'workhorse'. "I was sick of the teeny fame," he told Chris Roberts. "I wanted to make it serious, for us to be established as a 'proper' group." As early as the summer of 1982, Rowland had outlined plans to Paolo Hewitt of undertaking a new approach. "There's only so much you can say about yourself and I don't want to keep writing about myself."

"He knew back then where it was going," Hewitt insists. "He already had the next stage mapped out. And you knew that after *Too-Rye-Ay*, something different would be coming. You look at *Don't Stand Me Down* and that whole thing is a reaction to 'Come On Eileen', it really is. He had loads of money and it wasn't making him happy. It just wasn't a happy time for him."

Or as Rowland insisted to Phil McNeill in 1985: "I'm not trying to follow up *Too-Rye-Ay*, I'm trying to forget it."

Rowland knew that Dexys' management and accountants had access to the group's money. Yet he'd seen no sight of any bank statements or disclosure of account details. Regardless, he and O'Hara bought a flat. "I thought that would make me feel good," he told Daryl Easlea. "We ended up buying this video, when video machines had just come out. I thought, 'Great, we can watch films now.' We'd become this pop group, so let's have the rewards. White carpet in the bedroom, big video. After a few nights I thought, 'This is fucking shit! It felt like we'd sold out.'"

Shelton quit Dexys towards the end of the year, citing financial issues as one of the reasons behind his departure. Aside from a measure of personal grievances, Shelton took the lyrical procession of anti-middle-class rhetoric, a key signifier of the group's subsequent material, to heart. He also felt that Rowland and O'Hara's relationship had affected the group's touring lifestyle in the face of a 'no girlfriends' embargo.* Rowland's response was

---

* Ironically, Shelton later married O'Hara's sister, Kate.

146

telling. "I was trying to aspire to these impossible ideals for my good self and my name fellows and falling very short of the same," he told *Record Collector* in 2000. Significantly, Paterson returned to the fray. Wearing a raincoat and glasses disguise, Rowland had met the trombonist (with Blythe and Speare) at a Birmingham pub in late 1983, prior to their Odeon show as the TKO Horns with Elvis Costello.

Paterson accepted that the dynamic of his creative allegiance with Rowland had changed. He later told *Keep On Running*: "I'd made my decision to leave so I couldn't expect things to be like they had been. Helen and Billy were the new hub of the band with Kevin, and I didn't have any qualms with that. Playing the trombone is hard enough so I was quite happy."

Following a 12-week summer sabbatical, Rowland, Adams and O'Hara resumed work again in the early autumn of 1983. "After *Too-Rye-Ay* I thought, 'This is bullshit. What's real? What's important?'" Rowland recalled to Simon Price. "I was an angry boy."

"Kevin was searching for something that I don't think the rest of the band knew what it was to be absolutely honest," Nick Gatfield told Daryl Easlea.

Clive Langer agrees. "Kevin was looking for something. He wanted to make an Al Green record. Well, he's not Al Green, the musicians weren't, even if he used the same drummer, and the engineer's equipment had changed since the Sixties. We were using modern recording techniques, we weren't recording like they did in the Sixties in America."

Yet Rowland had struck upon a viable creative proposition. During the group's early hibernation, his burgeoning interest in republican Irish politics and socialism had begun to surface. Investigating old family ties in County Mayo, he later visited Sinn Fein representatives in Belfast, a significant instalment in the unfolding lyrical plot. "I stayed indoors for a year, felt alienated, became obsessed with politics, particularly Irish ones, and started writing the next album," he told Jon Wilde. Little did he realise it would be two long years before his greatest artistic statement finally came to fruition.

In spirit, *Don't Stand Me Down* was conceived with March 1983's 'Reminisce (Part One)', where, during the song's fade-out, he championed Ken Livingstone's folk hero status. Rowland's growing socialist preoccupations were clear. He was serious, brushing aside his colleagues' mirthful responses. "I wanted people to hear it. I had a lot to express at that point and it all came out on this," he said in 1997.

"At that time, there was a lot of left-wing and right-wing politics going on," Hewitt recalls of the political landscape characterising the mid-

Eighties, "the Red Wedge thing and Thatcher, and there was a divide. But what Kevin was doing was actually challenging your kind of assumptions. Somebody would go, 'Fuckin' Americans,' and he'd go, 'Well, actually from America you get amazing clothes, amazing music. They're not all bad people.'" This stance would become clear when the group's new sartorial ethic was unveiled.

Devouring defiantly 'red' publications like *Morning Star* and *Socialist Worker*, Rowland resolved to demonstrate and rally in political fashion for various causes. Considering his later lyrical vehemence, one particular march that he and O'Hara embarked upon was, ironically, in honour of the CND organisation. Admitting support of their fundamental aims to *Melody Maker* in November 1985, Rowland described CND as a "totally ineffective organisation". He has since insisted he was actually attacking the people who advocated such causes, particularly the "pipe-smoking, real-ale liberal elite." Rowland did, however, want to ring the alarm bells.

"I saw someone dressed as a giant planet Earth with a sign saying 'Save Me'. I was trying to say, 'There's genocide going on now! In Ireland!' I wanted to shake them," he told *The Independent*'s Simon Price in 2002. Rowland outlined his growing fascination with the politics of unrest to some Sinn Fein representatives. "One of them, quite rightly, said to me in plain language, 'We don't want bullshit. We are living this. We have American actors and actresses coming over to sort things out for them,'" he told *Record Collector*.

Having devoured Kevin Kelly's book *The Longest War* during this period, Rowland felt duty bound to do something constructive. What became *Don't Stand Me Down*, Dexys' greatest work, was originally conceived as an overt political album. "I'd gone back to the Irishness in me, that was something that had some meaning," Rowland told Easlea. "I really felt I wanted to do something for Ireland." Upon the album's release, he would be accused by particular sectors of the music press of running scared from the issues closest to Ireland's heart (British military presence, nationalism, and republican hunger strikes). When promoting the album in late 1985, Rowland, wary of misrepresentation, was reticent to discuss the themes explored on the record.

He told the BBC in 2000: "I just thought, 'I'm gonna put everything in this that I know. Everything I want to say, I'm gonna put it in.' I didn't care. It was like that. It was a real passion. So driven. And I felt I had nothing to lose again funnily enough. I thought that all I'd experienced was crap, this is all that's important."

Distilling his original vision of a socio-political, consciousness-raising tract on the plight of Ireland and its attendant causes, *Don't Stand Me Down*'s broader canvas embraced humour, satirical punch, lovelorn reveries, pet obsessions and catholic redemption. It culminated in an astonishingly effective personal manifesto.

Rowland, O'Hara and Adams had spent upwards of three months developing new ideas separately over the summer. These were brought together as work began on a demo of their greatest composition, initially entitled 'What's She Like', in the early autumn of 1983. The song's opening vocal line was the original starting point. In a moment of twilight inspiration, Rowland taped his chorus idea on the spot. Devising a suitable melody the following morning, he and O'Hara began working on a basic structure. The conversational idea, of course, was already well in hand.

Almost nine months of writing sessions lasted into the spring of 1984. (Press stories, stating that September recording sessions would result in new, pre-Christmas material, proved highly premature.) Their old rehearsal space, Outlaw was used to audition suitable new musicians. The day after Burton informed Brennan his tenure in the group was over Rowland approached the violinist to play on the group's demo material as a well-paid session man. To his eternal regret, he was convinced by outside forces to turn Rowland down. "But if you say no to Kevin, that's it. You don't get a second chance. And I pestered him to get me in on it somewhere down the line. And he said, 'When we come to record you can do it, or when we go on tour.' My biggest regret about the whole thing is not playing on *Don't Stand Me Down*. There's something so conclusive about it. It's cinematic."

Rowland was also keen on capturing a real 'feel', an emotional quality that would translate well in the studio. With saxophonist Gatfield and bassist Edwards already on board, pianist Mick Boulton was recruited in February 1984. A hard-playing, spirited blues-based keyboardist was also sought. After three days of auditions, Atomic Rooster keyboardist, the late Vincent Crane arrived.*

Having just been offered a place in ex-Fleetwood Mac guitarist Peter Green's new band, the long-haired Crane was certainly distinguishable from previous applicants, clad in a cheesecloth shirt and flares. Sitting in on a beat-up piano, he, Adams and Edwards undertook a rendition of 'The Waltz'. On Rowland and O'Hara's arrival, they ran through the song again, before demoing a formative version of 'What's She Like'. Crane's personality and musical presence clearly struck a chord with Rowland.

---

* Most renowned for playing organ on The Crazy World Of Arthur Brown's 1968 hit 'Fire', Crane sadly passed away in 1989.

"He took his playing very seriously and had a great natural feel for the music," Adams recalled of Crane's attractive, deceptively effortless approach. With a greater emphasis on musicianship, right from the outset, Rowland was chasing something different. During the arduous process of assembling a recording group, he looked for a suitable, mid–Sixties groove for inspiration. He found what he was looking for in a Birmingham record shop. Drawing on his love of the classic Beach Boys and Bob Dylan 1966 cuts, 'God Only Knows' and 'Sad Eyed Lady Of The Lowlands' respectively, Rowland purchased *The Beach Boys Greatest Hits, Blonde On Blonde* and 1965's *Highway 61 Revisited*. Dylan had been a voice of inspiration at an impressionable age.

"He spoke for me at a particular time in my life, 19 or 20 years old; he was a true romantic," Rowland confided to *Mojo* in 1999.

Dylan's ground-breaking works would inform a shift towards a greater percussive flair and a more prominent guitar/organ influence. Mandolin player Julian Littman, steel guitarist Tommy Evans, drummer Crusher Green and organist Robert Noble were all eventually brought on board. "We soon realised the people who were right for the group were the ones we enjoyed playing with and who actually gave something to the music," said Adams. Players were auditioned as new songs were conceived, including 'Listen To This' and an overhaul of the jaunty, countrified 'Kevin Rowland's Band', one of his more anodyne lyrical outings.

"I didn't have anything else to write about because I didn't have a life outside the band," Rowland later explained.

With a permanent line-up complete, the rigours began. Breaking from intensive rehearsals with visits to greasy spoon cafés, Crane recounted how one young autograph hunter spied Rowland enjoying a cuppa. Her mother laughed off the young girl's excitable requests for his signature. 'Kevin Rowland wouldn't be seen dead in a place like this,' she chided.

Burton and Phonogram were left scratching their heads on exposure to the Outlaw demos of songs like 'The Waltz' and 'What's She Like'. "I mean they couldn't make head nor tail of it," O'Hara recalled to Radio Two in 2004. "That was the beginning really, of the sort of shock of what Dexys were about to reveal."

In early 1985, O'Hara assumed the mantle of Dexys' musical director. For Rowland, the prospect of bringing the album to fruition without both her and Adams' moral and musical support would have been unthinkable. "Billy was Kevin's sounding board – he was so honest, he was the rock," O'Hara told *Record Collector*, later comparing the convoluted recording process to assembling a jigsaw puzzle.

"I felt such a fraud. I didn't have the balls to confront 1985," Rowland told Chris Roberts. "I wasn't that guy who'd been taking everybody on earlier. I felt somehow beaten." Yet with rehearsals complete and a gifted coterie of sessioneers in tow, Dexys adjourned to Switzerland to begin recording. Housed at Montreux's Mountain Studios for a month, veteran Atlantic helmsman Tom Dowd initially represented an emissary of hope in Dexys' search for the right producer.

Having met the group in Birmingham, great things were in the offing, according to Rowland. "It all seemed so exciting, like the cavalry coming in – 'you don't need to be so confused, things are going to be better'," Rowland told Daryl Easlea. "'Fucking fantastic Tom, let's go!'" Aside from conceiving the beguiling album cover shot of the stylishly clad quartet (Rowland, Adams, O'Hara and Gatfield) staring solemnly into the camera, the fruits of their four-week labours comprised a solitary backing track to the life-affirming 'Listen To This', Dexys' most direct, heart-of-the-matter love song, later captured on film in a spirited Wembley studio performance.

Recorded live, its raw, energetic power was unmistakeable, yet capturing the 'feel' had proved problematic. "When we got to record, it wasn't working," Rowland added. "Tom said, 'I think we want to do it separately now.' In the end, we just ignored him."

Chasing a landmark album, (a *Dark Side Of The Moon*-sized *magnum opus* for the Eighties, no less), Rowland worried little over the time that elapsed in capturing the requisite spontaneity. "He didn't care," Adams told the BBC. "He did whatever it would take. It's always the way Kevin worked. He'd do whatever it would take to get it right."

Brennan acknowledged Rowland's creativity and imagination as an incredible blessing. "It was almost on terms of genius in knowing what he wants. And I think it is difficult to communicate those kind of things."

Rowland's eventual decision to relieve Dowd of his duties puzzled subsequent producer, Alan Winstanley. "If it sounded so good, why did he sack Tom Dowd and get me in? That version [of 'Listen To This'] wasn't used. I never heard any of it. It was all re-recorded." Former Smiths producer John Porter had also been tried out but lasted just a day at the helm. Having completed one satisfactory take of a new song and deciding to keep the tape running, he asked the group for another rendition. We've got enough tape, Porter assured a concerned Rowland. "So they got to the last chord of the song and the tape ran out!" Winstanley said, laughing. "That was the take. And what had happened, in true Dexys style, was they'd done that take maybe ten bars longer, so it ran out just as they hit the last chord!"

Porter was credited for his work on the 'lost' opening track 'Kevin

Rowland's Band', subsequently rechristened 'Kevin Rowland's 13th Time'. Rowland insisted that an out-of-sync drumbeat convinced him to discard *Don't Stand Me Down*'s five-minute entree.*

Rolling Stones producer Jimmy Miller was also 'auditioned'. During a creative impasse, the group committed a tender rendition of the Jerome Kern standard 'The Way You Look Tonight' to tape. Rowland deemed the song – featuring Trevor Burton (bass), Mick Boulton (piano), Robert Noble (organ) and, unexpectedly, ex-David Bowie's Spiders from Mars drummer Mick 'Woody' Woodmansey – as suitable single material. However, according to Gatfield, Miller lasted just one day. "Looking back, he was good," Rowland told *Mojo* in 2002. "But at the time I thought, 'What's the point of having him?' He just sat there, never suggested anything, just said, 'That sounds pretty good to me.' I couldn't comprehend a producer like that. He might have been alright, but I still don't know how he transmitted his ideas."

Resolving to scrap much of the early material and start again, Paul Burton suggested re-engaging Alan Winstanley. *Don't Stand Me Down* would be a swiftly recorded 'live' album, Burton and A&R man Roger Aimes stressed.

"They wanted to do a whole album in two weeks, record everything in the first week, do a bit of improving in the second week, and then a third week to mix it. And that was it," Winstanley recalled, smiling. "A *three week* album."

Dexys spent two weeks recording the bulk of the album live at Westbourne Grove's Marquis Studios in London. Day one proved an ominous portent of what was to come, as Winstanley recalled. "We were hanging around waiting for Woody [Woodmansey], and Kevin said, 'Do you think we could get going?' I said, 'Well, when's Woody gonna get here?' And Kevin said, 'He's not turning up until later in the week. I thought we'd do it a bit different this time.'

"There was a big live booth at the far end of the studio, which in my mind was where the drums were gonna be set up. So I put the horns in, tried to get a sound, and it just sounded a bit dead really." Roughly three days were given over to perfecting a suitable sound. In utilising only a modest-sized studio, by the time Woodmansey arrived, there was no space to accommodate his drum kit. Winstanley spent a day outside the studios constructing a makeshift sound booth from a three-by-two wooden frame and sheets of corrugated iron. "That's where the drums stayed."

---

* Retaining its original title, the track would not appear until the release of Rowland's solo single, 'Tonight' in 1988.

While his contributions to 'The Waltz' and 'The Way You Look Tonight' were retained, the former Spiders stickman was seen as surplus to requirements. A couple of weeks later, the drummer telephoned the studio. Winstanley asked Rowland: "Doesn't he know he's not in the band any more?"

"Kevin just said, 'Don't worry, I'll let him know at some point.' He was firing people left, right and centre. There were so many."

Clive Langer had just returned from a three-week cycling holiday with Madness singer Suggs, in the South of France. Expecting to find the project completed, he was surprised to find Winstanley still toying with a drum sound.

Steve Torch, of White & Torch, was belatedly credited for his inspiration on 'The Waltz', for which Edwards' soft, atmospheric bass took time to perfect. "I mentioned that he was playing the bass late," Winstanley recalls. "And Kevin said, 'No, that's the way it should be played, laid-back,' and I said, 'It's more than laid-back, it's *late*.' It went on and on all day. In the end, I just gave up and left Kevin to it. It was miles out of time.

"We came in the next day, put the track up, and the first thing Kevin did was turn round to John and say, 'It's fuckin' late! Let's do it again!' I said, 'I was trying to tell you that yesterday!'"

Dexys relocated to Westside Studios for a week of mixing. However, despite retaining a couple of tracks, the bulk of the album was dumped and re-recorded.

Chapter Twenty-One

AS Dexys working methods became clear, Winstanley suggested six months in the studio might prove beneficial. Rowland and the group insisted that a fortnight was adequate. Having recorded a handful of rhythm and horn tracks, the group would often uproot themselves again weeks later. Thus, the protracted recording sessions for *Don't Stand Me Down* have subsequently assumed legendary status.

Rowland was desperate to stretch his ambition beyond any pre-conceived pop boundaries. "It was me," he told Daryl Easlea. "It was very much my vision, although Billy and Helen helped. It's funny isn't it? Someone said the silence surrounding *Don't Stand Me Down* was deafening. That's how I felt."

In the process of Rowland leading his group through endless retakes, tapes began disintegrating in front of the producer's eyes. Boxes of tape reels (Winstanley estimated there were around 200) piled up high at the back of each control room. "People presume we spent ages wading through tapes, but we never got lost, did we?" Rowland asked *Record Collector*. "We never got lost on the album once. It wasn't chaos, as some people suggested, that we finally got something out of it. There aren't any gems hidden away. We focused on the best stuff, we knew what we were doing at the time. We were just being incredibly meticulous and it took forever."

Perplexed by the work being presented to them, Phonogram's enthusiasm and support for Rowland's Olympian sized dream gradually waned. "They must have had some faith to pump the money in. We had to keep going ahead with what we believed," O'Hara insisted to Easlea. "It was difficult, really hard. Nobody was on our side."

Rowland enlightened Mercury with Dexys' own marketing strategy for the forthcoming album. Their initial plan, according to Paul Burton, centred on conceiving a record of unassailable perfection. Like numerous self-respecting Seventies artists, they refused to issue any preview single in full support of the album. It might prove problematic, the company's managing director informed Rowland, but the proposal was tentatively accepted.

Yet the record's lengthy gestation meant the matter became almost non–negotiable by the middle of 1985. With a new director in charge of affairs, Rowland told *Record Collector*: "We said the same thing to him, and he said 'no'. So it became a battle of wills, and I was definitely not one for standing down in those days."

While Rowland was summoned to a court case involving Dowd's dismissal, Winstanley resolved to record O'Hara's violin parts in his absence. Her contributions were taped in a single productive day. "She was a really good musician, and easy to work with," Winstanley praised. "Kevin came back the next day, listened to everything, and apart from one phrase in one song, he liked everything." Conversely, the fabled brass took an eternity to perfect. With one sax player let go during the sessions, Gatfield ended up playing both alto and tenor parts. "The horns took forever," the producer recalls, "but Jim was there as well."

On the originally entitled 'My National Pride', brass parts were temporarily considered in place of Adams' rhythm guitar, while on the towering centrepiece 'This Is What She's Like', individual stringed instruments were favoured at one point over Adams' contributions. As on *Too-Rye-Ay*, his proficiency as a guitarist proved problematic, as Winstanley attested, "This was more Kevin's idea than mine, but we ended up doing it one chord at a time, stopping, re-tuning the guitar, and then dropping in for the next chord. We ended up doing it like that for the whole song!"

"Someone told me there were 120 versions of 'This Is What She's Like', Paolo Hewitt recalled incredulously. "Can you imagine making *Don't Stand Me Down*? I mean the hours that they put into that record. They worked so hard."

Undertaking basic acting lessons for the lengthy conversational takes, Adams endured a torrid time perfecting his parts. He also insisted there was an element of spontaneity. "The amount of takes it took – what Kevin put Billy through, really acting it out, walking through doors – real method stuff," O'Hara marvelled to *Record Collector*. "I'm surprised Billy put up with it!"

"What's even more incredible, and which gives some insight into how humorous Kevin could be, was the whole section of dialogue [the song's opening sequence] that he did with Billy that was based on paranoia. Those scenarios happened daily within Dexys," Brennan recalls. "And it was an incredible thing to live under."

The album's conversational thread appealed to critic Chris Roberts' theatrical tastes. "It reminds me of Beckett, Pinter and the great theatre of the absurd. It's almost like a play, and a very good one, about absurdity and the meanings of mundane stuff. That's an absolutely essential part of what makes *Don't Stand Me Down* such a unique and unparalleled record."

"That took a long time to get right," Winstanley admitted. "It was strange, and what ended up on the final album might have been re-recorded again after I'd left." With just a couple of tracks completed, a prospective August 1984 release date already proved optimistic in the extreme. In September, the group picked up the thread from the original Miller-mixed session and recorded 'The Way You Look Tonight', which remained unreleased until April 1988.

As time wore on, Winstanley felt that self-indulgence and quality control became a cause for concern. "The songs were not nearly as strong, which is why it took so long. They were too long. I know that a lot of people like that album, but I'm sure the record company were after something a bit more commercial!"

"They had had a massive hit with 'Come On Eileen' and they wanted another *Too-Rye-Ay*," Roberts suggests, "but the record company didn't help by not really getting behind it."

By December, Dexys were ensconced at the Townhouse Studios in Shepherd's Bush. Eight months into recording, the record company, Winstanley sensed, were understandably getting "a little nervous". Having made a handsome profit from more than three million sales of *Too-Rye-Ay*, Phonogram were counting on a similar commercial success. "They were obviously hoping he was gonna come up with another masterpiece, so they had given him a bit of slack," Winstanley insists.

With the record company growing frantic at the lack of progress, Rowland was feeling the heat over mounting studio costs. "We'd already spent enough to do two fucking albums, and we had two songs!" he told Easlea. "They wanted to release the thing in a few weeks. I thought we were going mad. They were telling *us* we were going mad!

"I was working my bollocks off. I could just about handle being locked away in the studio. But it was no life. Billy said he couldn't go through it again after that. I was just completely driven and obsessed. I still get like that sometimes and I just hate it," he admitted to Johnny Rogan. The recording process reached an impasse.

When Gatfield eventually left, Dexys' biggest problem centred on finding the right drummer. Having dispensed with both Woodmansey, and Crusher Green after his contributions on 'Listen To This', a procession of percussionists had been auditioned during the second half of the year. "No one we tried seemed to know what we wanted," Adams concluded.

Eventually, Rowland and O'Hara drew much needed inspiration from an Al Green show at the Royal Albert Hall at the turn of 1985. "He had this brilliant drummer – Tim Dancy. We'd been trying to get all these

English players to play like him," Rowland informed *Record Collector.*

Rowland stretched the group's spiralling recording budget even further in order to secure Memphis session man Dancy, who was sent demo versions for 'This Is What She's Like', 'One Of Those Things' and the latterly titled 'Knowledge Of Beauty.' His powerful empathetic style proved crucial. Almost inevitably, there were hold-ups. It allegedly transpired that the drummer had experienced problems with his work permit. On his arrival at Heathrow Airport, he had no choice but to return to the States, sort out his paperwork and fly in from Ireland. On arrival, Dancy approached Rowland and began singing a refrain from 'One Of Those Things'. With close attention paid to perfecting its innuendo-laden humour, the song provided a vital pressure release, according to O'Hara. "There was a lot of hilarity," she told Easlea. "There had to be this release at points. Some days there were a lot of jokes going on. Often at other people's expense. Alan Winstanley was great as well. We would have all cracked up if we'd taken it seriously. Kevin is very good at mimicking people, and that went through the sessions."

However, Rowland was wary of the group growing too indulgent. "We'd ask him [Dancy] if he wanted to start and he'd say, 'What tempo do you want that thing in?' He would walk round the studio, get in the groove and then he would begin. Then it fortunately all became very quick." The recording finally found some momentum, with 'One Of Those Things', 'This Is What She's Like' and 'Knowledge Of Beauty' being swiftly recorded. Dexys instinctively knew they had found their man in Dancy, whose skills also furnished 'Kevin Rowland's 13th Time' and 'The Occasional Flicker'.

After taking a welcome Christmas break and with the mixing close at hand, it seemed the end was in sight. Having visited New York during the festive season, Rowland resolved to mix the album there. "The mixing again took a long, long time and at one point he [Rowland] decided he had to record in America, and he went to New York," Burton told the BBC. "There was a lot of time, I think, there was over two months spent in America mixing, and he still wasn't too happy with the results." Roger Aimes' proviso was that all recording duties had to be completed prior to the team's relocation to the Electric Lady Studios.

"He [Aimes] didn't like the idea too much," Winstanley recalls, "because he thought the whole band was gonna traipse over there, and it was gonna cost more and more money. In the end, he agreed to let us go, as long as it was just me and Kevin."

Inevitably, O'Hara and Adams were asked to fly out to the Big Apple to undertake minor recording duties. Rough mixes of the forthcoming record were leaked to the music press, with *Smash Hits*, rather oddly, noting its overt 'rock'n'roll' tendencies. Winstanley had given Rowland advance notice of his intention to start work on Madness' new album in London in January. However, by Christmas, it was patently clear he would still be needed. Fortunately, Suggs and co appeared happy for their work to be postponed, as long as proceedings were under way by March 1. "There were all these pressures," Adams recounted to *Record Collector*. "Music is an art, yet people would never say to artists, 'This painting's got to be finished by March, and then you've got to be out promoting it.'"

Three weeks of mixing sessions were booked, commencing on February 1, but by the afternoon of February 28, Dexys were still at Electric Lady. "I flew out of New York," Winstanley recalls. "The whole album was basically mixed, but the last song was still on the board. And I just remember saying to Kevin, 'I've gotta fly back tonight to start this album tomorrow morning in London. Get a house engineer in. If you wanna make any changes to the mix, it's all set up.' And he seemed really happy with that."

Carrying with him most of the completed material, Winstanley touched down at Heathrow before journeying straight to AIR Studios on Oxford Street. Later that day, he took a break from Madness to pay Aimes a visit. "I went over to play him the mixes, and he loved them. He said it sounded great." Winstanley informed Aimes that the final track's mixing would involve one last day's effort. *Don't Stand Me Down* was now pencilled in for a spring release. Rowland later told fanzine editor Neil Warburton that the title originated from overhearing a similar lyric to a Bill Withers song 'Use Me Up', and also as a plea to Adams during one studio marathon.

Don't Stand Me Down's imminent arrival was now music press news. Three live London dates for a prospective TV show were also mooted. With the industry wheels in motion, pictures of the new Dexys image slowly filtered through to typical consternation among sections of the music press. Derogatory comments couched in smug disdain were targeted at the group. The latest instalment in their great sartorial saga, Dexys' new visual statement invited snide comparisons to Wall Street attorneys, fastidious chartered accountants, clean-cut American collegiates and strait-laced bank clerks. "It was actually an American Ivy League look," Rowland belatedly corrected his detractors in 1997. "I've admired those clothes since my teens and feel some of them are so beautiful they are works of art."

"It has to be put in context," stresses Chris Roberts. "Around that time, every band was doing things with clothes. It wasn't like they were the only band who had come out with a different image for their new album. It was quite normal for a band to appear with a brand new dress sense for every record. It was what was in vogue at the time. And Kevin did come up with a really different, original look, at a time when people were wearing all sorts of bizarre and surreal things."

Rowland felt that Dexys post *Too-Rye-Ay* profile and status demanded a suitably salubrious look. There was no longer a compulsion to dress down or scour second-hand clothes shops.

While on tour in New York in January 1983, Rowland had taken a stroll down Madison Avenue. "I still had the big hat with a feather in it, dungarees and a great big overcoat and pumps," Rowland informed Easlea. "I looked in Brooks Brothers' window, saw these Ivy League clothes. I went in and started buying them, and it just felt great. It also felt like going back to something that was good again."

Dexys spent the best part of a year returning to the store, questioning the staff on etiquette and appropriate hairstyles. Rowland encouraged Jack Hazan, director of the three promotional films for *Don't Stand Me Down*, to visit the same specialist barbershop near Grand Central Station. Curiously, Rowland wasn't unduly concerned with the ad-hoc aggregate of mid-Eighties fashion disasters assembled for the 'This Is What She's Like' performance shoot. "We decided the look didn't matter, we just wanted the best players, they didn't have to be part of the image," he told David Hutcheon. "We told them to wear what they liked. So in the videos they're wearing bandanas and Spandex, we're in Brooks Brothers."

Rowland felt comfortable in these simple, sharper threads. The attention to detail struck a chord with O'Hara. "I could understand what he was doing. The image was very strong. So many people have told me how unappealing it all was, so unattractive, unsexy. I rather liked it because of that."

"The image evolved, it wasn't all off the peg," Adams insisted to *Record Collector*. "Nobody had seen that evolution. We'd changed as people. We were changing and being true to ourselves." The group's subsequent television appearances raised a few eyebrows.

Typifying the general 'whaaa?' consensus was an October 4 interview conducted by a clueless Muriel Gray on Channel Four's *Bliss*. "What's with the double glazing salesmen look?" she enquired.

Rowland shot back: "*What* double glazing salesmen look?"

"Isn't it mad how just wearing a suit can cause such offence?" Rowland asked Easlea. "I was dying for the album to come out, so I could start wearing it. We'd been keeping it a secret. I thought somebody was going to nick it." He later regretted not making a more concerted effort in reappraising the group's image. "I've always loved clothes and I used to think I needed an excuse, like, I got to have a new record."

Having received no immediate feedback, Winstanley presumed no news was good news. A fortnight elapsed before the producer received an alarming update. "Suddenly I got a call from Roger saying, 'Did you know Kevin was still in New York, in Electric Lady?' He said, 'He's decided to remix the whole album!'"

Chapter Twenty-Two

WHILE stretching his visionary powers to their limit in bringing *Don't Stand Me Down* to fruition, Rowland lacked the necessary musical and technical proficiency to produce his own material. "It was desperation and ego again, I think," he confided to Phil Sutcliffe. "An ego the size of a house, I had. I'm still not good enough. I'm not well-versed enough in musical terms, not musical enough in any way."

As proceedings dragged on in New York, Rowland's loyal but frustrated right-hand man had reached the end of his tether. "I kicked the wall in the live room, after my bits of talking," Adams recalled to Daryl Easlea. "That was pretty much the end. It was too hard for me to be around. I was missing my home, my girlfriend, my motorbikes. I'd just been living in studios. I didn't know what was good or bad any more."

"Things were definitely more difficult in the studio for *Don't Stand Me Down*," said Winstanley, "and Kevin was even more of a perfectionist. I suppose he thought doing things over and over again was the way to make things better, which I don't think is always the case."

"He was often right when you'd do the 100th take or so, irritatingly so, sometimes!" O'Hara told *Record Collector*. "Everybody who's worked with him knows that's how it is. I thought I was a perfectionist until I met him!"

" 'When are you going to be finished?' was all I was hearing," Rowland told Easlea.

"This awful strain. Paul Burton said, 'Do you think it will *ever* be finished?' I then thought, 'I don't know,' because *everybody* was implying that to me . . . I didn't have a life. That was it. It was just this thing. I was so determined."

Two weeks into their New York mixing stint, the Electric Lady studio manager approached Winstanley. He informed the producer that the studio had been booked for the forthcoming two evening sessions. "He said, 'Have you got a lockout?' And we said, 'No.' The manager said, 'Don't worry, let 'em come in and I'll come in each morning and make sure it was all put back as it was.' So we did." New York studios in the mid-Eighties were an expensive proposition. Any group wanting to retain their set-up for the following day incurred a 'lockout' charge for a 14-hour session.

Aimes had told Winstanley not to bow to pressure. "He said, 'You can't just work eight hours and pay for fourteen.' It wasn't the end of the world and you were saving a lot of money."

Following Winstanley's departure, Rowland took control of the situation. "There wasn't that kind of craziness going on," he told *Record Collector*. "We always knew we were moving forward, it just took an incredibly long time." While the studio bosses allowed Dexys to continue mixing/recording, Phonogram New York, who were picking up the bills, refused to confirm the extra time. When the record company insisted they had no intention of settling Dexys' mounting debt, Electric Lady reputedly threatened to withhold the master tapes.

As the project crawled towards a dramatic conclusion, Winstanley was growing familiar with frequent calls of a frantic nature. The telephone rang. It was Aimes, enquiring whether the producer would consider flying to New York at his earliest convenience to help purloin the album master tapes. Burton, O'Hara and Adams were already there. "In the end, I didn't go. I remember telling Roger, 'Make sure he [Rowland] get's the floppy disk. And everything he needs if he's gonna come back and carry on mixing it in London.'" According to Winstanley, legend has it that the assistant engineer was sent out of the studio, enabling the group to enact their escape. The producer was told how "three or four of them allegedly grabbed the tapes, ran through the Electric Lady studio, straight through reception, and past the studio manager's office. They got to the car, and the chauffeur had gone off for a cup of coffee or something, y'know, the door was locked!" A studio employee reputedly foiled their getaway. After Phonogram had resolved the outstanding costs, the tapes were eventually released and sent to their New York offices. But this incident-strewn saga had one final twist.

"The next thing that happened was the office below the one they were stored in caught fire," the producer recalls. "The offices were evacuated for a week. So for seven days, no one knew whether the tapes were intact or not!" Consternation turned to relief when the tapes were eventually found and shipped to London. Initially working the record alone in the spring of 1985, Rowland eventually called in amiable engineer Pete Schwier for the final three months to complete the project. Having visited Outside studios in Reading before relocating to the capital, the saga closed at Kim Wilde's Selectsound studios in Hertfordshire.

Schwier's patience and dedication proved invaluable. "Without him, it wouldn't sound like it did," Rowland admitted to *Record Collector*. "I'd lost faith in the album by that point, right at the very end. I was thinking, 'What the fuck has this two years been about?'" Rowland offered praise to

Schwier for managing to "hold it together", considering that a suitably spontaneous quality had taken the best part of 18 months to perfect. Burton surmised that it's lengthy gestation and recording costs (estimated at more than half-a-million pounds) were totally unjustified in terms of subsequent record sales. Rowland's rigorous perfectionism had reached new levels as he pushed all involved to their limits.

"It was a horrendous experience," he told Phil Sutcliffe. "I stumbled through, wearing the group down. Maybe that works when you wear them down a little bit, but then you go on and wear them down completely 'til there's nothing left of them . . ."

Don't Stand Me Down was, Winstanley claimed, "a nightmare. But that [three-week 'live' recording schedule] was my brief, and in hindsight, I can't see that Kevin did want to do it like that. It seems hard to believe."

Apart from the odd moment of levity, Rowland admitted that the sessions had proved an exhausting affair, and he had no intention of repeating such an arduous process. "I was driven to do something really good, at the cost of everything else. I think I really enjoyed the fact that everyone else around, even some of the musicians, were saying, 'What's he doing? What the hell's going on?' "

In 1993, he proudly assured Q that *Don't Stand Me Down* had been a worthwhile struggle. "I can't help thinking this stuff was really good music and it is a shame it wasn't heard by people at the time. And it wasn't so leftfield that nobody would understand it. It was just good music, that I think if people had heard they would appreciate," Rowland enthused to Chris Roberts in 2002, who was mesmerised by its emotion and power. "There are so few records where you get a sense of individuality and someone testifying, telling it like they think it is, talking openly about their emotions." Another of the album's ongoing sagas involved its front cover. On the initial proof run of the sleeve, Rowland insisted the wrong shade of burgundy had been used bearing the group's name and the record's title. Proofs were reprinted in lighter and darker shades as record company patience and fiscal resources diminished before Rowland was happy.

"All Pete Barrett would reveal about the sleeve at the time was that it was 'anti-design'," recalled Paolo Hewitt. "Sleeves are meant to sell the record, and you've got four people just sitting there, very conservative, but that was part of the whole thing. People had no idea what Dexys were doing. On *Don't Stand Me Down*, the politics are radical, the statements are radical, but people thought, 'They look like bank managers!' I thought, 'But have you heard this record about the IRA and the PLO?' "

The sleeve's outward orthodoxy certainly concealed the album's experimental musical content. *Don't Stand Me Down* aspired to the majestic warmth of *Pet Sounds*, drew upon the poetic vernacular and exploratory compositions of *Astral Weeks*, reflected *What's Going On* for ambition and vocal experimentation and enjoyed a similarly rich, mercurial spirit to *Blonde On Blonde*. Upon *Don't Stand Me Down*'s reappearance in 2002, the new opening track was a herald for the cluster of epics that originally formed its opening side. 'Kevin Rowland's 13th Time' represented the unearthing of a lost treasure. With Noble's shuddering organ and Crane's trilling piano, Dexys rose to the occasion. Gatfield's steaming sax, Dancy's incisive percussion and O'Hara's haughty violin enacted a climactic battle. As Rowland snarled his lines, the band smouldered and sparkled, matching him growl-filled blow for blow. This headstrong, soul-stewed swagger and menace was reflected in a fiery lyrical bite. This opening salvo introduced the album's prevailing pathos, righteous belief and nonconformity. It's conversational thread unveiled an exploration of humour, Rowland firing his opening volley in a 'joke' about class, with Adams doing his utmost to sound tickled. Lyrically, the song now represented one of Rowland's most sophisticated, engaging entreaties.

Opening with reference to a wasted youth, the middle classes' tendency towards artistic pretence raised Rowland's hackles. "I'm proud of it, though lyrically my viewpoint has changed massively," he stressed in the album's new liner notes. On the enigmatically titled 'The Occasional Flicker', gentle humour was located in Rowland's admission of an intermittent sufferance with a "burning" sensation. He waved aside sympathy before initiating self-redemption. Addressing his own bitterness and contempt before reasserting a sense of conviction, one of the album's greatest, most memorable lines came in Rowland's opening, curled-lipped broadside against the act of compromise. His refusal to waver was never posited more succinctly. It was going to be a hell of a ride.

Stoking the coals, Paterson's trombone and Gatfield's wild-eyed sax evinced a soulful white heat. Dancy's percussion uncoiled into a spellbinding groove, the brooding plot thickened thanks to Edwards' bass and Crane's quicksilver piano. With Crane's inimitable presence taking *Don't Stand Me Down* to greater heights, he recalled the difficulty in perfecting the piano link at the heart of 'This Is What She's Like', a staggering, seamless emotional *tour de force*. With its fluctuating tempo and theatrical form, this 12-minute, wide screen epic remains a source of perpetual awe. Following mundane, intimate conversation coloured by Adams' curiosity and Rowland's procrastination, the song segued effortlessly into a soft, introductory croon. A coruscating opening movement then unfurled. A combustible mix, sparks flew as O'Hara's thrilling violin motifs formed a striking musical foil to Rowland's fiery ripostes, given their bite through his preoccupations with the *nouveau-riche* and middle-class, CND-baiting lyrics.

"That particular line [concerning the 'scum'-like Notting Hill and Moseley CND patrons] came from an experience of mine in Notting Hill. I saw this guy looking into a window. He had all the badges on, 'Nuclear Power, No Thanks', and all that and this tramp came up to him and asked him for ten pence and the guy just said, 'No', and walked off. I just thought, 'So pathetic, you know?'" Rowland was later embarrassed by the ferocity of his attack on the middle classes.

"The good thing about Kevin Rowland is that he recognises that every class on the social scale has its own clichés. And you don't necessarily have those things educated out of you," Peter Paphides maintains. "He was able to recognise the middle-class clichés that even the middle classes, for all their education, don't recognise for themselves. And that's one of the many reasons why 'This Is What She's Like' is such a great song."

According to Jack Hazan, Rowland's passionate, wordless exultations on his fractured love affair with O'Hara formed a basis for the subsequent video. Spliced with an electric studio ensemble performance, it was filmed on location on May 1, 1985, Labor Day in New York. Hazan was aiming to achieve something unique and at odds with the traditional promo approach. The incredible drama of a slow motion, long-shot camera sequence captured Rowland running through Manhattan utterly alone, the city resembling a ghost town. "When he's running down Fifth Avenue, absolutely deserted, how did they do that?" Hewitt wonders. "Dexys never let you down. Other groups let you down. Dexys never did."

A piano-led breakdown and lilting mandolin melted into a soaring, Beach Boys-inspired harmony interlude. As Rowland tantalises the listener with the beauty of his muse, the song reaches a percussive crescendo. It's sky-scraping ambition and emotional epiphanies were translated into one of the video's inventive passages. "We had some sort of crane and cut from shots of Kevin's feet above the ground and his head on this crane to look as if he's flying up in the air," Hazan told *Record Collector*. In the broadest sweep of the album's musical canvas, fat saxes, freewheeling guitar and mandolin, rolling piano and firework percussion orchestrated Rowland's hot-blooded exhortations.

Hewitt enthused over the song's inexpressible quality. "I love the fact that he's written a song about what she's like, and he can't tell you because it's so *above* everything. And every time he tries, Billy says, 'Come on, what's she like?'"

Overpowered, Rowland likened the emotional sensation to a "thunderbolt". "I'd fallen for Helen, see, and my brother said, 'I think the Italians have a word for it.'" Rowland had been inspired by Michael Corleone's post-restaurant shooting scene from *The Godfather*. "I must've liked the ring of it," he told *Uncut* in 2002. Kevin Pearce detected Oscar Wilde's influence in Dexys' use of a punctuating narrative, with other parallels drawn to Harold Pinter, James Joyce and Samuel Beckett. Even Rowland's characteristic fashion concerns weren't forgotten, expressing his distaste for the country's creased Levi-wearing constituency.

Critics who derided the album's supposed self-indulgence clearly over-looked its attendant humour and pathos. A suitably perplexed *NME* also failed to notice any of the sophisticated musical daring of 'This Is What She's Like'. "I remember thinking, 'It's good, and it's got everything in there,'" Rowland told *Uncut*. O'Hara found the song's semi-cinematic, emotional content particularly striking. Timeless, unrelenting and torren-tial, 'This Is What She's Like' remains unbowed.

Rowland's quest for redemption and fondness for his ancestral home-land was eloquently conveyed in the following track. Tempering his political fury over Ireland, 'My National Pride' was an awakening; a potent, emotional synthesis of love and anger, regret and honesty. The song's convivial warmth made it an ideal candidate as an alehouse air. Rowland had long dreamt of finding reassurance in his romanticised view of old Ireland. With past and parentage prevalent, it illustrated the sombre heart of a misplaced wanderer, a searcher devoid of ties and sense of belonging. Sadly Rowland lacked the courage of his original convictions. "I remember not calling 'Knowledge Of Beauty' 'My National Pride', because I thought it was too strong," he informed Easlea. "The line 'knowledge of beauty in these days rare' was originally 'they rot in prison cells over there'. It was about people in jail in Ireland. It felt like too much of a statement."

Seeking an authentically 'derelict' Irish setting for the accompanying promotional video, the quaint rustic villages Rowland seemingly yearned for had disappeared. "On that video he goes into the church, and it was all about the Catholic thing," Hewitt states. "I think it was all related to that, on a subconscious level. Dexys was about redeeming yourself."

Crane's gorgeously understated piano, clear and fresh as a Galway stream, ushers in a slow hymnal meditation, a sense of longing evinced in O'Hara's weeping violin and Tommy Evans' evocative steel guitar work. Gathering momentum, Rowland repents for the infliction of unnecessary anguish, while addressing something of the empty experience of attendant fame. Anger at his denial of his own roots emanates through the crashing piano chords that bring proceedings to a shuddering halt.

Melody Maker praised Rowland's rich Scott Walker-like croon, while

Steve Wynne was belatedly acknowledged for his chorus vocal idea. The song's melody, Rowland maintains, came from a subconscious source. 'One Of Those Things' wasn't quite so original in its melodic beginnings. A solid piano and bass bedrock gave Rowland ample room to manoeuvre, seeking to settle a score with the inanities of commercial radio. With Crane's giveaway opening piano sequence in mind, Rowland later admitted purloining the three-chord riff intro from 'Werewolves Of London' by Warren Zevon, who now owns a share of the song.*

Apparently, Mercury suggested making a case for the song's similarity to 'Sweet Home Alabama' instead. Under the pseudonym of Sid Jenkins, Rowland brought the playlist fare of Radio One DJ David 'Kid' Jensen into focus. He pointed to the derivative, faux-soulful, synthesiser-driven music predominating on the airwaves. Yet Rowland later underlined how impressed he'd been by Frankie Goes To Hollywood's enormous-selling, chart-topping single 'Relax' during the album's early gestation in January and February 1984. (It's probably no coincidence that producer Trevor Horn was another rumoured candidate to helm *Don't Stand Me Down*.) Redressing a more serious imbalance, Rowland compared banal chart output to the empty platitudes and left-wing rhetoric spouted by supporters of far-flung political causes. It reiterated his desperation at ignorance over The Troubles. Address matters on your own doorstep, namely Belfast, as Rowland told Simon Price, "I'd be talking to supposed socialists and I'd say, 'Do you know what's happening in Ireland?' And they'd say, 'What?' and I'd say, 'It's being occupied, by the army of this country!'" An incredulous Rowland reeled off a list of political causes to stack Ireland's woe against. Given his disillusionment and anger, the song roars and scolds. But the candid, comical dialogue Rowland conducted with Adams soothed the sting. It ends with a semi-resigned shrug of the shoulders.

As the sanguine sentiments faded, this beautifully sequenced record revealed the warmer connotations of Rowland's love-hate affair with UK radio in the reflective intimacy of 'Reminisce (Part Two)'. Sparked by a welcome encounter with The Fifth Dimension's 'Wedding Bell Blues', tender piano chords and a lightly woven acoustic guitar and bass accompany Rowland's inviting dialogue. Leading the listener through memories evoked by the soundtrack to his own summer of '69 (despite not charting until 1970), a suitably open-winged mandolin recalled John Denver's

---

* Ironically, Zevon had contributed to the soundtrack of critical flop *FM*, a 1978 film concerning a tussle between forward-thinking and backward-looking forces over the playlist of an American radio station.

'Leaving On A Jet Plane'. In a dreamy reverie, Rowland harked back to long, balmy evenings walking down Oxford Street with his sixteen-year-old squeeze. The Kinks' 'Lola' and Jimmy Ruffin's 'I'll Say Forever My Love' had captured their imaginations. Music was a nostalgic barometer of old emotions.

Peter Paphides recalls *Melody Maker*'s policy of not citing obscure singers' names in their reviews. "It was intrinsic to the regime: 'What's the point of referencing someone who the readers have never heard of?' But you only have to look back to Dexys songs to realise that it is absolutely justifiable. I went to a rare records shop in Birmingham, and deliberately searched out that [Jimmy Ruffin] record, so that I could enter the world of 'Reminisce (Part Two)'.

Narrating the fleeting nature of this gilded teenage bliss, Rowland's rich incantation of 'I'll Say Forever' emerges. A sumptuous counterpoint to trembling piano and spine-tingling mandolin, it was a tangible, eye-moistening moment. On an album filled with stirring vocal performances, this was an unforgettable demonstration of Rowland's prowess. "For me, he had one of the great white voices in music," Roberts freely admits. "In reviews I've often called him the white Al Green, but there is certainly more credibility and emotion in his voice than in a thousand other singers of his era. You just believe in his voice. When he sings, you really believe he means it. It's from the heart." 'Listen To This' (later retitled 'I Love You' in honour of his relationship with O'Hara) is positive proof. The traditional horn-led punch, brevity and passion of old excited the critics, quick to point out its suitability as single material.

Paolo Hewitt believes it would have rejuvenated Dexys' relationship with the UK charts. "It would have gone straight in, big time. But Kevin didn't want to [release it], and I don't blame him." A pulsing three-minute testimony, this was a lightning bolt of directness among the album's more ponderous material. Rowland's concerns were shrouded in obscure wordplay once more on the album's closing track, 'The Waltz'. Originally entitled 'Elizabeth Wimpole And Kathleen Ni Houlihan' and pre-occupied with fervent Irish sensibilities, Rowland appeared to relish drawing a lyrical veil, seeming to hint at the consequential effects and futility of attendant fame.

Beguiling introspection aside, this was a sincere protest. Registering his adolescent gripe with all things monarchical, Rowland criticised the British myth propagators for their historical fallacies built around "royal victories", evidencing his interest in republicanism. O'Hara's mournful viola strained against Littman's melancholic mandolin and Evans' arid steel guitar.

Lamenting the absence of beauty, Rowland sang of self-restraint as the music broadened its horizons. As elegiac strings ignited an elemental duel, earthy piano and winged mandolin held their ground: Green's percussion work doused Gatfield's roasting sax in a rousing coda.

"There were many times when we thought we'd never finish this album and when I listen to it now," Rowland confided with such satisfaction and gratitude in 1997, "I'm amazed at how beautiful it turned out."

Chapter Twenty-Three

WITH all the ways in prolonging the release of *Don't Stand Me Down* apparently exhausted, Phonogram's lawyer contacted Winstanley's counterpart to inform him that the group had asked for the producer's name to be removed from the LP credits. Later scrapped, the original inner sleeve credit was to read: 'Produced by Kevin Rowland – recorded by Alan Winstanley.' Winstanley's lawyer was told the group had taken this step because Dexys had been left to complete the record alone. The producer subsequently sought an injunction against the album's release. The September 7 *NME* news story 'Dexys Stood Up?' outlined the saga, pointing to a fateful release date of Friday the 13th. Following nine months' work on the record, Winstanley rightly argued it was unfair and wrong. The case went to court.

"My lawyer told me that the Phonogram lawyer felt it was unfair, but his hands were tied. He'd been told that this is what they were going to do. He informed us because he could see problems later when the record had come out, without the credit there. They had no case really. The judge ruled in my favour and they reprinted the sleeves. Their argument was, 'We've spent a fortune printing these sleeves,' but the credits were on the inner sleeve, which in comparison to the album sleeve cost peanuts. All I asked them to do was to pay my costs. I wasn't compensated money-wise."

Plugging the album on TV, Dexys barnstormed their way through a live rendition of 'Listen To This' on BBC1's *Wogan*. "That *Wogan* performance is just phenomenal," Peter Paphides enthuses. "The rest of the band look like they are miming but Kevin's singing live, and you can see that it's all been welling up inside him for two years. It's astonishing. I think he could have released 'Listen To This' and it would have been hailed as a real return to form." *Don't Stand Me Down* finally entered the charts with a muted fanfare at number 22. With Mercury having repeatedly wrung their hands in despair over it's lengthy gestation, (it was just over three years since *Too-Rye-Ay*'s release), they then washed their hands of the whole project as an expensive exercise in non-commercialism.

"We were silent for two years, but it takes time to be so good," Rowland argued to *The Hit* in 1985. "We don't produce any rubbish and we look better than anyone else too. We're unique."

"The automatic reaction was, 'Let's bury this project and move on quickly, cut our losses and get out of it,'" Nick Gatfield told *Record Collector* in 2002. "Combine a notoriously difficult artist with a challenging record and it's not necessarily a winning combination for a record company wishing to make their budget at that particular time! It's ultimately the consumer that determines whether this is a record of value, and I felt the same thing with *Don't Stand Me Down*."

The *NME*'s Sean O'Hagan felt the record was rather a perplexing, fruitless contrivance on behalf of a creatively moribund group. Paolo Hewitt begged to differ. "I remember at the *NME* they used to really wind me up, coming in saying, 'We've got the next radical group.' And I used to think, 'Well, you think that this stuff is so radical, yet you're laughing at this guy who's just made one of the most radical statements going but you can't fucking see it.'"

Confusion over the absence of immediacy in the music seemed to breed contempt. Barry McIlheney attacked Rowland's alleged reticence to address Ireland head on. But there were notable exceptions. Former *NME* deputy-head and editor of short-lived *The Hit*, Phil McNeill praised Rowland's vocal authority, a marked contrast to the frantically restless spirit of old, a man at peace with himself in the studio. Even *Smash Hits* awarded the album eight-and-a-half out of ten. *Record Mirror*'s Diane Cross gave the record full marks, also noting Rowland's burgeoning vocal prowess. Praising the breathtaking accomplishment of the American session men on board, she suggested that Dexys' third LP might just prove incomprehensible to the straggling faithful.

"It completely blew me away straight away," then-*Sounds* journalist Chris Roberts remembered. "It just stands out. It's not like you put it on and it sounds like anything else. It was so unique, so ambitious, so different, so intelligent, so inquisitive, and it comes from the heart. It completely knocked me sideways. And it still does, to this day. It rips the roof off. It's a ball of fire."

"I heard Robert Elms [*The Face* journalist, who noted a debt to early Seventies Beach Boys] saying that people loved that album right from the start. I'm a huge Dexys fan and it took me at least a month, two months for that record to finally make sense to me," Hewitt told the author. "It was just so removed from everything that had gone before, in terms of sound, in terms of song structure, and also in terms of what [Rowland] was writing about."

Having drained every ounce of passion in pursuit of his goal, Rowland's original vision had proved an incredible, time-consuming process. Yet the record's unique nature warranted such attention to detail. Rowland clung to the project like nothing else Dexys had dared to produce. He insisted that he'd just made the greatest LP of his career. "I never lost hope," he delighted in telling *The Hit* in 1985. "And having gone through the hardness, we've now got something for the future – not just the LP, but the group, everything."

Rowland contended with a sense of fear over *Don't Stand Me Down's* reception, convinced that the music press were eagerly anticipating its failure, although he admitted in 1997 that he'd drawn succour from those assuring him of its merits. "No one really said at the time that it was brilliant and when it failed, everybody gave me a million reasons," he confided to Johnny Rogan. "They got to me. You think these people are right because I just had a crisis of confidence." Observers outlined any number of faults. There wasn't an obvious single to promote it, its production had ruined the songs or it was a self-important, indulgent work that had taken too long to appear on the shelves. Rowland argued at the time that the greatest injustice was the fact that nobody knew the record was out. "That commercial failure felt very familiar. People were saying, 'You fucked it up because you did this, this and this,' and I pretended to take it on board, but secretly I was going, 'Fucking great!' I couldn't cope. I'd always felt like a failure. I was amazed I'd got as far as I got without anybody noticing," Rowland told Ted Kessler.

"The failure of *Don't Stand Me Down* really, really hurt Kevin," Hewitt told Radio Two. "Even though he'd been doing his best to sabotage its success, the fact that when he was successful in doing so, I think really knocked him."

Yet perversely, Rowland was also keen for the new material to be accepted and attain commercial as well as critical recognition. He asked Mercury to get *Don't Stand Me Down* played on radio. "They stuck it on their LP slots at 7 o'clock on a Thursday night and nobody heard it. It didn't work and that was my only miscalculation." Adams recalled the radio policy of not playing album tracks and the almost total absence of record company marketing and promotion as a "depressing, ludicrous" state of affairs. The year before its emergence from cult status into critical re-evaluation thanks to Creation's 1997 re-release, Q Magazine nominated *Don't Stand Me Down* as one of the 50 greatest rock follies of recent years, noting Rowland's bullish stubbornness as Dexys delivered their career-sinking third album. Their most incriminating *faux pas*, according to Q, was Adams and Rowland's "disastrous" attempt at humorous conversational narratives.

The passage of time and a fresh perspective on *Don't Stand Me Down's* merits has witnessed a shift towards general acclaim. Music journalists competed to deliver superlative-laden reviews for what was now being hailed as a modern masterpiece. "It's taken until now for *Don't Stand Me Down* to find its place," Rowland expressed, "but I'm glad it finally has.

"I suppose I never really acknowledged *Don't Stand Me Down* because I never had the confidence that it was a great work," he told *Record Collector* in 2000. "I never believed in it after that."

"But nobody can take that from me. No matter what happens I know I made this great record," Rowland proudly informed Ted Kessler.

Three weeks before the album's release, Dexys' promotional scoop of headlining a five-hour *Tube* show special was scuppered because of an industrial strike. A 10-date British tour was to follow in November. While Rowland had been in London applying *Don't Stand Me Down*'s finishing touches, O'Hara and Adams relocated to Nashville, Tennessee during the summer in search of new musicians. With Crane and Boulton still in the fold, guitarist Jerod Minnies was top of the wanted list. Through Minnies, drummer Duane Cleveland was soon on board. Bassist Jerry Preston and pedal steel player Penn Pennington completed the American contingent before trombonist Fayyaz Virji and saxophonist Pol Cousee were recruited in London. Their musicianship reaching new heights, Rowland worked the band hard during autumnal rehearsals in south London. A beautiful, set-opening rendition of Elvis Presley's 'Can't Help Falling In Love' and The Fantastics' 'Something Old, Something New' were added to the live repertoire.

Following a rare screening of the 'My National Pride' video and Rowland's interview appearance on *The Whistle Test*, the group finally played *The Tube* on October 11. They performed 'Listen To This' and a version of John McCormack's 1926 traditional Irish composition 'Kathleen Mavourneen', the B-side of Dexys' final single 'Because Of You'. "Maybe these days we're a bit more forgiving. But you had the bizarre sight of people wearing headbands and suits trying to lock into the groove of an old Irish folk song," Paphides recalls. "Two years later, when The Waterboys appeared on *The Tube* doing 'Fisherman's Blues', it kind of seemed a better idea."

Initially entitled 'Park Street South', Dexys' 'Coming To Town' tour opened to a half-full Edinburgh Playhouse on November 1, the hordes of 'Come On Eileen' devotees having long gone. At Manchester two nights later, a bare, 400-strong theatre crowd witnessed what a blinkered *Record Mirror* felt was a bland performance from a group whose career appeared to be going off the rails. "I remember having no confidence at those live shows," Rowland later admitted to Chris Roberts. "There were dance moves I wanted to do in my head, but my legs wouldn't move me. We'd finish a song and I'd be so paranoid of hecklers I'd rush the band into the next song quick." Rowland had refused to sanction a 12-inch release of 'This Is What She's Like' in full, unexpurgated glory prior to *Don't Stand Me Down*'s release; a missed opportunity for which he remained rueful in 2003. "I think it might have done for Dexys what 'Bohemian Rhapsody' did for Queen," he told Easlea.

Attempting to market what they considered an unwieldy follow-up to its three million-unit shifting predecessor, Mercury had been desperate for Rowland's co-operation. "In the end I sabotaged the record's chance of success by disallowing the record company from promoting it effectively," he revealed in 1997, unable to deal with the attendant pressure and in need of a break. As the group prepared for their Bristol Colston Hall performance on November 8, 'An Extract From This Is What She's Like' was belatedly released. The symphony had been severed in half on seven-inch, its flipside acting as a finale. "I think that while it was kind of sacrilegious to have edited 'This Is What She's Like' as a whole version which worked so brilliantly," Roberts opines, "there was a lot to be said for the shortened version. If the record company had got behind it and promoted it, it could have caught people's imagination." (A 12-inch version also appeared, featuring an instrumental of 'This Is What She's Like'. And with Adams a former Status Quo disciple and Edwards later to become their long-serving bassist, a cover of 'Marguerita Time' graced the 10-inch release.)

The group's final show in a three-night residency at the Dominion Theatre on November 13 proved to be Rowland's last major live stage performance for almost 14 years. It was one he'd never forget. "I fell over on the stage. It was an accident, but I was so stiff from nerves, from fear," he told Kessler. "That's when I decided to stop. I was so stressed with it, so tired. I had all these great ideas I couldn't bring to fruition. Outwardly I blamed everyone else. Inside, though, I blamed myself. I always did."

The attendant atmosphere was dispiriting, Paolo Hewitt recalls. "It was a quarter full. All the people who'd gone had come to see 'Come On Eileen', even the most devoted Dexys fans. But it was such a great show." The surreal humour of Adams dressed as a policeman, arriving on stage to question Rowland at length about his 'burning' disposition, simply bypassed critics, likened to "awkward pantomime" by *Melody Maker*.

"I'd never seen anything like it," Roberts attests. "It was a fantastic allegory of soul and passion and rebellion, of being a misfit and a proud individual. It was utterly compelling and so different to anything else. Just being able to hear 'This Is What She's Like' was transcendent. It dared you to ridicule it. Kevin was pushing people to question what a gig was about, daring to go into places other people daren't go."

"He was always thinking of things people had never done before in terms of presentation," Hewitt corroborates. "With all that conversation, it was a difficult record and it was difficult live. But they were so powerful on stage."

By this point Rowland felt exhausted from his relentless drive. "I felt like I had no armour left," he told Jon Wilde. "I'd have routines to dance but my legs wouldn't move. I was paralysed with fear. It's called stage fright. I didn't think I could tell anyone. That was the last time I was on stage professionally." That month, Rowland realised the *Don't Stand Me Down* era was finally over.

O'Hara cited record company apathy as one reason for the album's swift demise. "It was quite hard to deal with, particularly for Kevin," she informed *Record Collector*. "The main satisfaction was in having completed the thing." With financial resources at a premium and spirits low, Rowland refused to bow to his disappointment. "He wouldn't be self-pitying," she marvelled in 2002. "He was always ready to move on."

Having written new material during the early summer of 1986, the engaging, acoustic-guitar strut of 'Walk Away' was proposed as the next Dexys single. Earlier in the year, they'd also worked on 'You're Alright With Me', the theme tune to the forthcoming BBC sitcom *Brush Strokes*. Retitled 'Because Of You', the Arun Chakraverty-helmed single was a country-inflected, violin-led ode, boasting one of Rowland's most concise lyrical offerings and a beguiling vocal. Released in November and reaching number 13, he performed alone on *Top Of The Pops*. Sporting a goatee beard, sideburns and leather trousers, his reinvention as a solo artist was under way. He was snapped outside London's Limelight Club celebrating the single reaching the Top 20. "I remember meeting Kevin and saying, 'Wow, you're doing alright now!' like a hit record makes everything alright," Paolo Hewitt recalls. "But for him and for a lot of people, it's a horrendous experience. Even though you get the money, you're not happy with it. But it's about being able to live with yourself. And at that point, he couldn't."

In November, when the group appeared close to recording again, O'Hara revealed that any new Dexys work would comprise less violin-augmented material. Yet the tight nucleus of Rowland, O'Hara and Adams slowly parted company. "It broke up. I say that, I think we were broke," Rowland admitted in 2004. "It didn't so much end as fizzle out."

"There was never anything so definite as 'I'm leaving,'" O'Hara later insisted.

Keen to relocate to London, Rowland continued demoing new material. "I said [to Adams], 'Bill, y'know what, I think this is a solo album,'" he told Radio Two. "And he was sort of quite relieved when I said it."

O'Hara assisted Rowland on his new venture. "Dexys were finished really," she told Easlea. "It was never said or announced, but it was apparent. Then I started to go my own way."

Adams and O'Hara's presence had proved pivotal. "I couldn't have done what we did without them," Rowland conceded.

"For me, it worked for a while," Rowland told Adrian Deevoy in 1988. "I just woke up one morning a couple of years ago and realised that I don't need anyone else any more."

Chapter Twenty-Four

DURING the summer of 1987, Rowland relocated Stateside to record with Brazilian producer Eumir Deodato, who had previously worked with Roberta Flack, Aretha Franklin and Gwen Guthrie. Three months were spent "sweating blood" in New York. He told Geoff Deane he felt like "an apprentice who has spent years learning his craft." The long-in-gestation 'Walk Away' was initially planned for Rowland's debut solo single that autumn. When eventually released in April 1988, backed with 'Even When I Hold You', it failed to chart.

Appearing in June, *The Wanderer* sold poorly, peaking at number 67. The album, which also featured Jim Paterson's involvement, was a satisfying work reflecting some of Rowland's nostalgic, romantic tendencies; an economical set of sedate, "almost country and western" numbers. Clocking in at just 37 minutes, this 10-track affair blended warm pop pastiches and Fifties-inflected work, "paying homage to the art of the barroom ballad," in Chris Roberts' words. With Rowland's vocals now centre stage, its sparse feel, invariably dated production and monotonous instrumentation failed to stand it in great stead.

The doo-wop flavoured material included the confessional 'Age Can't Wither You' and 'I Am A Wanderer', while the clichéd "baby" refrain on 'I Want' represented the album's nadir. Also featuring an engaging cover of Harlan Howard's 'Heartaches By The Number' and breathy, piano-led 'When You Walk Alone', the slide guitar-spiced 'Remember Me' (co-written with O'Hara) was a sweet, wistful coda and was arguably the album's strongest moment. An enthusiastic *NME* voted 'Tonight' – a beguiling, sophisticated slice of late Eighties pop – Single Of The Week in August, but it only reached number 81. 'Young Man', featuring Rowland on suitably strong-voiced and reflective form, also failed to chart in October.

Eulogising both the lyrical thread of 'Young Man' and the familiar, middle class-directed vitriol of 'Tonight', *Q* also applauded the sassy 'I Want' for broaching new musical terrain. While Rowland's musical maturity on *The Wanderer* might disappoint devotees, his voice, they assured, had lost none of its rich allure. Jon Wilde felt the album constituted Rowland's most coherent work, coming to terms with musical limitations and age while unafraid to address his subject matter head on. Yet David Quantick lamented Rowland's subdued passion and absence of inspired lyricism, questioning why this record took almost two years to complete. Rowland acknowledged in 1999 that this solo venture, although far from a failure, was not a high point.

"It would have been better if Helen and Billy had been involved. I think I got a bit taken over by the producer, but there you go. It was where I was meant to be at that time."

Jim Irvin felt Deodato's involvement could have proved a revelation. "It should have worked, but it didn't. It was almost as if Kevin had lost confidence as well. There's something about that record that he didn't believe it either."

"Kevin was trying to find a new voice for himself as a solo artist," Roberts argues. "It was more of a mellow work, not as passionate or as contrary."

Paolo Hewitt also saw the logic in Rowland's flawed approach. "Woody Allen once said you think of something in your head, y'know, 'it's amazing', and then you write it down and it's lost 20 per cent. And then you try and tell someone and it's lost another 20 per cent. By the time the thing is finished, you're 60 per cent down. He didn't want to go through that [*Don't Stand Me Down*'s lengthy gestation] again."

Cutting a suave, Gaultier-jacketed figure, Rowland performed Chris Montez's 'The More I See You' on Jonathan Ross' *The Last Resort* TV show. He also planned to leave Phonogram after London Records made encouraging signs that they were willing to offer him a new recording contract. Yet despite their apparent interest and assurances, no formal deal materialised. London, according to Rowland, had "reneged" on their unwritten promise of an offer. "It was later resolved," he insisted to Johnny Rogan, "but privately."

Rowland was now in the unfortunate position of being left without a record deal. He told Phil Sutcliffe in 1993 that this major setback had played a large part in his ensuing bankruptcy, alongside the fact he'd been deprived of much of his Dexys-related earnings thanks to unnamed parties. Naturally, it hadn't been an easy time. "But probably easier than when I had loads of money and was desperately unhappy." From late 1987, Rowland admitted that his drug use had begun to steadily escalate. "Any money I did get went on cocaine," he later told *The Independent*'s Simon Price.

After acid house unfurled its day-glo tentacled grip on the nation in the summer of 1988, Rowland was frequently spotted at clubs, now "the guy with the stripy T-shirt and the sombrero," Hewitt recalls.

"And, for a while, it was good fun," Rowland told Jon Wilde. "When the honeymoon period came to an end, that's when I fell apart," he admitted, as a self-declared five- to six-year long "lost weekend" unfolded. However, following their meeting at a party in 1990, Rowland and Paterson resolved to revive their songwriting partnership. Tabloid reports in March found Rowland celebrating Dexys' re-formation. "We started writing again, much better songs than I can do on my own," he enthused to Phil Sutcliffe. "It's grown men doing their job, doing it well. I mean to be totally co-operative, totally realistic."

However these sporadic songwriting forays didn't prove successful. "We did some good stuff but I was impossible to work with," Rowland admitted to *Dazed And Confused*. While 1991 brought the release of Mercury's singles-oriented *The Very Best Of Dexys Midnight Runners*, Rowland contributed guitar and vocals the following year to Shut Up And Dance's 'Autobiography Of A Crackhead' after Heavenly Records financed new Dexys demo recordings in March. 'My Life In England' reflected Rowland's nostalgic fondness for rebel republican anthems and the Catholic social clubs of his youth. Ancestry was also addressed on 'My Rose', in part a heart-warming paean to his mother. 'Coming Home' signified a chugging halt to wandering instincts, while the vibrant, call-and-response 'You Can Get Your Own Free' resembled a Celtified 'Tell Me When My Light Turns Green'.

Acknowledging sadness and self-hatred on the fear-eschewing 'Manhood', 'She's Got A Giggle That Melts My Heart' was a sequencer-led, atmospheric ode to infatuation. The plaintive 'If I Ever', meanwhile, morphed into a fiery entreaty that articulated Rowland's amorous frustrations. With both Paterson and Rowland drawing unemployment benefit, demo funding proved difficult. "At the same time, the struggle is good. We don't take anything for granted. And we share the load," Paterson told *Q*. While rumours circulated of a proposed Fleadh Festival appearance in the summer of 1992, early discussions *had* taken place with Alan McGee's Creation Records.

Insisting he'd rejected record company offers, Rowland later admitted that tentative negotiations with the likes of Go! Discs and Heavenly had been hampered. "I'd sabotage it every time it got near to happening," he told Jon Wilde. But after two years' work on new material, Dexys were ready to return. "In a lot of ways, this will be like the first LP," Rowland suggested to Stuart Bailie. Optimism and expectation was raised with an appearance on Jonathan Ross' Channel Four show, *Saturday Zoo* on March 27. Flanked by a long-haired, leather-trousered Adams, a demure-looking Paterson and bearded, wildly tousled Rowland (also sporting leather cowboy chaps) served up a dual vocal idea on the string-augmented 'Manhood'. The trombonist turned co-frontman traded lines with Rowland on his battle with guilt and rejection. "And he talks about 'Have you got enough money for food?' because we're brought up to believe in society that success is all," Hewitt said.

On 'If I Ever', Adams strummed ebulliently before Paterson's regal solo yielded to a dramatic act: Rowland dropped to his knees, delivering a riveting flashback to the stage testimonies of old. Further work on five tracks in late 1993 included a lyrically overhauled 'My Life In England', its coda calling for British troops' withdrawal from Ireland. After live autumn dates had been mooted, the comeback trail then tailed off. Rowland admitted he had made several attempts to stop using drugs, including will-power, hypnotherapy, and even the Brahma Kumaris religious cult before he entered a Clapham residential treatment centre in 1994. He underwent an initial period of rehabilitation in a 12-step recovery programme. Eight months later, he attended a secondary treatment centre for whose help he offered sincere gratitude in his gradual recovery. "They helped me when no one else could. From then on I slowly started to get well due to the self-help groups which I still go to now," he told Jon Wilde in 1999, admitting he had been away from drugs for more than five years.

Rowland later began to undertake a process of confronting the past and atoning for his actions, confessing to Q in 1993: "He [Kevin Archer] was responsible for the *Too-Rye-Ay* sound, but it was credited to me. This is very important. As a result, he disbanded his group." Rowland professed to be "deeply ashamed" of his actions.

Ironically, it had been his brother, Pete, who eventually offered Archer's Blue Ox Babes a managerial contract back in 1988, prior to their signature with Go! Discs. Yet with Rowland busy launching his solo career, Archer intimated to music journalist Jonathan Romney (who pigeonholed The Blue Ox Babes as a "folk and western swing band") that he and Rowland were now firm friends. A reconstituted Babes line-up included drummer Pettitt, pianist Pete Wain, saxophonist Nick Smith, former Dexys bassist Wynne and violinist Brennan, with whom Archer co-penned their debut single 'There's No Deceiving You'. Released in March, and accompanied by a string driven rendition of Al Green's 'Take Me To The River', it failed to chart. Following the Babes' national tour support slot, Brennan featured on Scottish Dexys' aficionados The Proclaimers' second LP, *Sunshine On Leith*. He'd first met the Reid Brothers five years earlier at Rowland's flat.

"They [Charlie and Craig] were always talking about Kevin," Brennan stresses. "They loved him. And obviously they saw an aspect to Kevin that many people didn't see. Kevin was such an incredibly generous person, and he always had this sort of consideration which I've never heard anybody mention."

The Babes recorded their excellent (yet subsequently shelved) 10-track LP, *Apples And Oranges*, at Chipping Norton studios with Pete Wingfield and Barry Hammond. The Irish pipe-led title track, (subtitled as the *International Hope Campaign*), was released as a follow-up single, also failing to chart. A third single, the bullish, melodic Archer stomp 'Walking On The Line' was released, another slice of their early Eighties stockpile of material. Following poor record sales, The Babes, ever the perennial bridesmaids, soon disbanded once again.

While Archer relocated to Hamburg in the mid-Nineties, making an unsuccessful attempt to secure a recording contract, Rowland informed the music press in mid-1995 that he was fortunate enough to exercise his option not to record. "I value myself and my work, and I don't measure my dignity in how newsworthy I am to the *NME* or anyone else." Yet three years after initial discussions, Rowland met Alan McGee that summer. Six months later, he felt the time was now right to make music once again. Resolving to put an end to Rowland's wilderness years, McGee likened the singer's appearance to King Henry VIII in a full-length, flared fake fur coat. Playing a demo tape of new material, Rowland eventually stood and sang. A three-record deal was later finalised. A January 1997 Creation press release outlined work on his second solo album, *My Beauty*. "I was signed to Creation for my own material, but I knew I had to make this record before I could do anything else," Rowland later admitted.

Work had commenced back in 1996, with Paterson travelling to Brighton to work with Rowland on musical arrangements. He insisted it felt "completely natural" to still be working with Rowland, 18 years down the line. "Dexys is the only group that I can say I really felt part of," Paterson told *Keep On Running* in 1997. "I think we worked well together and I think musically we are quite a good partnership." Upon completion, work on a fourth Dexys album was promised. Significantly, Rowland's Creation press release also contained an admission of guilt over the theft of Kevin Archer's idea and influential soul-folk hybrid sound. He stated deep regret for having accepted the plaudits for 'Come On Eileen's success, apologising to fans, associates, and media alike. It also contained a heartfelt apology to his old colleague, stressing his envy of Archer's talents.

Archer responded in a *Daily Mail* interview that January, pointing at Rowland's apology and gesture of friendship while underlining his unhappiness and state of hardship. Insisting he'd contacted Rowland to outline his parlous financial position, Archer subsequently told Johnny Rogan that Rowland had awarded him his share of *Too-Rye-Ay* publishing royalties back in 1995. "And it was only when the press picked it up wrong, like the *Daily Mail* said I stole my friend's song," Rowland reiterated to Everett True, "I thought, 'Hold on a minute, I fucking wrote that song.'" In a subsequent counter-statement, he reaffirmed he'd not stolen any of Archer's lyrics, melodies or music.

"I know he will always be successful because he is talented and he has such charisma that people are drawn to him," Archer said, wishing Rowland well.

With *My Beauty*, Rowland had opted to narrate his own story through a reinterpretative set of ballads, standards and pop fodder from the Sixties and Seventies. He defended his decision in style. "Marlon Brando didn't have to write Tennessee Williams' words to be brilliant in *A Streetcar Named Desire*." Resonating deeply with Rowland at a crisis point in his life, the songs evoked a period of innocence, but also a rediscovery of what he simply coined 'beauty'.

Prior to Paterson and then engineer Pete Schwier co-helming Rowland's project, Pete Wingfield was approached to produce what was originally intended, he insists, as a new album of original Dexys material. "But that transmogrified into an album of covers," Wingfield admits, "and I think the choices were odd. We met up in a café and I said, 'I don't think it would be a good idea for me to produce it because we'll only fall out. And we don't wanna do that, do we?'" Wingfield subsequently joined a musical cast including, among others, former Kokomo and Roxy Music guitarist Neil Hubbard, drummers Andy Newmark and Blair Cunningham, bassist John McKenzie, pianist Chris Stainton and string arranger Fiachra Trench.

By February 1998, Paterson had ended his involvement on the album, after some two years. He revealed to fanzine *Keep On Running* that personal differences with Rowland following a studio incident proved decisive. Proud of his huge input and dedication, Paterson still felt vindicated in parting company.

"I was sad when he left, though I was being a bit of a drama queen, but we'd had much worse arguments than the one on the day he upped and went," Rowland admitted in July 1999, lamenting the fact that they hadn't spoken since. "He's very angry about *My Beauty*," Rowland told Johnny Rogan the following year, "and there's a lot of things he said in there that I didn't know he was feeling."

Under pressure, Rowland's labour of love became extreme. "I had no life outside of it," he later recounted. "I took it all so seriously, I got paranoid." Rowland insists he began to doubt Paterson and Schwier's talents. Rowland would also work on a Sixties-inspired romantic duet entitled 'Loving', with Tasha Lee McClumney.

Invited to Brighton to hear the *My Beauty* tracks in March 1999, Chris Roberts enthused: "I loved them. I'm sure he was pleased that someone was hearing them objectively and saying that this was good."

Rowland was clearly disappointed at Roberts' less enthusiastic reaction to photos of his yet-to-be unveiled new image. "I didn't think it was a good idea, and his face fell. I think he'd have preferred me to go, 'Yeah, this is a great idea.' But I thought I could only be honest, at the risk of offending him. I thought that journalists are just gonna pick up on that and not really focus on the record."

To a typically reactionary press, Rowland reappeared in a summer poster campaign replete in hitched-up dress, stockings, make-up, necklace and knickers. "This look is not something I've just decided on to promote a record. It's more important than that," Rowland argued, insisting he'd taken to wearing male dresswear a few years earlier.

"Here's this rock culture that's meant to be liberal and open to everyone," said Paolo Hewitt, "and here's a guy with a dress on. Kevin was challenging them and they couldn't handle it."

Prior to offending Creation employees' tastes and sensibilities with September's accompanying video to his interpretation of 'Concrete And Clay', Rowland pondered whether the company knew how serious he was about his career. "I want to make good records and be successful."

Rowland felt he had penned every line in this varied musical autobiography. "I'd sung every song to myself, at different ages," he told Glyn Brown. Previously dismissive of Whitney Houston's saccharine 'The Greatest Love Of All', Rowland played the song incessantly in 1990, reduced to tears over this lesson in self-love. Addressing his 11-year-old self, an astounding rendition of Frankie Valli's 'Rag Doll' followed. With stirring choir, Rowland implored the listener to shine, while the joyous, sultry samba of 'Concrete And Clay' was a 'thank-you' for its influence on 'Come On Eileen'. Childhood friend Little G appeared on an endearing, all-embracing 'Daydream Believer' before a keening take on the Burt Bacharach classic 'This Guy's In Love With You'. The wistful regret of Lennon/McCartney's 'The Long And Winding Road' ended in a victory for self-worth from a newly emergent Rowland, while Cass Elliott's 'It's Getting Better' was intoned with sweet, genuine resolve. The Hollies' 1970 cut 'I Can't Tell The Bottom From The Top' became a six-and-a-half minute scalding confessional. Against dramatic strings and soaring vocals, Rowland's voice wavered between shivering fear and bellowing warmth. As a tender, country-tinged interpretation of Squeeze's 'Labelled With Love', the pivotal 'I'll Stay With My Dreams' featured a flawless vocal in a candid account of a secluded cocaine nightmare. Stirring sadness, the gloriously crooned 'Reflections Of My Life' found Rowland bestowing the 1969 Marmalade original with poignant gravitas.

Envisaged as *My Beauty*'s penultimate track (although eventually omitted after Rowland failed to secure permission for lyric changes), 'Thunder Road' would have proved a sensitive, dynamic treatment of Bruce Springsteen's vein busting original. Offering graceful self-encouragement in a rousing finale with the *Carousel*/Kop anthem 'You'll Never Walk Alone', one of the great white British voices had reawoken. Borne from experience, this moving offer of warmth, honesty and intimacy was a triumph. "It was beauty," Rowland asserted. "I'd forgotten all about it. Welcome back Kevin."

Battling with awful stage fright, a London Jazz Café show occurred days before Rowland's first, nerve-wracking major live performance in 14 years at Reading Music Festival's main stage on Saturday, August 28.

Attracting music press opprobrium as a 15-minute karaoke farrago, 'You'll Never Walk Alone' attracted mirth, missiles and catcalls. Rowland discarded his sarong to reveal a white mini-dress and stockings before undertaking a provocative dance routine with two female dancers during 'Concrete And Clay'. Struck by a bottle, Rowland addressed the crowd during 'The Greatest Love Of All': "Who wants to hear me sing?" He was buoyed by the response.

Rowland was eventually vindicated once an 11-year, between-album hiatus had ended. *My Beauty* had a predictably polarising effect upon its release in October. Garry Mulholland urged Creation to dissuade Rowland from his questionable new path, citing a lack of interpretative powers underscored by anodyne accompaniment. However, 'I Can't Tell The Bottom From The Top' and 'Reflections Of My Life' were applauded. 'This Guy's In Love With You' and 'It's Getting Better' aside, the rest, *Mojo* mused, was a mixed blessing as the music cushioned Rowland's weighty valedictions.

Peter Paphides also considers *My Beauty* something of a misjudgement. "I think Kevin had made the mistake of thinking that using better musicians would produce better music. There was nothing wrong with it, it was just too pretty." The *NME* considered Rowland somewhat bereft of his old fire, hedging their bets on an impressively voiced, compelling return. With a harsh eye on image, *Q* praised *My Beauty* and Rowland's reinterpretative vocal powers.

"It's fantastic interpretations of great songs," says Chris Roberts, "and it's sung with such passion and conviction at a time when it wasn't fashionable to do that. If he'd come back with a different image, that album would have been received very, very differently and more favourably." Rowland cited lack of TV and radio play for 'Concrete And Clay' as the primary reasons for disappointing record sales.

Following hurtful press scorn during the autumn, and despite having just offered some of the finest vocal performances of his career, Rowland outlined the extent of its effect upon him. "It makes me feel like not wanting to be in the music business," he told Johnny Rogan the following year. "The thought of going in and doing another album like that fills me with . . . it just makes me feel lousy. Like why bother? I don't want to do it."

Chapter Twenty-Five

AS the controversy over *My Beauty* demonstrated, Rowland had lost none of his singular passion for daring sartorial expression. Undertaking a lengthy, detailed oratory on Mod couture and American styling in a reading session from author Paul Gorman's book *The Look* at an Islington pub in August 2001, he later performed renditions of 'This Guy's In Love With You' and 'I Love You (Listen To This)'.

That same month, Pete Williams launched his new band, Basehart, at a songwriter's festival at Ronnie Scott's in Birmingham. "The response so far has been very encouraging and it feels good and right," he told Carrie Shearer a few months later. A soundtrack to his film *Bent Nickels, Wooden Dimes*, shot while working in Los Angeles in 1999 with Andy Growcott, was also in progress. The following year, Williams admitted to the BBC he still "yearned" for the feeling he'd experienced as part of Dexys.

As an artist, the prospect of a Dexys reunion based on financial gain was untenable to Rowland. Any fresh activity would have to be for the right reasons. Part of the aim would be to redress 'Come On Eileen's pre-eminence over the group's legacy. This might involve rejecting possible financial incentives or advances from advertisers, he told *The Independent On Sunday*'s Simon Price. Part of Rowland's *mea culpa*-spirited process of atonement involved contacting his former Dexys colleagues, he admitted to William Shaw in 2003. "It was a few years ago, I suppose I had come to address some things from the past. And – you know – that sort of necessitated getting in touch with some people." (For original members Growcott, Paterson, Saunders, Spooner and Williams, that now incorporated a quarterly cheque from EMI, after Rowland had subsequently assigned his own share of future Dexys royalties to be divided between the five men.) "And the idea of getting Dexys back together occurred to me."

Kevin Archer, not involved in writing music at the time, had briefly discussed a reunion with Rowland early in 2000. Although not totally dismissive of the concept, they had certainly rejected tempting offers to board the Eighties nostalgia tour bandwagon. Simon Price broached the subject in 2002, ahead of *Don't Stand Me Down: The Director's Cut*'s release. Nothing was planned, Rowland informed him. "A lot of bands just do a greatest hits show, but there would have to be a new record. It would have to be relevant to now."

In April 2003, that criteria was partially fulfilled. An announcement was made of the newly recorded, decade-old 'Manhood' and 'My Life In England (Part One)'s inclusion on an imminent EMI compilation. The news which sparked real fervour was the intention to stage a long-anticipated tour, the first in almost 18 years, entitled 'To Stop The Burning'. Following his beloved Wolves' promotion to the English Premiership, Rowland thanked Dexys devotees for two decades' worth of dedication in a letter to *Mojo* in June. Q Magazine also bestowed their Classic Songwriters accolade upon the group. 2003 rapidly became Dexys' *annus mirabilis*. "It seemed the right time," a 50-year-old Rowland suggested to David Hutcheon that autumn. "I met up with some people who used to be in the band and came away with the thought that I could just see it working. And I knew there was a willingness from Pete Williams, so it had to be Dexys." Bringing the group full circle, Rowland envisaged a new take on their original co-vocalist configuration.

"I've not really been in contact with Kevin," Williams admitted on *It Was Like This* in a 2003 interview. "Kevin made contact with me about three years ago, not to talk about the band, it was about something quite different. But he broached the subject of the band, and we've kind of stayed in touch since then."

Maintaining contact, the topic of a reconstituted Dexys arose around the turn of 2002. If it proved "creative and fulfilling," Williams was interested. Corresponding ideas for songs and travelling to Rowland's Brighton home, tour preparations began in April. Coincidentally, Williams had travelled to North Shields, near Newcastle with Steve Spooner early the previous month. They had convened with a keen Mick Talbot, trombonist Paul Taylor and singer Archie Brown following fans encouragement for a group reunion of The Bureau. Feeling suitably emboldened to pursue former paymasters Warners for the belated UK release of their eponymous debut album, this enjoyable, low-key summit proved significant in trombonist Taylor and 'musical director' Talbot's recruitment.

"I had been approached a few years later [after the original split] by Kevin's manager to be part of a later line-up of Dexys," Talbot recalled in 2003, "but I was busy doing something else. The timing wasn't right. There was something else going on. I thought, 'Well, maybe third time lucky.'" Other former members were contacted in light of Rowland's decision. Fellow Bureau colleague Jeff Blythe was unavailable, while Andy Growcott, now a record producer in Los Angeles, was sadly out of playing commission after years of strenuous drumming. Having not played sax since 1982 and having lost touch with his former bandmates, Cornwall-based Spooner's musical past reared its head. After travelling back from a meeting in London with Warners about The Bureau LP, he was then called by Rowland and asked if he'd be interested in accepting a place on tour. He initially refused.

After discussing the prospect with Williams, Spooner agreed in principle. Returning from Brighton after meeting Rowland, he sensed it was a viable option. Weeks later, Spooner undertook rehearsals in London with Taylor. He was pleased with his performance. In diplomatic fashion, Rowland subsequently disclosed that his services would not be required after all. "Kevin had said the management decided there wasn't the finance to have as big a band as they wanted." Hopes for swathes of strings and a full complement of brass were dashed. With Adams, O'Hara, Paterson and Shelton notable absentees, Pete Saunders received a telephone apology from Rowland for being given any impression that he would be involved. Having considered the offer to tour, Mick Billingham contacted Rowland to accept the invitation, although his place never materialised. Paul Speare was told in June that budget restrictions ruled out his inclusion. He admits he would have seized the opportunity to play, hoping to put unresolved issues over credit for his work and loyalty to rest.

In the event, Taylor was the sole brass presence in a nine-strong line-up, comprising viola player Lucy Morgan of Celticana, former Galliano drummer Crispin Taylor, ex-Incognito bassist Julian Crampton and Spear Of Destiny keyboardist Volker Janssen, who provided sax and string augmentation. Rowland was thrilled at having guitarist Neil Hubbard's presence on stage among a group of musicians embodying artful subtlety and spirited composure. In conversation alongside Williams with Radio Two's Mark Goodier in August, Rowland insisted previous propositions to resurrect Dexys just hadn't felt appropriate. "It would have always been a way of just recreating the past," he insisted. Recorded on September 17 and broadcast on October 8, Dexys made their first live TV appearance in 18 years on *Top Of The Pops 2* to promote forthcoming single 'Manhood'. Its recent lyrical "revamp" now offered a positive outcome and a solution. With Rowland full of presence and strong of voice, Williams proved an eager foil, offering a positive insight into what was to come.

While bringing the Dexys tale up to speed, and despite promotional CD singles being circulated, neither 'Manhood', nor 'My Life In England', ever surfaced. With David Ditchfield credited for his songwriting contributions on both these Mike Hedges engineered cuts, Pete Saunders had undertaken keyboard duties. He found the Wessex studio vibe one of cordiality. "It was really pleasant. With Pete it was like seeing an old school friend, someone I hadn't seen for years. Kevin was very charming, on his best behaviour. I managed to prove to him that I wasn't the right piano player. I'd only heard the tracks the day before and they had piano on it. I put some bits on, but Kevin probably felt I was far too jazzy. He was probably right on that score."

He found Rowland's vocal presence startling. "I was so impressed. There's no one else who sings like it. It's a really big, warm voice. And Pete Williams is a fantastic singer. He can sing with Kevin, no problem." Their dual vocal role took time to ferment.

"It was quite hard. Kevin's register doesn't sit that comfortably with mine. It took a lot of working, but I think we got there. I really enjoyed it. I think we did some good work." With half the album later aired live, an 18-track overview of Dexys' entire career, *Let's Make This Precious: The Best Of* was released on September 22. Rowland admitted that a double album would have been more appropriate. Sequenced to emphasise the hits, the preponderance of *Too-Rye-Ay* offerings was hardly surprising. *Don't Stand Me Down* material aside, the album's strongest artistic move was the inclusion of BBC Radio One session versions of 'Until I Believe In My Soul' and 'Let's Make This Precious'.

Five-star reviews proliferated in the music monthlies. Contentious omissions were inevitable, notably firebrand debut 'Dance Stance' and the superlative 'I Couldn't Help If I Tried'. Although 'Plan B' thankfully surfaced, would fans have objected to the absence of the endearing yet hardly exemplary 'Let's Get This Straight (From The Start)'? Meanwhile, Dexys' 20-date theatre tour promised an atmospheric musical occasion. Talbot had hinted that humorous, Pinter-esque patter would also prevail, a warm repartee reprising the surreal dialogue that Adams and Rowland had undertaken back in 1985. Offering a reappraisal of previously overlooked album material, Rowland's lyrical revisions also gave a fresh perspective on his old work. 'Soon' was given an exquisite new poignancy, while 'Until I Believe In My Soul' featured a police-uniformed Williams enquiring into Rowland's confession of wrongdoings between 1971 and 1993. A breathless segue into 'Tell Me When My Light Turns Green' found Rowland singing of life as a 49-year-old man in a song penned 25 years earlier. Conversely, the chorus of 'Liars A To E' reverted to its 1978-vintage, Killjoys-oriented lyrics. Now more strut than swagger, Rowland reclaimed 'Geno' in a stage monologue awash with memory. Emblematic of this new outlook, the caustic lyrics to 'This Is What She's Like' were soothed of some of their sting.

Dexys flew to Dubai for a pre-tour festival; a humid midnight show in Saudi Arabia being an unusual way to kick off proceedings. On October 4, the group recorded a short, semi-unplugged three-song set in Newcastle for Radio Two. These dapper, elegantly suited pop statesmen were now resplendent in Twenties French gangster/*Dirty Rotten Scoundrels* garb, designed by Soho tailor Mark Powell.

Their opening UK show at Portsmouth Guildhall on October 21 was watched by, among others, *Mojo* reviewer Pat Gilbert, who waved aside suggestions of nostalgic reverie, noting the group's intention of redrawing Dexys' image as one of subtle artistry. Slow-burn opener 'The Waltz' evinced a touching moment of chemistry between Rowland and Williams, who urged "don't stand him down."

"This was my protest, this was my protest," Rowland responded, a moving moment for many. His dextrous voice won admiration, while Williams' policeman routine got the popular vote. 'I Love You (Listen To This)' and 'Liars A To E' were momentous. A 20-minute rendition of 'This Is What She's Like' was unsurpassable. This was the genuine article.

'My Life In England' audibly whetted appetites for more new material from a Leeds crowd. Compared to an "Eighties opera" by one fan, their Liverpool Royal Court Theatre show was filmed for posterity. Following a jubilant Northampton set, Dexys' rapturous welcome at London's Royal Festival Hall certainly impressed Talbot. Shaking a clench-fisted salute as the group returned for a rapturous encore, Rowland's gesture was comparable in victory to that of a prize fight-winning heavyweight boxer. Undertaking the set's sole cover of The Commodores' 'Nightshift', Rowland was busy eulogising over Jackie Wilson and Marvin Gaye. In his *Evening Standard* review, John Aizlewood believed the Wolverhampton maverick would be worthy of a similar plaudit-strewn legacy as one of the greatest white soul singers of his age. Chris Roberts felt similarly inspired. "When he did the line on 'Liars A To E' about the 'voice of experience', that was really touching, with Dexys coming back from all their ups and downs and trials and tribulations."

While some former colleagues were pleased to see the unguarded power of Rowland's presence, Spooner felt somewhat underwhelmed by the Plymouth show. "I thought it was totally passionless. And although it was my mates in the band and I wouldn't fault any of the musicians, they were too restricted to play with any flair. They were just going through the motions. And I thought that especially of Kevin. I was thinking, 'You're playing a part,' which I guess was part of the plan."

"I thought, 'It's not going to be anything like it was.'" Brennan corroborates. "I've got good memories of some of those older songs and I thought, 'I don't want to hear them done any other way. I'll just leave it as it is.'"

Saunders, meanwhile, spoke admiringly of Rowland's achievements. "He can pull stuff out the bag occasionally like that last tour which is fantastic. And he's done gigs where I've never seen anyone do a gig like it." One fan noted Williams' angelic voice and Rowland's powerful delivery in the wake of a phenomenal Dublin show. This was a 'reunion' venture of genuine merit, an enthusiastic *Irish Times* chorused.

"Dublin was fantastic, it always is," Williams acknowledged later that year. "It's a very warm city. The feeling that I got off the crowd there was immense." A four-date Scandinavian sojourn ended in a tremendously received, freezing cold finale in Gothenburg.

Any fears that the crowds would not embrace the reinterpretations of Dexys classics proved unfounded. Rowland had even apologised on stage for the ubiquitous place 'Come On Eileen' occupied in the group's folklore after 21 years. Dexys' music still represented something uniquely powerful to their fanbase. Having not performed on stage with a full group for almost 18 years, Rowland had returned to reclaim his rightful musical position. "I loved it. I loved it. It just all worked for us," he enthusiastically told Radio Two. "We made it relevant to now, 'cos I started to remember, 'Oh yeah, I used to really enjoy that feeling of working with the band,' and maybe giving some direction, and it really clicking in some sort of spiritual way."

"Kevin is as driven as he always was," Williams said that year. "And he's been through a lot. We've all been through a lot, one way or another. It would be good to do this again, to see where it could go."

"Perhaps having Pete there did free up Kevin in a way to go for the flourishes and to go on tangents that he wouldn't have gone for otherwise," Roberts surmises. "It's really good that he's come through some really difficult years to have a good, positive attitude about the whole of Dexys."

"I think he's still got the same fire in his belly that makes him perform in the same way that he does," Talbot declared in an end–of–year interview. "I think essentially, deep down, he's the same person. I think the essence of his character, as much as I did know him from the early days, seems fairly intact."

While Rowland stressed that the tour was the initial creative focus, fans and critics eagerly discussed the prospect of future new studio material. The possibility of a live album release (Dexys' equivalent of *It's Too Late To Stop Now* perhaps?) would surely have sated appetites in the interim. While Talbot undertook a British tour with Sixties and Seventies soundtrack-influenced, instrumental collective The Players, Rowland featured in a Swedish radio/film festival public interview in Gothenburg in late January 2004. "It's a pity Kevin only wants to be a pop star," Pete Saunders told the author. "The idea of doing small gigs doesn't seem to interest him at all. It would be interesting if he did do some intimate gigs with just piano and voice."

In May, Rowland appeared onstage in Sweden at a small Stockholm club gig, performing renditions of 'This Is What She's Like', 'Tell Me When My Light Turns Green' and 'Come On Eileen'. Speaking to Williams in October 2004, he admitted to being hopeful of Dexys performing live again. "I take deadly serious what I do," Rowland had said. "It's very important to me to be an individual. I don't care if people laugh. That's what Dexys Midnight Runners is all about. Showing your feelings and not giving a damn what other people think. People will always laugh at Dexys. That's fine. But I know that what I'm doing is totally honest. I believe in myself. I will pin up my soul on the wall and let people read it. They can laugh, they can cry. It's up to them. I really don't mind."

In the wake of the tour, Williams discussed the essence of Dexys' enduring appeal with one interviewer. "It obviously lights a spark in so many people. Does it sound too pretentious for me to say it's a real honesty? There has to be good music, that goes without saying. But there's an openness and a rawness, lyrically and musically as well. And that's it. That's the thread, the honesty and the intensity that's in it."

"To have been a soul group in the Eighties," a decade invariably looked upon as a triumph of style and technique over content and inspiration, "is really something to be proud of," Kevin Archer told Everett True.

"Most people can say, 'I want to make music that'll last forever.' But they don't put the work in," Hewitt insists. "Kevin was so precious about the whole thing, that he'd sacrifice for his art. But it was quite self-destructive as well. And you can only do it as a young man. You have to be obsessed. He couldn't understand why people would keep on going on, putting the same album out."

Casting his eye over the compact Dexys canon, Talbot asserts: "Those three albums are spaced out over five years, and they always dragged their audience along with them. It's not like the same album time and time again. If it had existed and carried on for 20 years I think there might have been artistic dips. It's always moved on."

Arguing the case for the original incarnation, Saunders believes Rowland's intention was to make the "big explosion". "We were like The Sex Pistols who were immortalised in summing up everything to do with punk in that way, and never went on to be The Clash making *Combat Rock*."

"So many records are just bland and run-of-the-mill," opines Chris

Roberts. "But I think we can safely say, love them or hate them, Dexys records are extremely individualistic and you can't really confuse them with any other band."

"You wouldn't find another group with the same career shape as Dexys," says Jim Irvin. "The change of labels is one thing, and to have a number one single two or three singles into each deal is amazing. The air-punching catchiness of 'Come On Eileen' is comparative to 'Geno', but they had two number one records that are so diametrically opposed in a way, yet that are so similar."

"For me, it's about Kevin at the end of the day," Roberts adds. "You can put great musicians with someone else and it wouldn't lift off. But with Kevin's ideas, voice and lyrics, it's the combination of those things that really makes this band elevate."

"Playing in the group and playing those songs was the most important thing in your life at the time," Brennan freely admits. "It left a tremendous impression on me. It was a long way from playing Puccini, that's for sure!"

Despite what he considers a wealth of "self-hype" constructed around the group, Paul Speare also admits Dexys were unique. "Kevin was more unique than most. He spent all that time and effort, losing friends everywhere in the process, struggling to chase the success which eventually led to his downfall. It's a salutary tale. We all put so much of ourselves, and our lives, into Kevin's eventual success, even though he didn't find it to his liking."

"I often wonder what it would have been like if I'd been this relaxed character who just sort of let things happen," Rowland told Jim Irvin. "You see those bands who get together, smoke a bit of dope or have a drink and, 'Okay, anyone got any ideas?' I wonder what it would have been like. I've no fucking idea, because our group was the total opposite of that."

Irvin insists it was Rowland's innate genius for galvanising Dexys' music into such an original shape that helped set them apart. "I persevered with all the off-shoots, and that's what made me realise how brilliant Kevin was. However hard to work with this guy is, he's got something or he does something that brings these strange records together. That makes them coalesce, and has the vision and makes them work, against all the odds."

"A lot of the icons and singers that people come to love have a questing spirit," defines Paphides, "and Kevin had that, this kind of restless, perpetual itch that they need to scratch. You recognised he was driven by things that even he didn't understand. Dexys had a leader you could believe in, and Kevin was very good at creating this world, and you wanted to be in the band. You bought into it wholesale, and that set

Dexys apart. Ironically, it didn't make him a very happy person."

"When I look back now, I didn't enjoy it," Rowland admitted five years ago. "I could have had a good time. It would have been nice. When I look back and see the Beatles and the Stones and we were all like, 'Oh no, we're not gonna talk to other bands, we're gonna do this and that.' It was all so intense, and so uptight. I wish that I hadn't been like that. I missed out on an awful lot. Having said that, the music was unique, that was the good thing about it, but a very big price, y'know, very big price."

"But Kevin did what he set out to do," Hewitt says in summation. "He said, 'I'm gonna make records that last.' And he did."

Postscript

Tuesday, November 16, 2004

A YEAR to the day after the revived Dexys ended their penultimate UK tour in Belfast, Pete Williams is holding court in the intimate studio theatre surroundings of Birmingham's burlesque and comedy venue, The Glee Club. The erstwhile Dexys bassist had been immersed in raising the profile of his three-year-old Basehart project. During the autumn of 2004, he'd busily undertaken studio work, having previously demoed a handful of tracks including 'The Bottle', 'Heartbeats', 'People' and 'Nothing Going To Stand In Our Way'. The ever youthful-looking 45-year-old admits he finds his work difficult to categorise, although he feels certain that he's got a "great record" within his grasp. Williams played over an hour-long set to support the previous day's release of 'Black', with 'Trust Me' and 'Said I'd Be The One', on Basehart Recordings, which is being playlisted by Radio Two's Dexys champions Mark Lamarr and Jonathan Ross.

Admiring the talented singer-songwriter's performance from the back of the small auditorium was former Dexys organist, Mick Billingham. "Ask any of them. We were all proud to have been a part of the group," he insisted. Billingham regrets the fact that he'd not had the fortune to play alongside the unrivalled Runners' rhythm section of Williams and Growcott: "The greatest drummer in the world" was the exact compliment he paid to the man they called Stoker. He also spoke fondly of his friend Kevin Archer, being mightily impressed upon hearing The Blue Ox Babes demos back in the early Eighties. Also in attendance and seated to the left of the stage was Williams' former Dexys compatriot, Jeff Blythe. Alongside Jim Paterson, he had played on Archer and co's 'lost' album from 1988. Blythe had long since relocated to New York, a part of the powerfully eclectic Irish-American Black 47 musical collective since the early Nineties.

Tuesday, February 22, 2005

Just over three months and barely three days' worth of rehearsal later, Williams and Blythe stand in nervous anticipation inside the same

195

Birmingham venue's dressing room. Alongside them are Steve Spooner, Mick Talbot, and Crispin Taylor, whose percussive duties were used on the re-formed Dexys tour sixteen months earlier. The fleeting reunion of The Bureau has attracted an expectant 200-plus audience, gathered to witness their first UK show in 23 years.

Some group members were a little disconcerted by the fact that their 'ex-Dexys' tag was used as a means of advertising The Bureau's return. Perhaps in number, personnel and spirit, this was a closer approximation to the original Dexys ethos than the acclaimed 2003 re-formation. Even tour manager Chris Gray's role had proved significant in bringing these two shows to fruition. However, concerns were raised after one day's full rehearsal that this might prove a difficult proposition. "The next night, we had a rehearsal studio booked and the whole band went in there without a drummer," Spooner recounts. "It still sounded like, 'Is this going to come off?' The next day, Crispin turned up. It was like a revelation. Having that powerful drum thing brought it together. We left that second rehearsal thinking, 'We might be able to pull this off.' And the next night was the gig.

"It was difficult to describe the feeling of being back onstage. I welled up. It made me feel great. It was fantastic to be back playing with Jeff again. There was an electricity between us all. I could sense it from all eight of us, including Crispin, that excitement. The chemistry was still there. Right until we got up there, I wasn't sure if we were going to pull it off. But we did. We've all left it on a real high."

Lamarr was in attendance at The Bureau's Borderline club gig in London four days later. He'd already trumpeted the group's imminent live return on his Radio Two breakfast show the previous Saturday, although he was unable to enlighten listeners as to the finer details due to a lack of effective promotion.

The Bureau's 24-year-old debut LP finally appeared on February 28. It included a bonus live CD of their first show at London's Forum in 1981. Their twin objective had been achieved. Group members dispersed to work on new ideas, with the hope of venturing into a studio and recording a clutch of new material. Securing a choice summer festival slot had also been an ambition.

Following Dexys' long-awaited, overdue renaissance in 2003, the need for new material, as Williams insists, was clearly a proviso for any future revival. After sharing a Liverpool club stage with Madness singer Suggs at a reunion show for Seventies art-rockers Deaf School in March, Rowland has been busy crafting new material. At the time of writing (June 2005), Rowland revealed to Radio Two that an unconfirmed Dexys line-up had just reconvened in the studio to record fresh material for a fourth album, their first in 20 years.

Characteristically, he stressed that there would be no rush to complete new work while the group were seeking a record deal. Rowland admitted he was under no illusions. "I don't think things are going to be incredibly easy," he told the BBC. "There aren't as many doors open as there were in the past. In any event, I wanna make the songs really good. I get pride from that, I feel good. I wanna do my best."

Should that old creative flame be rekindled once again, long may it burn.

Appendix

What follows is a brief overview of former group members' post-Dexys involvements and recent musical activities or occupations, not directly addressed in the book's main narrative. Thanks to the unofficial msn Dexys website and fanzine *Keep On Running* for additional information.

Kevin Adams
Following his role in Dexys' televised reappearance in 1993, Adams retained his long locks for a guitar-wielding role in Rowland's 1999 video 'Concrete And Clay' before contributing to a spate of documentaries. He is understood to have embarked on a lifestyle of travel.

Kevin Archer
Having reappeared alongside Kevin Rowland in a round of 2000 interviews after years away from music, it's believed he is not making music at present.

Mick Billingham
Having spent months playing alongside Andy Growcott in General Public during the mid-Eighties without realising their mutual Dexys connection, Billingham is currently busy lecturing in musical theatre and musical theory at Dudley College in the West Midlands.

Jeff Blythe
Still adding his muscular experience to the potent Celtic blend of New York's Black 47, the city's premier house band released their latest album, *Elvis Murphy's Green Suede Shoes* in the spring of 2005. Following stints working as the TKO Horns with Squeeze's Chris Difford and Glenn Tilbrook and with Nick Lowe, he and Paterson played on a selection of Pete Williams' These Tender Virtues material in the mid-Eighties. The pair ventured into Funkadelic/George Clinton/Prince-inspired terrain with Neighbourhood in the late Eighties. Blythe has also worked on TV and film music, classical compositions and made playing appearances on film.

Steve Brennan (né Shaw)

Having maintained his working rapport with The Proclaimers, the violinist also played with Deacon Blue's Ricky Ross and Birmingham band Lucky Luciano. However, a shoulder complaint has left Brennan unable to play, precipitating what he called an enforced retirement. He has not been involved in music for the last two years.

Brian Brummitt

Having met with Paterson and Speare in late 2004 for the first time in many years and with tentative plans to play together again, Brummitt currently lives in Eton Wick near Slough, employed at Heathrow Airport. He's now relishing his relocation to France.

John Edwards

After 20 years service, he remains solid as a rock as bass player with Status Quo.

Spike Edney

Currently heading his own group, Spike's All Stars Band.

Nick Gatfield

Now in the esteemed position of Managing Director at Universal (UK).

Andy Growcott

Now a record producer working in Los Angeles. Following his Dexys and Bureau tenures, Stoker also drummed with Tin Tin before joining General Public. He has now built an incredible portfolio as a record engineer/producer in the States, working with Sting and Pato Banton among others, having also undertaken a wide array of work on TV/film music. He was awarded 1990 Alternative Producer of the Year Award in Philadelphia, and has hosted his own TV show in the States.

Andy Leek

Recorded an LP with George Martin in 1989 before studying classical music at Cardiff University. He later recorded a couple of singles and an album's worth of material in the mid-Nineties, entitled *Say Something*, in Germany. Currently busy with his group The Blue Angels and Dexys II tribute band.

Roger McDuff (né Huckle)
Following his brief tenure, the classically trained violinist is now understood to be working for a radio symphony orchestra in Iceland.

Helen O'Hara
Following studio and tour work with Tanita Tikaram, O'Hara embarked upon a solo career, investigating New Age/instrumental music that blended classical and popular forms. Worked with Nicky Hopkins, BJ Cole, Robert Noble and Mick Woodmansey on her 1990 LP *Southern Hearts*, before releasing a more traditional 1998 follow-up entitled *A Night In Ireland*. She is now married with children.

Jim Paterson
Spent much of his post *Too-Rye-Ay*, pre-*Don't Stand Me Down* involvement playing alongside Blythe, Brummitt and Speare as part of the TKO Horns. Following a plethora of session work, he briefly joined the Jamiroquai-influenced group Pure Junk. Currently living in west London and attempting to land a record deal, during 1999, Paterson undertook co-writing duties with Pete Rowland and singer Amee Panchal following his involvement on *My Beauty*.

Pete Saunders
Following a brief tenure with The Damned, Saunders worked with Vic Godard, Carmel, Jake Burns and recorded numerous John Peel sessions with Norwich group Serious Drinking, who counted future *Loaded* mogul James Brown as their 17-year-old tour mascot during the mid-Eighties. Now living in Islington, north London, he fronts the New Originals, a Dr John-meets-Tom Waits-meets Randy Newman affair, who have been playing for four years and have recorded one LP, *Who's Been Talking*. Saunders hopes to undertake further recording during 2005.

Seb Shelton
Shelton gave up drums after leaving Dexys in 1983. (His colleagues, who found it hard to ignore his obvious organisational and telecommunication skills, daubed a red telephone on the wall of their rehearsal space with the words 'Seb's Office' next to it.) Also a keen cod fisherman, Shelton soon moved into artist management, working with the likes of Adrian Sherwood and Julian Cope and what he later called "alternative", rather than commercially driven, artists. Still running Seb Shelton Management in London.

Paul Speare

Speare cites his involvement with Jerry Dammers on The Special AKA's 'Nelson Mandela' single in 1984 as one of his proudest musical moments. A session player until that year, he then set up a recording studio in Tamworth. He worked at a further education college while pursuing session and TV work for a house music label in Birmingham. Having run a nine-piece band for several years, Speare relocated to London in 1995 to begin full-time college work. Currently Curriculum Leader of Music Technology at a college in Oxfordshire.

Steve Spooner

A self-confessed "city boy with a country heart", Spooner moved to Cornwall in 1988. Now living in St. Keverne, just outside Helston, he is currently a window cleaner.

Mick Talbot

Spent the rest of the Eighties in The Style Council alongside Paul Weller. Talbot continues to tour with a busy schedule through a variety of musical ensembles.

Pete Williams

Following his These Tender Virtues work in the mid-Eighties and prior to his emergence with Basehart, Williams has never stopped writing, despite involvement in numerous occupations outside the music industry. He also worked as musical director for a clutch of Midlands theatre companies and enjoyed his involvement in film and animation work.

Acknowledgements

Firstly, special thanks for their time, co-operation and memories to group members Mick Billingham, Brian Brummitt, Pete Saunders, Steve Shaw, Paul Speare and Steve Spooner. I am particularly grateful to Steve Spooner for access to the group's first ever demo recordings, to Pete Saunders for his Dexys scrapbook and paraphernalia and to Brian Brummitt for his European tour photographs and live video footage. Although he didn't contribute directly to the book, thanks also to Pete Williams for his time and interest. A big thank-you to record producers Clive Langer, Pete Wingfield and Alan Winstanley and to journalists Paolo Hewitt, Jim Irvin, Peter Paphides and Chris Roberts for their enthusiastic contributions. I am also heavily indebted to Dexys' photographer, Mike Laye, for his excellent contributions at such short notice.

I must also extend my gratitude to Chris Charlesworth at Omnibus Press for his help and advice during the course of my writing this book and Andy Neill for editing the manuscript; to Manchester music journalist Mick Middles for his initial encouragement and suggestions, without which, I doubt the book would have gotten written; to Barney Hoskyns at rocksbackpages.com for his provision of contact details, and to Clive Whichelow at Backnumbers for his invaluable supply of music magazines and weekly press papers. I am also sincerely grateful to the enthusiasm, interest and co-operation on the part of many dedicated Dexys fans. Thanks to Neil Warburton for supplying copies of his excellent *Keep On Running* fanzine and an assortment of press reviews from his encyclopaedic collection, to Vincent Cain for his efforts, to Ian Jennings for his assistance, and to Stuart Cranston for his scrapbooks and images.

Thanks also to John Annals, Eddie Cooney, Clive Gray and Tim Webb who operate a clutch of Dexys fan websites/forums. A number of these guys have assisted in forwarding obscure and hard-to-locate press cuttings and CDs. Their comprehensive websites serve the group extremely well. I must also tip my hat to Tony Beesley, David Brindley, David Innes, James McMurtry, Richard Nash and Paul Watson. Aside from in-depth interviews with group members, record producers, journalists and fans' memories, I have drawn upon an assortment of documentary/TV footage, fan club newsletters, fanzines, newspapers, press cuttings, press releases, rare demo/live/promo material, radio/web interviews, tour programmes and video footage. I should also reference Dexys' *It Was Like This* – Live DVD (ILC Music) interview footage with Mick Talbot and Pete Williams, who also features in a glittercritter.com web interview with Carrie Shearer.

I'm also particularly indebted to Paolo Hewitt and co-author Mark Baxter's book *The Fashion Of Football: From Best To Beckham, From Mod To Label Slave* (Mainstream) which offered a wonderful insight into Kevin Rowland's adolescent passion for, well, fashion and football. In terms of group-specific reference material, I have drawn upon chapters on Dexys and Kevin Rowland in both John Aizlewood's *Love Is The Drug* (Penguin) and Kevin Pearce's *Something Beginning With O* (Heavenly). I have also dipped into Q Magazine's *25 Years Of Two Tone Special*, the excellent *Sent From Coventry: The Chequered Past Of Two Tone* by Richard Eddington (IMP) for a perspective on Dexys' brief association with the phenomenon, *NME Rock and Roll Years* (BCA) edited by John Tobler, and *This Is Uncool: The 500 Greatest Singles Since Punk And Disco* by Garry Mulholland (Cassell).

I must also acknowledge my debt to a number of journalists/writers whose interviews, features and retrospectives covering the various stages of the group's career have proved particularly useful: Daryl Easlea, Paolo Hewitt, Jim Irvin, Ted Kessler, Gavin Martin, Chris Roberts, Johnny Rogan, Phil Sutcliffe, Everett True and Jon Wilde. I'd also like to acknowledge those journalists who I have referred to and/or referenced in the course of my research and writing: Harry Adams, John Aizlewood, Stuart Bailie, Max Bell, Chris Bohn, Glyn Brown, Danny Buckland, Garry Bushell, Keith Cameron, Roy Carr, Jamie T. Conway, Mark Cordery, Martin Culverwell, Debra Daley, Stephen Dalton, Paul Davies, Geoff Deane, Adrian Deevoy, Fred Dellar, Barry Egan, Mark Ellen, Paul Evers, Helen Fitzgerald, Tony Fletcher, Simon Frith, Pat Gilbert, Ian Gittins, Stephen Gordon, Jonathan Hope, David Hutcheon, Colin Irwin, Danny Kelly, Nick Kent, Tom Lappin, Jackie Lee, Spencer Leigh, Alan Lewis, Jan Libbenga, Richard Lowe, Liam Mackey, Paul Mathur, Dave McCullough, Barry McIlheney, John McKenzie, Phil McNeill, Garry Mulholland, John Mulvey, Mike Nicholls, Sean O'Hagan, Peter Paphides, Simon Price, Gill Pringle, David Quantick, Paul Rambali, Ian Ravendale, Dave Sefton, Victoria Segal, William Shaw, Anne Shooter, Paul Simper, Daniela Soave, Mike Stand, Terry Staunton, Dermot Stokes, Adam Sweeting, Sam Taylor, Adrian Thrills, Mick Wall, Jane Wilkes, Kevin Wilson, and Lois Wilson.

On a more personal note, I can't stress enough my gratitude to Mum,

Dad and Nicola for their thoughtful assistance, invaluable support and encouragement over these long and winding months. It has been much appreciated.

I'd also like to raise a glass to my old soul brother Andrew Panter, in memory of the music, the fun and some unforgettable Friday nights at The Blarney Stone, and to my friend Gerard Vance, the Leeds music man. Proof that, despite living in Yorkshire, it *does* apply . . .

Dexys Midnight Runners Discography

Thanks to Martin Strong (editor, *The Great Rock Discography*, 6th edition, Canongate, 2002) the unofficial Dexys msn website, Clive Gray, Richard Nash, Neil Warburton and Tim Webb.

SINGLES

November 1979

Dance Stance / I'm Just Looking (7″) EMI/Oddball Productions R 6028 (UK 1979); EMI/Oddball Productions R 6028-DJ demo (UK 1979)

March 1980

Geno / Breaking Down The Walls Of Heartache (7″) EMI/Late Night Feelings; R 6033 (UK 1980)

July 1980

There, There, My Dear / The Horse (7″) EMI/Late Night Feelings R 6038 (UK 1980); EMI/Late Night Feelings R 6038 demo (UK 1980)

Thankfully, Not Living In Yorkshire It Doesn't Apply / The Horse (7″) Parlophone 2C 008-07.402 (France 1980)

Seven Days Too Long / unknown (7″) (Canada 1980)

November 1980

Keep It Part Two (Inferiority Part One) / One Way Love (7″) EMI/ Late Night Feelings R 6042 (UK 1980)

March 1981

Plan B / Soulfinger (7″) EMI R 6046 (UK 1981)

Soulfinger Parlophone R 6046 B-1 (One-sided handwritten white label test pressing – UK 1981)

July 1981

Show Me / Soon (7″) Mercury/Phonogram DEXYS 6 (UK 1981), Mercury/Phonogram DEXYS 6 paper label with insert (UK 1981), Mercury/Phonogram DEXYS 6 plastic label with insert (UK 1981)

November 1981

Liars A To E / And Yes, We Must Remain The Wild Hearted Outsiders (7″) Mercury/Phonogram DEXYS 7 (UK 1981)

March 1982

The Celtic Soul Brothers (More, Please, Thank You) / Love Part Two (7″) Mercury/Phonogram DEXYS 8 card label (UK 1982), Mercury/Phonogram DEXYS 8 paper label (UK 1982)

The Celtic Soul Brothers (More, Please, Thank You) DJ edit / **The Celtic Soul Brothers (More, Please, Thank You)** Mercury DEX DJ 8 DJ promo (UK 1982)

June 1982

DEXYS MIDNIGHT RUNNERS & THE EMERALD EXPRESS

Come On Eileen / Dubious (7″) Mercury DEXYS 9 card label (UK 1982); Mercury DEXYS 9 paper label (UK 1982)

Come On Eileen / Liars A To E (Too-Rye-Ay version) / Dubious (12″) Mercury DEXYS 9-12 (UK 1982)

Come On Eileen DJ edit / **Come On Eileen** Mercury DEXYS DJ 9 promo (UK 1982)

Come On Eileen / Liars A To E Mercury 7PP-83 (Japan 1982)

Come On Eileen (long version) / **Come On Eileen** (short version) Mercury 76189 DJ promo (USA 1982)

Come On Eileen / Let's Make This Precious Mercury 76189 (USA 1982)

Come On Eileen / T.S.O.P. (The Sound Of Philadelphia) / Let's Make This Precious Mercury MDS 4021 (USA 1982)

September 1982

KEVIN ROWLAND & DEXYS MIDNIGHT RUNNERS

Jackie Wilson Said (I'm In Heaven When You Smile) / Let's Make This Precious (7″) Mercury DEXYS 10 paper label (UK 1982), Mercury DEXYS 10 plastic label (UK 1982), Mercury DEXYS 10 (B-side incorrectly titled as 'Howard's Not At Home') (UK 1982)

Jackie Wilson Said (I'm In Heaven When You Smile) / Let's Make This Precious (7″) Mercury DEXYS 10 / **The Celtic Soul Brothers (More, Please, Thank You) / Love Part Two** (7″) Mercury DEXYS 8 seven-inch double pack (UK 1982)

Jackie Wilson Said (I'm In Heaven When You Smile) / Let's Make This Precious / T.S.O.P. (The Sound Of Philadelphia) (12″) Mercury DEXYS 10-12 (UK 1982)

Jackie Wilson Said (I'm In Heaven When You Smile) German 7″ promo

Jackie Wilson Said (I'm In Heaven When You Smile) Master Room one-sided acetate (UK 1982)

Jackie Wilson Said (I'm In Heaven When You Smile) / Jackie Wilson Said (I'm In Heaven When You Smile) Mercury 814 002-7 DJ promo (USA 1983)

November 1982

KEVIN ROWLAND & DEXYS MIDNIGHT RUNNERS

Let's Get This Straight (From The Start) / Old (7″) Mercury DEXYS 11 (UK paper label 1982), Mercury DEXYS 11 plastic label (UK 1982)

Let's Get This Straight (From The Start) / Old (live) / **Respect** (live) (12″) Mercury DEXYS 11-12 (UK 1982), Mercury DEXYS 11-12 DJ advance DJ copy (UK 1982)

March 1983

KEVIN ROWLAND & DEXYS MIDNIGHT RUNNERS

The Celtic Soul Brothers (More, Please, Thank You) / Reminisce (Part One) (7″) Mercury DEXYS 12 (UK 1983), Mercury DEXYP 12 with wrap-around poster (UK 1983)

The Celtic Soul Brothers (More, Please, Thank You) / Reminisce (Part One) Mercury DEXYP 12 with poster sleeve (UK 1983)

The Celtic Soul Brothers (More, Please, Thank You) / Reminisce (Part One) / Show Me (Live) (12″) Mercury DEXYS 12-12 (UK 1983)

The Celtic Soul Brothers (More, Please, Thank You) / The Celtic Soul Brothers (More, Please, Thank You) Mercury 811142-7 DJ promo (USA 1983)

March 1984

Dance Stance / There, There, My Dear (7″) (EMI Golden 45s series) Gold G455 (UK 1984)

November 1985

DEXYS MIDNIGHT RUNNERS

An Extract From This Is What She's Like / This Is What She's Like Finale (7) Mercury DEXYS 13 (UK 1985)

An Extract From This Is What She's Like / This Is What She's Like Finale / Marguerita Time / Reminisce (Part Two) Mercury DEXYD 13 gatefold double 7″ pack (UK 1985)

This Is What She's Like (DJ edit – short version) / This Is What She's Like (DJ edit – 7″ single version) Mercury DEXDJ 13 radio promo (UK 1985)

This Is What She's Like (full version) **/ Marguerita Time** (10″) Mercury DEXYS 13-10 (UK 1985)

This Is What She's Like (full version) **/ This Is What She's Like** (instrumental) **/ Reminisce (Part One)** (12″) Mercury DEXYS 13-12 (UK 1985), Mercury DEXYS 13-12 white label test pressing (UK 1985)

This Is What She's Like / One Of Those Things / Knowledge Of Beauty Mercury DMR 2 radio sampler (UK 1985)

One Of Those Things / The Occasional Flicker (12″) Mercury DMR 1 radio promo (UK 1985)

This Is What She's Like / Listen To This Mercury white label test pressing (UK 1985)

This Is What She's Like (edit) / This Is What She's Like / One Of Those Things Mercury PRO 387-1 promo (USA 1985)

November 1986

DEXYS MIDNIGHT RUNNERS

Because Of You / Kathleen Mavourneen (7″) Mercury BRUSH 1 (UK 1986)

Because Of You / Kathleen Mavourneen / The 'Sometimes' Theme (instrumental) (12″) Mercury BRUSH 112 (UK 1986)

October 2003

Manhood / Manhood (radio edit) promotional CD release EMI PRODEXYS 2003

Re-issues:

Come On Eileen / Jackie Wilson Said (I'm In Heaven When You Smile) (7″) Old Gold OG 9900 (UK 1989)

Come On Eileen / The Celtic Soul Brothers (More, Please, Thank You) / Jackie Wilson Said (I'm In Heaven When You Smile) / Liars

A To E (CD video) Mercury 080 628-2 (UK 1989)

Come On Eileen / Because Of You (7″) Mercury MER 347 (UK 1991)

Come On Eileen / Because Of You (CD single) Mercury MERCD 347 (UK 1991)

Come On Eileen / Because Of You / Let's Get This Straight (From The Start) (12″) Mercury MERX 347 (UK 1991)

Geno / There, There, My Dear (7″) Old Gold OG 9996 (UK September 1992)

Geno / There, There, My Dear / Dance Stance (CD) Old Gold OG 6176 (UK September 1992)

ALBUMS

July 1980

DEXYS MIDNIGHT RUNNERS

Searching For The Young Soul Rebels

Burn It Down (formerly Dance Stance); Tell Me When My Light Turns Green; The Teams That Meet In Caffs; I'm Just Looking; Geno; Seven Days Too Long; I Couldn't Help If I Tried; Thankfully, Not Living In Yorkshire It Doesn't Apply; Keep It; Love (Part One); There, There, My Dear. EMI/ Parlophone LP/cassette: SW-17042/ TCPCS 7213; EMI/Parlophone CD CDP 7464482 (UK 1980).

Re-issues:

EMI Fame LP/cassette FA 3032 (UK 1982); Budget re-issue LP Mercury PRICE 89 (UK 1986); CD re-issue (CZ 31) (UK January 1988)

20th Anniversary digitally enhanced remastered edition released in 2000. Track-listing as original UK album, featuring videos for Geno and There, There, My Dear plus a picture gallery full of extras including artwork, lyrics, credits, slides and audio facilities to play original Dexys UK Parlophone releases. EMI CD 7243 5 25600 0 4 (UK 2000); EMI ECD DEXYS 20 promo with colour photograph and press release (UK 2000).

July 1982

KEVIN ROWLAND & DEXYS MIDNIGHT RUNNERS

Too-Rye-Ay

The Celtic Soul Brothers (More, Please, Thank You); Let's Make This Precious; All In All (This One Last Wild Waltz); Jackie Wilson Said (I'm In Heaven When You Smile); Old; Soon (not listed); Plan B; I'll Show You;

Liars A To E; Until I Believe In My Soul; Come On Eileen. Mercury LP/ cassette MERS/ MERSC 8 (UK 1982); Mercury white label test pressing (UK 1982).

Re-issues:

CD issue – Mercury CD 810 054-2 (UK January 1983); Mercury LP PRICE 89/cassette PRIMC 89 (UK July 1986)

Remastered CD released in March 1996 boasting original UK album track listing plus eight extra tracks: The Celtic Soul Brothers (More, Please, Thank You) (US Mix); Jackie Wilson Said (I'm In Heaven When You Smile) (Live); Come On Eileen (Live); Marguerita Time; Respect (Live); Dubious; Love Part Two; T.S.O.P. (The Sound Of Philadelphia). Mercury 514 839-2 (UK 1996).

Digitally remastered enhanced edition released in 2000. Track listing as original UK album also featuring videos for The Celtic Soul Brothers and Come On Eileen, a gallery of photographs, records and sleeves plus an interview with Billy Adams. Mercury CD 542 961-2 (UK 2000).

September 1985

DEXYS MIDNIGHT RUNNERS

Don't Stand Me Down
The Occasional Flicker; This Is What She's Like; Knowledge Of Beauty; One Of Those Things; Reminisce (Part Two); Listen To This; The Waltz. Mercury LP/cassette MERH 56; Mercury CD 822 989-2 (includes additional track This Is What She's Like (instrumental) (UK 1985); Mercury white label test pressing (UK 1985). Remastered re-issue released in June 1997 with track listing as original UK album, except Knowledge Of Beauty (now re-titled My National Pride) and Listen To This (re-titled I Love You (Listen To This). Includes bonus tracks Reminisce (Part One) and The Way You Look Tonight. Creation CRECD 154 (UK 1997).

Don't Stand Me Down: The Director's Cut
Released in April 2002. Track listing is identical to 1997 Creation CD issue, but minus previous bonus tracks and including additional opening track, Kevin Rowland's 13th Time. Limited edition run includes DVD of three videos: This Is What She's Like, My National Pride and I Love You (Listen To This). (EMI UK promo does not include bonus DVD.) EMI 7243 5 537 0130 0 7 (UK 2002).

COMPILATIONS

1983

Geno
Geno; Plan B; Breaking Down The Walls Of Heartache; Dance Stance; The Horse; There, There, My Dear; Keep It Part Two (Inferiority Part One); One Way Love; I'm Just Looking; Soulfinger. EMI LP EMS 1007 (UK 1983).

Re-issues:
Track listing as original UK album. EMI LP/cassette: ATAK 72/ TC ATAK 72 (UK October 1987). Track listing as original UK album. EMI CD: CDFA 3189 (UK June 1988).

June 1991

The Very Best Of Dexys Midnight Runners
Come On Eileen; Jackie Wilson Said (I'm In Heaven When You Smile); Let's Get This Straight (From The Start); Because Of You; Show Me; The Celtic Soul Brothers (More, Please, Thank You); Liars A To E; Geno; There, There, My Dear; Breaking Down The Walls Of Heartache; Dance Stance; Plan B; Keep It Part Two (Inferiority Part One); I'm Just Looking; Soon; This Is What She's Like; Soul Finger. Mercury LP: 846 460-1/CD: 846 460-2/cassette: 846 460-4 (UK 1991).

Re-issues
Track listing as original UK album CD (UK July 1992).

May 1993

Because Of You
The Celtic Soul Brothers (More, Please, Thank You); Show Me; Liars A To E; An Extract From This Is What She's Like; Let's Make This Precious; Soon; Reminisce (Part One); Because Of You; Let's Get This Straight (From The Start); Old; All In All (This One Last Wild Waltz); This Is What She's Like (Finale); Dubious; The Occasional Flicker. Spectrum Music/Karussell CD/cassette: 550 003-2/4 (Germany 1993).

May 1996

It Was Like This
Breaking Down The Walls Of Heartache; Tell Me When My Light Turns Green; The Teams That Meet In Caffs; Dance Stance; Geno; I'm Just Looking; Thankfully, Not Living In Yorkshire It Doesn't Apply; Seven Days Too Long; I Couldn't Help If I Tried; Respect (Radio One Session version); The Horse; Keep It; Love Part One; There, There, My Dear; Keep It Part

Two (Inferiority Part One); One Way Love; Plan B; Soul Finger. EMI Premier PRMU CD1 7234 838 122 2 6 (UK 1996).

1996

Dexys Midnight Runners – Mercury Master Series
Jackie Wilson Said (I'm In Heaven When You Smile); The Celtic Soul Brothers (More, Please, Thank You); Show Me; Come On Eileen; Let's Make This Precious; Let's Get This Straight (From The Start); Because Of You; Kathleen Mavourneen; Reminisce (Part Two); Old; Liars A To E; Knowledge Of Beauty; The Waltz; The Occasional Flicker; Dubious; Love Part Two. Mercury CD 532 219-2 (UK 1996).

September 2003

Let's Make This Precious: The Best Of Dexys Midnight Runners
Geno; The Celtic Soul Brothers (More, Please, Thank You); Come On Eileen; Jackie Wilson Said (I'm In Heaven When You Smile); Because Of You; Manhood; Tell Me When My Light Turns Green; Breaking Down The Walls Of Heartache; There, There, My Dear; Plan B; Show Me; Let's Make This Precious (BBC version); Until I Believe In My Soul (BBC version); Let's Get This Straight (From The Start); This Is What She's Like; My National Pride; I Love You (Listen To This); My Life In England (Part One). EMI CD 7243 5 72680 2 6 (UK 2003).

RADIO

BBC Radio One John Peel Session (February 26, 1980)
The Horse; Tell Me When My Light Turns Green; Breaking Down The Walls Of Heartache; Geno.

BBC Radio One Live In Concert (Paris Theatre, London: May 20, 1981)
Spiritual Passion; Tell Me When My Light Turns Green; Soon; Plan B; Burn It Down; Respect; Until I Believe In My Soul; Show Me; There, There, My Dear; Your Own.

Netherlands live radio broadcast (Brouwershaven, Holland: June 30, 1981)
Spiritual Passion; Tell Me When My Light Turns Green; Burn It Down; Breaking Down The Walls Of Heartache; Soon; Plan B; Geno; Respect; Until I Believe In My Soul; Show Me; There, There, My Dear; Your Own.

BBC Radio One Richard Skinner Show (July 20, 1981)
Spiritual Passion; Your Own; Let's Make This Precious; Until I Believe In My Soul.

BBC Radio Transcription Disc – In Concert 287 (Exhibition Park, Newcastle: June 6, 1982)

T.S.O.P. (The Sound Of Philadelphia); Burn It Down; Let's Make This Precious; Jackie Wilson Said (I'm In Heaven When You Smile); Come On Eileen; Respect; Soon; Plan B; Geno; Old; The Celtic Soul Brothers (More, Please, Thank You); There, There, My Dear; Show Me. (NB: omits I'll Show You.) BBC Transcription Services CN 4076/S (UK 1982). Released as BBC Radio One Live In Concert (Windsong International WINCD 047 UK, November 1993). Re-issues: Griffin Music GCD-334-2 (UK 1995).

BBC Radio One Live In Concert (Royal Court Theatre, Liverpool: March 16, 1983)
Geno; The Celtic Soul Brothers (More, Please, Thank You); Let's Get This Straight (From The Start); All In All (This One Last Wild Waltz); Tell Me When My Light Turns Green; Plan B; Let's Make This Precious; There, There, My Dear; Come On Eileen; Until I Believe In My Soul; Respect.

July 1995

1980–1982 The Radio One Sessions
Tell Me When My Light Turns Green; Let's Make This Precious; Dubious; Until I Believe In My Soul; Liars A To E; Jackie Wilson Said (I'm In Heaven When You Smile); All In All (This One Last Wild Waltz); Old. Nighttracks CDNT 009 (UK 1995).

VIDEO

The Bridge (edited live performance at the Shaftesbury Theatre, London: October 10, 1982)
Old; All In All (This One Last Wild Waltz); Let's Make This Precious; Until I Believe In My Soul; Jackie Wilson Said (I'm In Heaven When You Smile); Respect; Come On Eileen; Kevin Rowland's Band; The Celtic Soul Brothers (More, Please, Thank You).
Polygram Video SPC 00062/ VHS Laserdisc (PA84081) (UK 1983).

Re-issue: Budget videocassette: Polygram Video 083 310 3 (UK 1991).

DVD

It Was Like This – Live (performance filmed at the Royal Court Theatre, Liverpool: November 7, 2003 – includes set-list, group member and fan interviews)
The Waltz; Old; Let's Make This Precious; (I Love You) Listen To This; I Couldn't Help If I Tried; Liars A To E; Soon; Geno; My Life In England (Part One); Until I Believe In My Soul; Tell Me When My Light Turns Green; Until I Believe In My Soul (Reprise); Come On Eileen; Because Of You; This Is What She's Like; Nightshift; Manhood.
(ILC Music Ltd DVD2444 UK 2004).

BOOTLEG RECORDINGS

Camden Electric Ballroom, London: December 27, 1979
The Horse; Tell Me When My Light Turns Green; Thankfully, Not Living
In Yorkshire It Doesn't Apply; Breaking Down The Walls Of Heartache;
The Teams That Meet In Caffs; Geno; Dance Stance; I'm Just Looking;
Respect; Hold On I'm Comin'; Big Time Operator.

Groningen Sterrebos, Holland: August 17, 1980 (highlights)
Seven Days Too Long; Geno; There, There, My Dear; I Couldn't Help If I
Tried; Burn It Down; Breaking Down The Walls Of Heartache; Respect.

Cologne Funkhaus, Germany: October 11, 1980
The Horse; Tell Me When My Light Turns Green; Thankfully, Not Living
In Yorkshire It Doesn't Apply; Breaking Down The Walls Of Heartache;
The Teams That Meet In Caffs; Geno; Burn It Down; I'm Just Looking;
Respect; There, There, My Dear; Seven Days Too Long; Soulfinger; Big
Time Operator; One Way Love. (Bandido Records B 021).

Playhouse, Nottingham: August 16, 1981 (edited highlights)
Show Me; There, There, My Dear; Soon; Plan B; Respect; Liars A To E;
I'm Just Looking.

Old Vic Theatre, London: November 14, 1981
Old; Spiritual Passion; Tell Me When My Light Turns Green; Let's Make
This Precious; Jackie Wilson Said (I'm In Heaven When You Smile); Soon;
Plan B; Burn It Down; Oh Eileen, Yes Let's; Respect; Until I Believe In My
Soul; Show Me; There, There, My Dear; Liars A To E; Soulfinger; Keep It
Part Two; I'll Show You; Seven Days Too Long.

Ashton Tameside Theatre, Manchester: September 30, 1982
Old; Geno; The Celtic Soul Brothers (More, Please, Thank You); Let's Get
This Straight (From The Start); All In All (This One Last Wild Waltz); Tell
Me When My Light Turns Green; Plan B; Let's Make This Precious; I
Couldn't Help If I Tried; Until I Believe In My Soul; Kevin Rowland's
Band; Jackie Wilson Said (I'm In Heaven When You Smile); Respect;
There, There, My Dear; Come On Eileen; Show Me; I'll Show You.

Haarlem, Holland: October 27, 1982
Old; Geno; The Celtic Soul Brothers (More, Please, Thank You); Let's Get
This Straight (From The Start); All In All (This One Last Wild Waltz); Tell
Me When My Light Turns Green; Plan B; Let's Make This Precious; I
Couldn't Help If I Tried; Until I Believe In My Soul; Respect; There,
There, My Dear; Seven Days Too Long; Come On Eileen; Show Me; I'll
Show You; Kevin Rowland's Band.

Eldorado Théâtre, Paris: November 13, 1982
T.S.O.P. (The Sound Of Philadelphia); Plan B; Until I Believe In My Soul;
Jackie Wilson Said (I'm In Heaven When You Smile); Geno; There, There,
My Dear; Come On Eileen.

Berlin, Germany: November 19, 1982
Old; Geno; The Celtic Soul Brothers (More, Please, Thank You); Tell Me
When My Light Turns Green; Plan B; Let's Make This Precious; I Couldn't
Help If I Tried; Jackie Wilson Said (I'm In Heaven When You Smile); Seven
Days Too Long; Come On Eileen; Respect.

Essen, Germany: April 16, 1983
Geno; The Celtic Soul Brothers (More, Please, Thank You); Let's Get This
Straight (From The Start); Plan B; Let's Make This Precious; There, There,
My Dear; Come On Eileen; All In All (This One Last Wild Waltz); Jackie
Wilson Said (I'm In Heaven When You Smile); Tell Me When My Light
Turns Green; Until I Believe In My Soul; Respect; Kevin Rowland's Band;
Keep It Part Two (Inferiority Part One).

Dominion Theatre, London: November 12, 1985
Can't Help Falling In Love; Let's Get This Straight (From The Start); Kevin
Rowland's 13th Crime; Tell Me When My Light Turns Green; Come On
Eileen; Something Old, Something New; One Of Those Things;
Knowledge Of Beauty; This Is What She's Like; The Waltz; The Occasional
Flicker; Respect; Plan B; Listen To This; Marguerita Time; Burn It Down;
Kathleen Mavourneen.

Straight From The Heart – The Rarities Collection (compilation
including assorted Dexys, Kevin Rowland and Killjoys tracks)
Thunder Road; Kathleen Mavourneen; A One Way Ticket To Palookaville;
Kevin Rowland's Band; Manhood; If I Ever; Until I Believe In My Soul;
And Yes, We Must Remain The Wild Hearted Outsiders; There, There, My
Dear; Even When I Hold You; Liars A To E; Tonight; Merry Xmas
Everybody; Big Time Operator; Johnny Won't Get To Heaven. (Dastardly
Records DR 006.)

KEVIN ROWLAND

SINGLES

April 1988

Walk Away / Even When I Hold You (7″) Mercury DEXYS 14 (UK
1988)

Walk Away / Even When I Hold You (7″) German promo

**Walk Away / Even When I Hold You / The Way You Look Tonight
/ Because Of You** (CD single) Mercury DEXCD 14 (UK 1988)

**Walk Away / Even When I Hold You / The Way You Look Tonight
/ Walk Away (Instrumental)** (12″) Mercury DEXYS 14-12 (UK 1988)

Walk Away / Even When I Hold You / The Way You Look Tonight / Walk Away (Instrumental) (12″) gatefold sleeve with Kevin Rowland biography Mercury DEXYB 14-12 (UK 1988)

Walk Away (12″ promo) Mercury DEXYSDJ 14-12 (UK 1988)

August 1988

Tonight / Kevin Rowland's Band (7″) Mercury ROW 1 (UK 1988)

Tonight / Kevin Rowland's Band / Come On Eileen / The Celtic Soul Brothers (More, Please, Thank You) (CD single) Mercury ROWCD 1 (UK 1988)

Tonight (Midnight Mix) / Tonight (3AM Mix) / Kevin Rowland's Band (12″) Mercury ROW 112 (UK 1988)

Tonight (Dance Mix) / Tonight (New York Dub Mix) / Come On Eileen / Kevin Rowland's Band (12″) Mercury ROW 1122 (UK 1988)

October 1988

Young Man / A One Way Ticket To Palookaville (7″) Mercury ROW2 (UK 1988)

Young Man / A One Way Ticket To Palookaville / Show Me / Jackie Wilson Said (I'm In Heaven When You Smile) (CD single) Mercury ROWCD 2 (UK 1988)

Young Man / A One Way Ticket To Palookaville / Jackie Wilson Said (I'm In Heaven When You Smile) (12″) Mercury ROW2-12 (UK 1988)

September 1999

Concrete And Clay / I Can't Tell The Bottom From The Top (cassette) Creation CS 322 (UK 1999)

Concrete And Clay / I Can't Tell The Bottom From The Top (CD single) Creation SCD 322 (UK 1999)

Concrete And Clay (three track promo CD) Creation SCD 332P

ALBUMS

June 1988

The Wanderer

Young Man; Walk Away; You'll Be The One For Me; Heartaches By The Number; I Am A Wanderer; Tonight; When You Walk Alone; Age Can't Wither You; I Want; Remember Me.

Mercury LP/cassette/CD: MERH 121/ MERHC 121/CD 834488-2 (UK 1988)

October 1999

My Beauty

The Greatest Love Of All; Rag Doll; Concrete And Clay; Daydream Believer; This Guy's In Love With You; The Long And Winding Road; It's Getting Better; I Can't Tell The Bottom From The Top; Labelled With Love (I'll Stay With My Dreams); Reflections Of My Life; You'll Never Walk Alone.

CD CRECD 216 (UK 1999)

My Beauty promotional CD (including Thunder Road) CRECD 216P

THE BLUE OX BABES

SINGLES

There's No Deceiving You / The Last Detail (7″) GOBOB1 (UK 1988)

There's No Deceiving You / The Last Detail / Take Me To The River (12″) GOBOB112 (UK 1988)

Apples And Oranges (The International Hope Campaign) / Pray Lucky (7″) GOBOB2 (UK 1988)

Apples And Oranges (The International Hope Campaign) / Pray Lucky / Yes Let's / Russia In Winter (12″) GOBOB212 (UK 1988)

Walking On The Line / Four Golden Tongues Talk (7″) GOBOB3 (UK 1988)

Walking On The Line / Four Golden Tongues Talk / What Does Anybody Ever Think About / Thought As Much (12″) GOBOB312 (UK 1988)

ALBUMS

Apples And Oranges

It Could Have Been Love; Walking On The Line; Apples And Oranges; Bedlam; East To West; She's So Strong; Gregory Right; There's No Deceiving You; Thought As Much; Ballad Of The Blue Ox Babes.

(Unreleased LP UK 1988.)

THE BUREAU

SINGLES

March 1981

Only For Sheep / The First One (7″) WEA K18478 (UK 1981)

Only For Sheep (double sided mono/stereo US promo version) Atlantic 3861.

May 1981

Let Him Have It / The Noose (7″) WEA K18753 (UK 1981)

Let Him Have It (Sweet Revenge) / The Carpetbaggers (7″) WEA 100181 (Australia 1981)

ALBUMS

February 2005 *(posthumous UK Warners release of original 1981 LP)*

The Bureau

Only For Sheep; The First One; Sentimental Attachment; Got To Be Now; Looking For Excitement; Let Him Have It; Find A Way; Bigger Prize; The Carpetbaggers; Helpless. **Bonus tracks:** The Noose; Hitman; Sorry I Spoke; The Horse; Only For Sheep (CD-Rom video).

Bonus disc: Live (London Forum concert, 1981) The Horse; The First One; The Noose; Got To Be Now; The Bigger Prize; Only For Sheep; Find A Way; Helpless; Sentimental Attachment; Looking For Excitement; Let Him Have It. WEA CD LC2828 (UK 2005).